AF249105

STUDENT ATHLETES

MERGING ACADEMICS AND SPORTS

STUDENT ATHLETES

MERGING ACADEMICS AND SPORTS

Frank P. Jozsa Jr.
Pfeiffer University, USA

NEW JERSEY · LONDON · SINGAPORE · BEIJING · SHANGHAI · HONG KONG · TAIPEI · CHENNAI · TOKYO

Published by

World Scientific Publishing Co. Pte. Ltd.

5 Toh Tuck Link, Singapore 596224

USA office: 27 Warren Street, Suite 401-402, Hackensack, NJ 07601

UK office: 57 Shelton Street, Covent Garden, London WC2H 9HE

British Library Cataloguing-in-Publication Data
A catalogue record for this book is available from the British Library.

STUDENT ATHLETES
Merging Academics and Sports

ISBN 978-981-3275-04-1

For any available supplementary material, please visit
https://www.worldscientific.com/worldscibooks/10.1142/11123#t=suppl

Desk Editor: Sandhya Venkatesh

Typeset by Stallion Press
Email: enquiries@stallionpress.com

Printed in Singapore

*To college and university student athletes who
successfully merged academics and sports*

ABOUT THE AUTHOR

Frank P. Jozsa Jr. is a former college and semi-professional athlete with an undergraduate degree in accounting and a masters' degrees in business administration and economics, and also a doctorate in economics. He is the author of several books on team sports in professional baseball, basketball, and football, and another on intercollegiate sports programs at American colleges and universities. His memoirs, *A Hoosier's Journey: Athlete, Student, Teacher, and Author,* were published by Dog Ear Publishing in 2011.

Besides books, Jozsa has written several articles published in journals, magazines, and newspapers. His dissertation — "An Economic Analysis of Franchise Relocation and League Expansion in Professional Team Sports, 1950–1975" — was completed in 1977 at Georgia State University in Atlanta, Georgia. After teaching undergraduate and graduate courses in business administration, economics, finance, and statistics for more than three decades, Jozsa retired from Pfeiffer University in 2007.

ACKNOWLEDGEMENTS

While researching, writing, and editing the manuscript for this book during 2017, a few individuals provided assistance, ideas, and information for it and thus helped me in different ways. Most important to my project, Pfeiffer University's library director and assistant professor of library science Lara Little found numerous readings about student athletes and their schools' sports programs in such publications as the *Chronicle of Higher Education*, *Diverse Issues in Higher Education*, *Journal of College Student Development*, *Journal of Intercollegiate Sport*, *Journal of Sport Management*, and *Journal of Sport and Social Issues*, and then promptly forwarded them to me.

I appreciate Lara's conscientiousness, professionalism, and her commitment to spend time and obtain articles, reports, and studies for me regarding topics in the book. Undoubtedly, Lara is a valuable employee and superstar librarian for the University's administration, faculty and staff, and especially for the school's undergraduate and graduate students.

Besides Lara, various officials from the National Collegiate Athletic Association, National Association of Intercollegiate Athletics, and National Junior College Athletic Association mailed me historical data including reports based on their organizations' affiliation with institutions in higher education and these schools' number of male and female athletes and their type of sport or sports by academic year, division, and season.

Thanks to each official who responded to my questions and also requests for reports and other documents.

In Chapter 6 — "Academics–Sports Controversies" — there are useful and valid but succinct comments, opinions, and/or viewpoints from a group of current and former professors and professionals in education. They voluntarily responded to my question: "From an academic and/or sports perspective, what are some important issues/topics regarding student athletes and their current/future role on college and university campuses?"

These individuals, in no specific order, were Catawba College Associate Professor and Chair of Sport Management, Dr. Duane Aagaard; Winthrop University Professor of Economics and Director of the Center for Economics Education, Dr. Gary Stone; University of Michigan Professor of Sport Management, Dr. Rodney Fort; Pfeiffer University President, Dr. Colleen Keith; South Florida State College President, Dr. Tom Leitzel; University of South Carolina Distinguished Professor Emeritus, Dr. Roger Sargent; University of Dallas Associate Professor in the College of Business, Dr. Scott Wysong; and Terry Parker High School Economics Teacher, Pat Curran. Special thanks to each of them for their insightful remarks about the status of student athletes.

My fiancé and best friend Maureen Fogle — who first recommended I author a book on student athletes — allowed me to use her computer to organize and write a manuscript for this book. She understood how important this project was for me to complete and then submit a professional copy of it to World Scientific Publishing Company on or before the due date of my contract. Once again, thanks to Maureen for her cooperation, patience, and support particularly since my retirement as a business administration/economics/statistics professor from Pfeiffer University in 2007.

Frank P. Jozsa Jr.

ABBREVIATIONS

ACC	Atlantic Coast Conference
ACT	Admission College Test
APR	Academic Progress Report
APRs	Academic Progress Reports
ASR	Academic Success Rate
ASRs	Academic Success Rates
CAPR	Coaches Academic Progress Rate
CBS	Columbia Broadcasting System
CNN	Cable News Network
COA	Cost of Attendance
CoA	Committee on Academics
CSAT	Collegiate Student-Athlete Protection Act
CT	Connecticut
D.C.	District of Columbia
DG	Drake Group
D-I	Division I
D-II	Division II
D-III	Division III
ESPN	Entertainment Sports Programming Network
FBS	Football Bowl Subdivision
FCS	Football Championship Subdivision

FGR	Federal Graduation Rate
FGRs	Federal Graduation Rates
GA	Georgia
GPA	Grade Point Average
GSR	Graduation Success Rate
GSRs	Graduation Success Rates
HED	Heavy Episodic Drinking
IAAUS	Intercollegiate Athletic Association of the United States
IPEDS-GRS	Integrated Post-Secondary Data System Graduation Rate Survey
IN	Indiana
IRS	Internal Revenue Service
M	Men
MA	Massachusetts
MD	Maryland
ME	Maine
MI	Michigan
NA	Not Applicable
NAC	National Administrative Council
NAFCAR	National Association of Faculty for Collegiate Athletic Reform
NAIA	National Association of Intercollegiate Athletes
NCAA	National Collegiate Athletic Association
NCSU	North Carolina State University
NFL	National Football League
NH	New Hampshire
NJ	New Jersey
NJCAA	National Junior College Athletic Association
NY	New York
Pac-12	Pacific 12
SA	Student Athlete
SAs	Student Athletes
SAT	Scholastic Assessment Test
SEC	Southeastern Conference

T&F	Track and Field
UCLA	University of California-Los Angeles
UH	University of Hawaii
UK	University of Kansas
UNC	University of North Carolina
UND	University of North Dakota
U.S.	United States
W	Women

CONTENTS

About the Author   vii
Acknowledgements   ix
Abbreviations   xi

Chapter 1   Introduction   1
Chapter 2   Schools Sports Programs   7
Chapter 3   Student Athlete Population   43
Chapter 4   Student Athletes Academic Performances   83
Chapter 5   Athletics Environment   121
Chapter 6   Academics–Sports Controversies   159
Chapter 7   Reforms: Academics–Sports   195
Chapter 8   Summary   229

Appendix: Tables   235
Bibliography   253
Index   267

Chapter 1

INTRODUCTION

PURPOSE

For decades in America, the number of athletic programs in most but not all small, mid-sized, and large colleges and universities have increased in size in order for these institutions to assemble and organize rosters and provide teams that compete to win games and perhaps titles and championships during fall, winter, and spring sports seasons. Besides additional assets, equipment, facilities and also resources and other types of investments, these programs and their teams required competent, non-professional, and qualified players. Being student athletes (SAs), practically all of them graduated from high school and were or were not awarded a full or partial scholarship to enroll in and attend a school in higher education.

Applying concepts and using data and other information from various sources in the literature, including suggestions and recommendations from coaches, academic colleagues, and friends, this book reveals and examines the role — behavior, contribution, influence, and/or impact — of SAs on campuses of colleges and universities in the United States (U.S.). It highlights and discusses, in part, their progress academically while they improved their skills and allocated time to participate on teams in one or more of their schools' sports programs in Division I, II, and/or III of the National Collegiate Athletic Association (NCAA), or in divisions of the National Athletic Intercollegiate Association (NAIA), or National Junior College Athletic Association (NJCAA).

LITERATURE REVIEW

Throughout the twentieth and early twenty-first centuries, sports column-ists, editors, and journalists and also such scholars as academic econo-mists, historians, and researchers studied and have authored a variety of articles, books, and other types of literature about men (male) and women (female) players and their participation on athletic teams sponsored by colleges and universities. Since many of these readings were important, relevant, and useful references to my project, the following reviews repre-sent a sample of books with respect to SAs and their merging of academ-ics and sports in intercollegiate sports.

College Knowledge for the Student Athlete was written to support the academic success of SAs — whether at a large or small university or col-lege, whether team or individual sport, whether women or men, whether on scholarship or not. While all college students must learn to negotiate the complex transition from high school to college, male and female SAs face unique challenges, including the complicated set of regulations set out by the NCAA and individual conferences that determine eligibility. The current environment in college athletics makes it even more critical that SAs understand what they need to do academically and how to avoid potential situations that could jeopardize their athletic careers.[1]

In *The Student-Athlete Playbook: Success in the Classroom, Sports & Life*, Barry Brown emphasizes SA character education and the developing of habits to achieve positive focus and mindset and make proper decisions at the right time. He, Brown, highlights the importance of understanding that the effort and passion put into a particular sport is the same as learn-ing and everything else done in life. His book shares information about whom and what a SA is and how he or she must grow and conduct them-selves. It also provides life plays and habits to achieve goals when they focus and put forth maximum effort to make great things happen for them and their team.[2]

---

[1] David Schoem and Shelly Kovacs, *College Knowledge for the Student Athlete* (Ann Arbor, MI: University of Michigan Press, 2011).

[2] Barry Brown, *The Student-Athlete Playbook: Success in the Classroom, Sports & Life* (Atlanta, GA: Bar-Red Entertainment Group, 2009).

Besides SAs, Brown's book is a gem for teachers, coaches, principals, parents, and athletic directors. It provides students with motivation, inspiration, and the desire to excel in the classroom, sports, and life in general. The book discusses the key notion that the passion you have in your classroom is the same you will have in sports and also in your whole life in order to achieve your goals. Get the most out of it by employing the practical approaches highlighted in its pages, which will surely be your ticket to progress, growth, and success in your career as an SA.[3]

Julie Cheville's *Minding the Body: What Student Athletes Know About Learning* describes how sites of learning within a single institution can require distinct, sometimes conflicting, ways of knowing. Over a two-year period, Cheville observed key episodes in the athletic and academic learning of members of a single intercollegiate basketball team. Their testimony highlights the influential partnership of mind and body. On the court, the SAs depended upon ritualized bodily activity to enter into relational knowing. In the classroom, where learning was often characterized by the transmission of information, cognition was detached from concrete activity and interaction.[4]

Dispelling the myth that language is the sole determiner of thought, Cheville explores the implications of academic settings that ignore or devalue the conceptual significance of the body and notes the effect of fragmented institutional sites. Among a host of recommendations, Cheville suggests the need for writing instruction in classrooms and academic support programs that minds the body by assisting students to draw upon their situated experiences of being and knowing for the purposes of critical inquiry.

Authored by Carl Fertman, *Student-Athlete Success: Meeting the Challenges of College Life* is an important guide for undergraduate students and also coaches, parents, and athletic directors who prepare to work with SAs at the college or secondary level. This reader-friendly text provides comprehensive coverage of the many challenges SAs face and the skills

---

[3]For a review of Barry Brown's book, see "The Student-Athlete Playbook — Book Review," https://seriousreading.com cited 3 August 2017.

[4]Julie Cheville, *Minding the Body: What Student Athletes Know About Learning* (Portsmouth, NH: Heinemann, 2001).

needed to address their unique needs and anxieties. Utilizing a positive voice, Fertman focuses the text on athletes' personal capabilities and accomplishments in the classroom and during athletic competition before discussing different types of challenges likely to be encountered. The text emphasizes the techniques needed to accurately assess an individual's health behavior and provides the resources to ensure athletes remain successful on the playing field and in the classroom.[5]

Out of Bounds: When Scholarship Athletes Become Academic Scholars explores the trajectories and challenges of exceptional men and women athletes who later became outstanding academic scholars. The book reports findings from participatory, qualitative research, and problematizes ways to think about the separation and integration of athletic and academic practices — embodied in both institutions and individuals, and reflected through intersecting categories and experiences of race, gender, and social class. Through the provocative and surprising narratives of gifted athletes who became prolific scholars, it offers significantly new ways of thinking about the connections, contradictions, and possibilities of sports and schools.[6]

Because of what Andrew Zimbalist reveals in *Unpaid Professionals: Commercialism and Conflict in Big-Time College Sports*, college sports is really a massively commercialized industry and based on activities that are often irrelevant and even harmful to education. Zimbalist combines empirical research and a talent for storytelling to provide a firm, factual basis for the many arguments that currently rage about the goals, history, structure, incentive system, and legal architecture of college sports. He paints a picture of a system in desperate need of reform and presents bold recommendations to chart a more sensible future.[7]

My book, however, greatly differs from these five publications because most of them are different analytically and/or do not specifically

---

[5] Carl Fertman, *Student-Athlete Success: Meeting The Challenges Of College Life* (Burlington, MA: Jones & Bartlett Learning, 2008).

[6] Jabari Mahiri and Derek Van Rheenen, *Out of Bounds: When Scholarship Athletes Become Academic Scholars* (New York, NY: Peter Lang Inc., International Academic Publishers, 2009).

[7] Andrew Zimbalist, *Unpaid Professionals: Commercialism and Conflict in Big-Time College Sports* (Princeton, NJ: Labyrinth Books, 2008).

use and apply gender, race, and sponsorship data from the NCAA, NAIA, and NJCAA; second, some focus primarily on practical ways for SAs to prepare for and succeed in college; and third, they do not generally or specifically discuss topics in my book from a historical and quantitative or empirical perspective.

BOOK OVERVIEW

Besides Abbreviations and Acknowledgements being the front matter and an Appendix: Tables, Bibliography, Index, and an About the Author page as back matter, *Student Athletes* consists of an Introduction and then six core chapters and a Summary. While the Abbreviations and Acknowledgements are self-explanatory, the Appendix includes tables of data to further measure, supplement, and understand the most important and relevant topics in the chapters. Then, the Bibliography includes articles, books, and Internet sources from the literature, and the Index lists keywords and their location in the text. Except for the front and back matter and Introduction, the following is an overview of the chapters.

Titled "Schools Sports Programs," Chapter 2 reveals the types of men and women sports programs that existed among American colleges and universities (schools) in Divisions I, II, and III of the NCAA and also in any of the NAIA and NJCAA, and highlights primary differences and similarities between them. The programs relate primarily to these schools' 2000 (2000–2001), 2010 (2010–2011), and 2015 (2015–2016) academic years.

Chapter 3 — "Student Athlete Population" — discusses and analyzes the number, distribution, and trend of SAs by gender, race, and sport in schools as of their 2015–2016 academic year and interprets how the population has changed, for example, since 2000–2001. This and other raw data were published in pamphlets, reports, studies, and tables by the three associations.

The fourth chapter, "Student Athletes Academic Performances" identifies and analyzes SAs' academic performances including their progress and graduation success and retention and eligibility rates at American colleges and universities. Furthermore, Chapter 4 compares results of these players' performances academically by sport. This information was published in reports and other documents by the NCAA.

Chapter 5, "Athletics Environment," denotes, in part, different commercial, economic, and financial aspects of college sports programs including the generated revenues, costs, and net revenue derived from them. Other topics in male and female SAs' environment are the benefits of sports events and facilities and also education standards according to rules established by the NCAA, NAIA, and NJCAA, and benefits of these sports players' grants, scholarships, and stipends. These are important subjects highlighted within the chapter.

Chapter 6, "Academics–Sports Controversies," reveals and critiques different types of problems and other issues that affect or may affect athletes while being students in school and currently playing on one or more of their college's and university's sports teams. These include such historical subjects as pay-for-play, players' behavioral crimes and scandals, and men and women SAs' stipends and subsidies. Among the group, some special topics are legal and illegal actions and activities that perhaps involved the athletes' classmates, families, friends, and/or teammates.

Chapter 7, titled "Reforms: Academics–Sports," examines actual reforms that schools and the NCAA have adopted and also those potentially considered to improve SAs' academic performances and increase their graduation rates yet maintain their ethical standards and social behavior. For example, whether to change the amount of time players allocate between academics and sports per semester or week? In addition, should schools be required to invest more resources in mental, psychological, and social well-being services of their sports athletes?

Based on data and other contents within previous chapters, Chapter 8 is a Summary. It highlights and includes the primary results of my research as depicted in Chapters 2–7 of the book. This information is necessary and important because it focuses on the key topics in each chapter for general readers and especially for professionals, researchers, and scholars in the primary audience.

Chapter 2

SCHOOLS SPORTS PROGRAMS

From the mid-to-late 1800s, American colleges and universities began to financially subsidize and support their students' physical activities besides those in intramural and recreational sports. The most prominent activity was their athletic teams' games and matches. Being competitive and also exciting for students to participate in, these contests became increasingly popular among such groups as athletes' family and friends, alumni and faculty, school officials, and journalists in the media. While local newspapers contained articles about them, various events appealed to people in the community including sports fans of all ages and even politicians.[1]

In higher education, schools gradually established budgets and allocated funds to finance their sports programs, and also decided collectively to organize conferences and leagues. This required officials of these groups to schedule games between member schools and adopt and enforce regulations to govern the behavior, conduct, and performances of athletes. Some college and university team sports in that era, for example, included baseball, crew, gymnastics, ice hockey, rugby, soccer, tennis, and track and field.

---

[1]As a reference, see "College Athletics — History of Athletics in U.S. Colleges and Universities," http://www.education.stateuniversity.com cited 28 March 2017; Ellen Staurowsky, "A Brief Historical Perspective on Intercollegiate Athletics." http://www.humankinetics.com cited 28 March 2017; Frank P. Jozsa Jr., *College Sports Inc.: How Commercialism Influences Intercollegiate Athletics* (New York, NY: Springer, 2013).

Although progress continued, sports on school campuses experienced different problems and risks. Some of these involved rules governing athletes, games, and conferences and/or leagues especially regarding those in football. In fact, many injuries, several deaths, and numerous violations occurred among athletes from mass formations and gang tackling in games, professional athletes being hired and compensated to play on schools' football teams, and gamblers who bet on college games and frequently paid players to underperform and then lose them. Although intercollegiate sports programs continued to expand geographically across more American schools particularly during the 1850s through 1890s, there was a variety of complex and unique cultural, ethical, financial, and social challenges and issues to confront and resolve by decision makers who led these institutions.

Despite problems particularly in football and men's basketball programs, intercollegiate athletics and sports games became more competitive, entertaining, lucrative, and otherwise popular and successful throughout the 1900s. To protect student athletes (SAs) from dangerous life-threatening injuries, exploitation, and gambling — which frequently occurred in the late 1800s and early 1900s — representatives from a group of colleges and universities met in New York City in 1906 and founded the Intercollegiate Athletic Association of the United States (IAAUS). Four years later, the IAAUS changed its name and became known officially as the National Collegiate Athletic Association (NCAA).[2]

After forming discussion groups and rules' committees in the 1910s, the NCAA adopted and enforced reforms to curb abuses of college and university athletes, schedule new sports events including postseasons, and do other things. The organization, for example, established national

---

[2] For information about the organization's history, there is "National Collegiate Athletic Association." http://www.britannica.com cited 28 March 2017 and "National Collegiate Athletic Association: History." http://www.thefreedictionary.com cited 28 March 2017. Two books about aspects of the association, including its controversies and operations, are Joe Crowley, *In the Arena: The NCAA's First Century* (Indianapolis, IN: National Collegiate Athletic Association, 2006) and Brian Porto, *The Supreme Court and the NCAA: The Case For Less Commercialism and More Due Process in College Sports* (Ann Arbor, MI: University of Michigan Press, 2012).

championships in several team sports, implemented guidelines for schools in higher education when they recruited athletes and also monitored their scholarships and financial aid, and approved legislation to control the distribution of national television broadcast rights primarily regarding the revenue from football and men's basketball games.

Despite being a non-profit organization, the NCAA periodically restructured itself into divisions and subdivisions, strengthened SAs' academic standards while enrolled in school, and encouraged, approved, and administered the growth of college and university women's athletics programs, services, and representation. In short, NCAA's executive directors led their organization in its mission to establish, govern, and sanction championships, finances, and rules for men and women team sports in intercollegiate athletics.

Between the early 1980s and 2000s inclusive, numerous athletic departments of schools experienced a variety of fiscal, management, and personnel problems that evolved from forming, launching, and operating their sports programs. While the NCAA increased pressure on school officials to establish, promote, and maintain academic standards and the integrity of their male and female athletes, some major college and university sports programs became increasingly dependent on outside sources for their assets, funds, resources, and services. In other words, they had to finance and expand their facilities and add or reduce a number of programs and teams, earn and invest revenue from exposure on television and in the media, become increasingly more competitive in games and tournaments, and compete each season to win conference and league titles and national championships.

During this period, however, several American sports economists, researchers, and prominent scholars and educators in academia studied the decisions and roles of officials and groups affiliated with schools including their chancellors and presidents, alumni associations, boards of trustees, athletic directors, and coaches. As such, these people analyzed controversial topics and subjects related to higher education and sports, and then performed studies and also authored articles, books, and reports about them. That literature, in part, dealt with the academic performances of SAs, increasing commercialization of collegiate sports programs and compensation of head coaches, and ability of the NCAA to govern the behavior, conduct, ethics, and strategies of its member institutions and the operations of their athletic programs.

Because of these research efforts, major and minor reforms were published by the media in order to expose, justify, and support or otherwise condemn, criticize, and denounce any relationships between commercialism and intercollegiate athletics. Besides reforms from current and former administrators and faculty of NCAA Division I, II and III schools, there were various models, proposals, and recommendations to reallocate revenue from games and tournaments among university sports programs and to improve operations of collegiate sports from three Knight Commissions and such organizations as the Collegiate Athletes Coalition. Although the types of reforms were different among officials of these groups, in some way, each proposal or recommendation contributed new concepts, ideas, and/or principles of how to maintain the academic integrity of male and female athletes while minimizing and regulating the influences of commercialism of sports programs within colleges and universities.

Thus far, this section of Chapter 2 briefly highlighted why and how intercollegiate athletics in America emerged and developed from the mid-to-late 1800s to early 2000s. During each period of this era, there were specific financial, ethical, and social problems that involved schools' athletic directors, coaches, and their SAs. Consequently, campaigns by college and university officials and their public relations departments were necessary to obtain assets, donations, and money from alumni, business organizations, communities, and government in order for these schools to finance and operate their teams, especially in such revenue-producing sports as football and men's and women's basketball, and also to subsidize athletes' performances and the seasons of non-revenue sports like bowling, cross country, field hockey, rowing, tennis, track and field, and volleyball.

In the next part of this chapter, the contents reveal, highlight, and compare differences and trends among NCAA men and women team sports that occurred within United States (U.S.) colleges and universities mostly during the 2000s. As a result, readers of this book understand and realize, in part, how schools have operated and managed their intercollegiate athletics programs and thus why some of them might temporarily or always struggle to be more competitive and successful relative to others within divisions of their conference.[3]

NCAA

Since the late 1940s, the NCAA periodically surveyed its members (schools) and reported such information to the public as their participation in and sponsorship of various athletic programs. As a result, data from these organizations' website denotes the number and type of sports sponsored and played by college and university teams in Divisions' I, II, and III for selected academic years.

Some schools' sports have schedules that extend into different months during parts of two calendar years. These include, for example, such team sports as football and also men's and women's basketball and track and field. Other college and university sports teams, however, play their seasons and postseasons during a single calendar year. A few of these are men's and women's cross country and volleyball in the fall, fencing and skiing in the winter, and lacrosse and tennis in the spring.

It is interesting to note that, for various reasons, the NCAA did not establish and maintain a consistent, comprehensive, and uniform system of data collection and reports until the fall of 1981. Indeed, that was the beginning of the 1981 college/university sports season during these schools' 1981–1982 academic year. As such, this section includes two tables of sports data specifically for schools' academic years of 1981–1982, 1990–1991, and 2000–2001 each for their fall, winter, and spring seasons. To access the data, it is contained in Tables A2.1 and A2.2 of the Appendix.

Historically from academic years 1949–1950 to 1969–1970, the total number of NCAA active, affiliated, allied, and associate members

---

[3] Besides the NCAA, this chapter includes the NAIA and NJCAA. Since they are relatively small organizations with fewer sports and conferences, Chapter 2 excludes the United States Collegiate Athletic Association (USCAA), National Christian College Athletic Association (NCCAA), Association of Christian College Athletics (ACCA), California Community College Athletic Association (CCCAA), and other associations, leagues, and conferences in individual sports.

(i.e., school sponsorships) almost doubled to 720. In size, the largest group of them was active members followed by allied, affiliated, and associate members. Then in academic year 1970–1971, the NCAA combined men and women sports and ranked 24 of the group according to the total number of schools in the NCAA's university division and college division that sponsored any of them.

The three most and least common sports during that academic year were, respectively, basketball, baseball, and golf, as compared to rugby, squash, and volleyball. Furthermore, football ranked seventh with 448 teams, soccer tenth with 346, and sailing twenty-first with 37. Financially, the two NCAA divisions' total expenses exceeded total revenues by $40 million, a deficit that required funds from sources other than these schools' athletic departments such as alumni, donors, government agencies, and even business and community organizations.

Sports Period I

In Table A2.1 of the Appendix are the number of school sponsorships by NCAA Division and Sport for the 1981 sports season (academic year 1981–1982) and 1990 sports season (academic year 1990–1991), and in Table A2.2 for the 2000 sports season (academic year 2000–2001). Based on information contained in the two tables, what is important to remember about intercollegiate athletics during these seasons and also what was different between the three divisions relative to the types and distribution of their team sports and sponsoring schools?[4]

First, the total number of team sports sponsored by schools across three NCAA divisions and 20 academic years increased from 11,615 in 1981–1982 to 16,390 in 2000–2001. In other words, there was a net increase of 4,775 sponsorships or approximately 41 percent. For various reasons, the number of such fall sports as men's water polo and women's field hockey actually declined during this period as did men's and women's fencing in the winter and also men's and women's crew in the spring.

---

[4] "NCAA Sports Sponsorship and Participation Rates Report 1981–82 — 2015–16." http://www.ncaa.org cited 13 March 2017 and "Sport Sponsorship, Participation, and Demographics Search." http://www.web1.ncaa.org cited 8 March 2017.

In addition, schools in Division I, II, and III eliminated a number of unpopular team sports between the 1981 and 2000 seasons. These included men's rifle and women's badminton in the winter and men and women's crew in the spring. Alternatively, Title IX provided an opportunity for some schools to expand their athletic departments during the early 1980s to 2000s by adding new sports like women's archery and temporarily rugby in the fall, rifle mixed in the winter, and women's rowing and sand volleyball in the spring.

Second, from academic years 1981–1982 to 2000–2001, there were major and minor changes among the total number of school sponsorships between the three NCAA divisions. Due to differences in budgets of athletic departments and such factors as Title IX, popularity of various team sports, revenue from commercial sources, and growth in student populations and their athletic fees, the total number of Division II and III school sponsorships each increased, respectively, by 47 percent and 59 percent while surprisingly those in Division I expanded by only 1,040 or 21 percent. From the early 1980s to 2000s, perhaps the latter group of schools allocated proportionately more assets and resources from budgets and outside sources to financially support their highest revenue sports of football and men's basketball, while schools competing in Divisions' II and III simply subsidized their new and also existing team sports more equitably and responsibly between sexes.

Third, across NCAA divisions, the number of school sponsorships by seasons increased from academic years 1981–1982 to 2000–2001. Specifically, these changes were 2,236 or 72 percent in the fall, 320 or 8 percent in the winter, and 2,216 or 49 percent in the spring. Thus, the number of sponsorships and their percentage increases varied greatly between fall, winter, and spring of academic years. This occurred, in part, because the NCAA approved such new athletic programs as women's bowling, equestrian and rowing, and because small and midsized liberal arts schools — especially in Division III — decided to adopt and finance additional non-revenue men's and women's sports programs. Moreover, schools' athletic directors received permission from college and university administrators and trustees to inflate their annual budgets, increase expenditures and perhaps debt balances on sports, request cash and loans from such outside sources as businesses, financial institutions, and other local organizations, and invest increasing amounts into existing and new team sports and also athletic facilities.

Fourth, there were variations in the number of sponsors in sports seasons of NCAA Divisions I, II, and III. From 1981 to 2001, for example, Division III schools added more sponsors in the fall than Divisions I and II. In contrast to them, during winter and spring sports seasons, the largest increase in sponsorships of athletic programs were in Division I. Apparently, such fall sports as men's and women's cross country and football, and women's volleyball were particularly appealing activities to expand in Division III schools. Meanwhile, during winters of 1981 and 2000, the most popular sports in Division I schools were men and women's basketball. But in the spring, they were men's tennis and golf in 1981 and women's tennis and men's golf in 2000. Despite the risks and increasing costs of operating college sports programs during the 1980s to early 2000s, a majority of NCAA Division I schools gradually shifted a portion of their athletics department's resources and funds from men to women sports in order to diversify their types of programs for students and spectators, and also because of equity and gender standards or goals established by Title IX.

Fifth, across three NCAA divisions in the fall, winter, and spring of academic year 1981–1982, the team sports with most college and university sponsors were equally men's and women's basketball and then men's tennis, golf, cross country, and baseball. Then in academic year 2000–2001, four NCAA team sports each had more than 900 sponsors. Ranked numerically, these were women's and men's basketball and then women's volleyball and cross country. Except for football and men's basketball in the majority of Division I and a few Division II schools, the other sports did not earn enough revenue to operate in their seasons at a surplus.

Sixth, for divisions and seasons stated previously, the eight NCAA sports with fewer than 20 sponsors each in academic year 1981–1982 were men's bowling, squash, and sailing, and women's badminton, bowling, ice hockey, rifle, skiing, squash, and sailing. However, 20 years later, team sports with the least number of sponsors were men's archery, gymnastics, squash, bowling, and sailing and also women's archery, bowling, and squash. Since they were not popular sports among college students or exciting activities to participate in by SAs, interest in and number of men's badminton and bowling and women's team handball each declined at schools, and thus the NCAA eliminated them. The others, meanwhile, continued to exist as sports because they receive subsidies to operate primarily from football and men's basketball programs, funds from alumni, donors, and student fees, and perhaps money and resources from companies in the private sector. In addition, they satisfy Title IX requirements.

Seventh, from academic years 1981–1982 to 2000–2001, the number of sponsorships across NCAA divisions in football increased by 127 or 25 percent and in men's basketball by 250 or 33 percent. Although these two team sports generate much more revenue for schools than others do, they are expensive to operate because of expenses to locate, recruit, and sign high school athletes and to pay for their equipment, scholarships, services, travel and tutors, and to afford the salaries and fringe benefits of coaches and their staffs. Consequently, relatively few schools and small proportions of them within each NCAA division refused to assume responsibility and the financial risk to launch and schedule new football and men's basketball programs after the early 2000s.

Eighth, across the three NCAA divisions in academic year 1981–1982, there were four different men's and women's sports in the fall, 11 each men's and women's teams in the winter, and eight men's and seven women's sports in the spring. In academic year 2000–2001, six different men's and five women's sports existed in the fall, and 10 men's and nine women's clubs in the winter. In comparison to them, during the spring, seven men's and eight women's sports teams performed for their schools. In addition to those sports, men's bowling competed that academic year, but did so in no specific months or seasons.

Based on the types of data in Tables A2.1 and A2.2, various colleges and universities dropped a few NCAA sports but added others from the 1981 to 2000 season. At the end of the period, however, overall results denote that the number of them expanded by three or 37 percent in the fall, decreased by two or 9 percent in the winter, and remained constant in the spring. In short, the number of sports within these divisions was not significantly different throughout these schools' 20 academic years.

Sports Period II

Between 2000 and 2016, there were several important changes in the NCAA's emerging sports programs across academic years. In 2000–2001, for example, women's ice hockey and water polo were removed from the list of emerging sports and the Association sponsored a national collegiate championship in these team sports. One year later, Division III established women's ice hockey as a divisional championship while Divisions I and II continued to participate in a national collegiate championship. Furthermore, women's rowing national collegiate championship was reclassified and also championships established in the sport for Divisions' I, II, and III.[5]

During 2002–2003, women's rugby was added as an emerging sport in each NCAA division and then in 2004, women's bowling was removed from the list of emerging sports and the association sponsored a national collegiate championship in that sport. In 2009, women's archery, badminton, synchronized swimming, and team handball were removed from the list of emerging sports in all NCAA divisions due to lack of growth in sponsors. Then in 2010, the NCAA added women's sand volleyball to the list of emerging sports in Divisions I and II.

As reflected in Table 2.1, the total number of sports sponsorships by Division I, II, and III schools combined increased by 2,731 or approximately 16 percent from the 2000–2001 to 2015–2016 academic year. Among groups, men's sports sponsorships expanded by 988 or 12 percent and women's by 1,743 or 20 percent. Because of such things as Title IX, their growing popularity on campuses, and actual economic costs and student demand, more colleges and universities added women rather than men's sports.

Regarding those in the fall season, men and women cross county, soccer, and volleyball each significantly increased during the 15-year period along with men's football and rugby and also women's field hockey. While men's rowing declined from 2011 to 2015, archery was dropped by four schools prior to 2010 because of poor attendances at

---

[5] "NCAA Emerging Sports Timeline." http://www.ncaa.org cited 21 March 2017 and "New Guide Released for Emerging Sports." http://www.ncaa.org cited 21 March 2017.

home and away matches and also SAs' lack of enthusiasm to participate in the sport.

Despite its ability to generate revenue for schools' athletic department, football grew from 624 to 674 sponsors or only 8 percent as a fall sport. Besides of costs for equipment, insurance, and uniforms, the sport is simply too expensive to operate by many colleges and universities and it usually requires an investment in — and maintenance of — a stadium to attract fans to their home games from nearby communities and metropolitan areas.

Although they had different numbers participating from 2000 to the 2015 academic year, both men and women sponsorships expanded almost equally at 14–15 percent. In other words, the table roughly indicates the number of sponsors of these eight sports for three academic years and their growth individually and as a group.

With respect to the winter season of three academic years as depicted in Table 2.1, schools had the opportunity to play in and financially support from zero to 12 sports. Among sponsors, while men's increased by 221 or almost 9 percent, women's rose even faster at approximately 16 percent or by 383. These differences occurred because of such factors as Title IX and growth in student populations.

From the 2000–2001 to 2010–2011 winter season, for example, some men and women sports combined had fewer sponsors including fencing, rifle, and skiing, but alternatively the numbers in basketball, ice hockey, swimming, and indoor track were each greater in the period. While women's but not men's bowling and gymnastics also expanded, wrestling declined by 11 or 5 percent among the group.

After 2010–2011, there were some important numbers and changes in them regarding sports sponsorships across NCAA divisions. Accordingly, men's and women's basketball, indoor track, and swimming programs were, by far, the most popular sports while the least attractive included bowling, rifle, skiing, and squash. For both groups, such sports as basketball, ice hockey, squash, swimming, and indoor track had more sponsors but not men's bowling, fencing, rifle, and skiing or women's gymnastics, ice hockey, rifle, and skiing. Meanwhile, wrestling reversed its downward trend and added 8 or 4 percent new sponsors. Consequently, in 2015–2016, women's winter sports exceeded men's in growth and total

Table 2.1. Men and Women Sports Sponsorships, NCAA Divisions I–III, Selected Academic Years.

Sport	2000–2001		2010–2011		2015–2016	
	Men	**Women**	**Men**	**Women**	**Men**	**Women**
Fall						
Archery	1	3	0	0	0	0
Cross County	860	923	952	1,026	999	1,075
Field Hockey	0	248	0	264	0	274
Football	624	0	644	0	674	0
Rowing	60	0	60	0	56	0
Rugby	0	0	1	0	3	0
Soccer	730	851	794	984	833	1,035
Volleyball	83	975	95	1,039	124	1,072
Winter						
Badminton	0	3	0	0	0	0
Basketball	991	1,020	1,051	1,072	1,092	1,109
Bowling	1	25	1	62	1	70
Fencing	52	46	34	41	34	43
Gymnastics	26	90	17	83	16	83
Ice Hockey	132	63	135	87	142	99
Rifle	45	45	28	34	2	9
Skiing	44	48	32	35	32	34
Squash	26	30	30	29	32	30
Swimming	385	470	410	524	427	544
Track/Indoor	553	593	616	694	701	795
Wrestling	235	0	224	0	232	0
Spring						
Baseball	860	0	922	0	952	0
Beach Volleyball	0	0	0	0	0	59
Equestrian	10	47	7	46	1	34
Golf	750	437	811	575	833	664

(Continued)

Table 2.1. (*Continued*)

Sport	2000–2001		2010–2011		2015–2016	
	Men	**Women**	**Men**	**Women**	**Men**	**Women**
Lacrosse	208	238	280	357	365	485
Rowing	0	138	0	142	0	145
Rugby	0	0	0	5	0	12
Sailing	25	0	23	0	4	0
Softball	0	877	0	969	0	1,006
Tennis	774	891	758	921	767	927
Track/Outdoor	659	696	722	778	800	883
Triathlon	0	0	0	0	1	4
Water Polo	46	50	43	60	45	59

Note: Sponsorships are schools' number of teams. NCAA is the National Athletic Association. Swimming includes diving and synchronized swimming. Rowing and Rugby are men's sports in the fall and women's in the spring.

Source: "NCAA Sports Sponsorship and Participation Rates Report 1981–1982 to 2014–2015." http://www.ncaa.org cited 13 March 2017 and "Sports Sponsorship, Participation and Demographics Search." http://www.ncaa.org cited 8 March 2017.

number of sponsors mostly in such activities as bowling, gymnastics, swimming, and indoor track, and also in fencing and rifle.

With respect to spring sports during the three academic periods in Table 2.1, the gap between the number of men and women sponsors grew larger from 2000–2011 to 2010–2011 and then from 2010–2011 to 2015–2016. In the middle period, for example, only men's golf, lacrosse, and outdoor track had more sponsors than before while eight women's sports expanded and zero declined in numbers. In addition, men's equestrian, sailing, tennis, and water polo each decreased from 2000–2001 to 2010–2011. Besides Title IX, these changes reflect such factors as the growing popularity among sponsors of rowing, rugby and softball — which were not men's sports — but also baseball.

After 2010–2011, there were more sponsors in seven men and nine women spring sports. The biggest improvements occurred in women's beach volleyball, golf, lacrosse, softball, tennis, and outdoor track. Even so, equestrian and water polo fell as did men's equestrian and sailing. Such other women's sports as rowing, rugby, and tennis had marginal changes along with men's baseball, golf, tennis, and water polo. In other words, from 2010–2011 to 2015–2016, colleges and universities sponsored women's spring sports to a greater extent than men's because the former group were becoming more competitive as athletes and also succeeded as students in their classes.

Table 2.1 denotes, in part, that from 2000–2001 to 2015–2016 in the winter and spring seasons, women sports sponsors doubled men's on a percentage basis. Besides cross country, field hockey, soccer, and volleyball in the fall, there was growth across winter and spring seasons in basketball, ice hockey, squash, and several other women's sports. These differences in sponsoring team sports occurred because of changes in college and university student populations, better opportunities for women athletes to play and compete in games, decline of cultural barriers between the sexes, and improvements in preparing SAs to excel academically in higher education.

Based on total and individual sponsorships in Table 2.1, the next section reveals how men's sports programs changed specifically within and between the NCAA's Division I, II, and III during a 17-year period. This data denotes which sports dominated their rivals while others failed to expand and become less rather than more prevalent in colleges and universities.

MEN'S SPORTS PROGRAMS

Division I

Within the 2000 to 2015 academic years, the number of men's teams — including provisional members — in this division ranged alphabetically from low to high by sport and season. During the fall, these included archery 0–1; cross country 296–314; football 234–251; rowing 22–28; rugby 0–1; soccer 195–204; and volleyball 21–23. Thus, archery and rugby had the lowest number of teams in the fall season with the highest being in cross country and then football.[6]

---

[6]Among the three NCAA divisions, Division I schools generally have the biggest student bodies, manage the largest athletics budgets, and offer the most generous number of

In the winter season, men's teams varied as follows: basketball 321–346; bowling 0–1; fencing 19–22; gymnastics 15–21; ice hockey 58–60; rifle 17–31; skiing 11–14; squash 8–12; swimming 134–149; track/indoor 240–260; and wrestling 76–90. Among these team sports, bowling had the least number of members and basketball the most, followed by indoor track and swimming.

For the smallest to largest number of teams in the spring season, they consisted of baseball 284–297; equestrian 0–1; golf 285–298; lacrosse 54–69; sailing 7–11; tennis 256–278; track/outdoor 240–260; triathlon 0–1; and water polo 21–23. While equestrian and triathlon had the lowest membership, the highest number played golf and then baseball and tennis.

To count and analyze the number of member schools that sponsor Division I men's teams, Table 2.2 includes data about them for seasons of the 2000–2001, 2010–2011, and 2015–2016 academic years. The table includes seven sports that existed in the fall, 11 in the winter, and nine in the spring. Next are highlights of the data and its significance within and across years in the periods.

Because of economic, school-specific, sport and other reasons, the total number of NCAA Division I men's teams increased by only 13 or less than 1 percent from academic years 2000–2001 to 2015–2016. Nevertheless, as of the beginning of the 17-year period in comparison to the end of it, there were changes among schools' sports programs each season with 25 or 3 percent more teams added in the fall, 27 or

---

scholarships. Schools who are members of Division I commit to maintaining a high academic standard for SAs in addition to a wide range of opportunities for athletics participation. With nearly 350 colleges and universities in its membership, Division I schools field more than 6,000 athletic teams and provide opportunities for more than 170,000 SAs to compete in NCAA sports each year. Division I is subdivided based on football sponsorship. Schools that participate in bowl games belong to the Football Bowl Subdivision. Those that participate in the NCAA-run football championship belong to the Football Championship Subdivision. A third group does not sponsor football. The subdivisions apply only to football; all other sports are considered simply Division I. For data on this division, see "Division I." http:www.ncaa.org cited 23 March 2017 and Erin Irick, "Report: National Collegiate Athletic Association." http://www.ncaa.publications.org cited 23 March 2017.

Table 2.2.   Men Sports Teams, NCAA Divisions I–III, Selected Academic Years.

Sport	I			II			III		
	2000	**2010**	**2015**	**2000**	**2010**	**2015**	**2000**	**2010**	**2015**
Fall									
Archery	1	0	0	0	0	0	0	0	0
Cross Country	305	307	311	230	257	283	325	388	405
Football	236	238	252	157	168	174	231	238	248
Rowing	28	28	28	6	3	3	26	29	25
Rugby	0	0	1	0	0	1	0	1	1
Soccer	198	201	202	171	190	216	361	403	415
Volleyball	22	23	21	19	16	25	42	56	78
Winter									
Basketball	321	337	346	288	302	322	382	412	424
Bowling	0	0	0	1	1	0	0	0	1
Fencing	22	20	20	7	2	2	23	12	12
Gymnastics	21	16	15	1	0	0	4	1	1
Ice Hockey	58	58	59	7	6	7	67	71	76
Rifle	27	18	2	2	3	0	16	7	0
Skiing	12	11	11	9	6	6	23	15	15
Squash	8	11	12	0	0	0	18	19	20
Swimming	149	136	132	52	69	73	184	205	222
Track/Indoor	252	251	260	107	134	167	194	231	274
Wrestling	90	80	76	41	56	60	104	88	96
Spring									
Baseball	285	293	295	232	255	272	343	374	385
Equestrian	0	0	1	3	0	0	7	7	0
Golf	293	292	298	188	226	239	269	293	296
Lacrosse	55	60	69	30	41	66	123	179	230
Sailing	8	10	2	1	1	0	16	12	2
Tennis	278	256	258	180	175	175	316	327	334
Track/Outdoor	270	273	281	150	176	215	239	273	304
Triathlon	0	0	0	0	0	0	0	0	1
Water Polo	23	22	23	6	7	7	17	14	15

Note: NCAA is the National Athletic Association. Academic years were actually 2000–2001, 2010–2011, and 2015–2016. Swimming includes diving.

Source: "NCAA Sports Sponsorship and Participation Rates Report 1981–1982 to 2015–2016." http://www.ncaa.org cited 13 March 2017 and "Sports Sponsorship, Participation and Demographics Search." http://www.ncaa.org cited 8 March 2017.

approximately 3 percent less in the winter, and 15 or 2 percent more in the spring. Based on that distribution, here is an interpretation of the data in the table and its effects each season in Division I.

As of fall 2010, for example, there were more squads than 10 years earlier in cross country, football, soccer, and volleyball, one less in archery, same number in rowing, and zero in rugby. Five academic years later, only the number of volleyball teams declined while all others besides archery and rowing experienced growth. Thus, during these seasons, Division I sports programs expanded overall but especially football by 16 or almost 7 percent. Although expensive to operate as a program, this is an important, popular, and revenue-generating sport for schools particularly those in the major conferences.

Of 11 sports in the winter season, approximately 60 percent of all men's teams were in basketball plus indoor track with relatively a few of them in skiing and squash and zero in bowling. From the 2000–2001 to 2010–2011 academic year, seven sports had fewer teams while more played basketball and squash but none in bowling. As of 2015–2016, numbers continued to decline in gymnastics, rifle, swimming, and wrestling but also increased in basketball, ice hockey, squash and indoor track, and remained the same in bowling, fencing, and skiing. Because of higher costs to operate and perhaps students' lack of interest, there were fewer total winter sports in 2015 than in 2010 especially in gymnastics, rifle, swimming, and wrestling.

Spring sports combined had approximately 41 percent of all Division I men's teams in each period as depicted in Table 2.2. While baseball, lacrosse, sailing, and outdoor track each expanded from academic year 2000–2001 to 2010–2011, those in golf, tennis, and water polo dropped with zero of the group in equestrian and triathlon. Five academic years later, seven sports grew marginally larger but not sailing or triathlon. In other words, the number of sports programs fell from 1,212 in 2000 to 1,206 in 2010 but then increased to 1,227 in 2015 primarily in baseball, lacrosse, and outdoor track.

In comparing the three groups across years, men's fall sports had the largest growth both in numbers and percentages of the three seasons in NCAA Division I schools. Alternatively, winter sports declined from 2000–2001 to 2015–2016 due to funding problems, lack of interest among fans, school officials and students, higher costs to operate some sports with few teams, and other factors. Besides cross country, football, and soccer in the fall, basketball and squash in the winter, and baseball, lacrosse, and outdoor track in the spring, there was uneven growth or worsening trends among other Division I sports programs during the 17-year period.

Division II

Throughout the fall seasons, five men's team sports were active and existed in this division during 2000–2001 and 2010–2011 and six in 2015–2016. As a group, they increased by 119 or approximately 20 percent within the period. From 2000 to 2010, for example, such sports as cross country, football, and soccer had impressive growth in numbers while rowing declined by 50 percent and volleyball by 14 percent, yet no schools adopted archery. By the 2015 academic year, teams in cross country, football, and soccer continued to expand, volleyball increased by 9 or 56 percent and rugby by 1 or 100 percent, and rowing did not change with three teams. Consequently, fall in the 2000–2001 to 2015–2016 academic years was an expansionary period in Division II history and more so than in Division I.[7]

In total, men's winter sports in NCAA Division II increased by 122 teams or 23 percent during the 17-year period. From 2000 to 2010, in fact,

---

[7] Division II is a collection of more than 300 NCAA colleges and universities that provide thousands of SAs the opportunity to compete at a high level of scholarship athletics while excelling in the classroom and fully engaging in the broader campus experience. This balance — in which SAs are recognized for their academic success, athletics contributions, and campus/community involvement — is the core of the Division II philosophy.

Each NCAA division emphasizes athletics and academic excellence for their SAs since the NCAA's overall mission is to make athletics an integral part of the educational experience at all member schools. The differences among the divisions emerge primarily in how schools choose to fund their athletics programs and in the national attention they command. Most Division I institutions, for example, choose to devote more financial resources to support their athletics programs, and many are able to do so because of the large media contracts Division I conferences are able to attract, mostly to showcase the publicly popular sports of football and men's basketball. See "Division II." http://www. ncaa.org cited 23 March 2017.

growth in such sports as basketball, rifle, swimming, indoor track, and wrestling more than offset fewer teams in fencing, gymnastics, ice hockey, and skiing. Meanwhile, bowling and squash remained constant.

Then during years 2010–2015, 58 new teams joined the group led by those in basketball, ice hockey, swimming, indoor track, and wrestling. However, bowling, fencing, gymnastics, rifle, skiing, and squash were least popular of the 11 sports. Consequently, more schools in Division II were aggressive, consistent, and successful in the winter season by adding one or more basketball, ice hockey, swimming, indoor track, and wrestling teams to their athletic departments despite more costs and other problems associated with these types of sports programs.

In spring seasons, NCAA Division II schools expanded their programs by 91 clubs or 11 percent from 2000 to 2010. Besides growth in baseball, golf, lacrosse, outdoor track, and water polo, fewer teams existed in equestrian and tennis, but the same number in sailing and triathlon. After 2010, men's spring sports increased in size by approximately 10 percent led by the same group as before while four others did not change. For the two periods combined, 184 teams joined the Division in the spring. Because of more funds and also increasing interest among students and fans, schools decided to offer additional sports during March to May of these academic years.

In contrast to changes in Division I, there was a significant boost in athletic programs within Division II from academic years 2000–2001 to 2015–2016. Of 27 total sports, only rowing, bowling, fencing, gymnastics, skiing, equestrian, and sailing declined numerically. Financed partly by student fees and donations from various sources, the budgets of many schools increased to support their new teams.

Division III

During the 17-year period in Table 2.2, the number of NCAA Division III teams increased from 1,330 in 2010 to 1,567 in 2015 or almost 18 percent. As of 2010 in the fall season, all men's sports had added new members except for archery. Five years later, four sports continued to expand while rowing declined and rugby remained the same with one team. With an increase in teams from 985 to 1,172 or approximately 19 percent in the fall, the division experienced significant growth because of SAs' participation particularly in cross country, football, soccer, and volleyball.[8]

In the division's winter season, the number of men's teams expanded from 1,015 to 1,061 or 4 percent during 2000–2010 and then five years later increased to 1,141 or 7 percent. Besides basketball, the most popular sports included ice hockey, swimming, and indoor track. Alternatively, such sports as fencing, gymnastics, rifle, skiing, and wrestling had fewer teams. For various reasons such as their appeal to students and fans and perhaps faculty and school officials, most winter sports in both Divisions' II and III were more prominent on campuses after 2000.

Except for equestrian, sailing, and water polo, the other Division III men's sports added members in the spring season from 2000–2001 to 2015–2016. For example, lacrosse increased by 107 teams or 86 percent and outdoor track by 65 or 27 percent. Besides them, baseball and golf each grew by more than 10 percent. Of the three groups in the table, Division III sports had the most teams in the spring seasons of 2001, 2011, and 2016. Because schools did not award athletic scholarships, some SAs likely received financial aid and grants while others fully paid for their education.

To summarize results in Table 2.2, Divisions' II and III men's sports programs increased in size during the fall, winter, and spring seasons from 2000–2001 to 2010–2011 and 2015–2016. The same results occurred for programs in Division I except in the winter season and spring (2000–2010) when the number of team sports fell among the group.

For several or more schools in Division I, it simply cost too much to operate and sustain such men's sports as fencing, gymnastics, rifle, skiing,

---

[8] More than 180,000 SAs at 450 institutions make up Division III, the largest NCAA division both in number of participants and number of schools. The Division III experience offers participation in a competitive athletic environment that pushes SAs to excel on the field and build upon their potential by tackling new challenges across campus. Academics are the primary focus for Division III SAs. The division minimizes the conflicts between athletics and academics, and helps SAs' progress toward graduation through shorter practice and playing seasons and regional competition that reduces the time away from their academic studies. Participants are integrated on campus and treated like all other members of the student body, keeping them focused on being a student first. See "Division III." http://www.ncaa.org cited 23 March 2017.

swimming, and wrestling in the winter and sailing and tennis, for example, in the spring. Furthermore, athletes had little success competing against rivals in their conference, teams failed to attract enough fans to home games and matches, more schools increasingly invested in women's sports, and schools' programs did not get sufficient financial support from organizations within their local communities.

Women Sports Programs

Division I

Within the 2000–2001 to 2015–2016 academic years, the number of women's teams in the division — including provisional members — ranged alphabetically from low-to-high by sport and season. During the fall, these included archery 0–3; cross country 318–343; field hockey 76–79; soccer 274–328; and volleyball 308–329. Thus, archery had the lowest number of teams in the fall season with the highest being in cross country and then volleyball and soccer.

In the winter season, women's teams varied as follows: basketball 318–344; bowling 22–36; fencing 9–20; gymnastics 61–67; ice hockey 27–36; rifle 21–34; skiing 12–16; squash 7–11; swimming 185–198; and track/indoor 279–322. Among these team sports, squash had the least number of members and basketball the most, followed by indoor track and swimming.

For the smallest to largest number of teams in the spring season, they consisted of beach volleyball 0–48; equestrian 9–20; golf 206–261; lacrosse 71–110; rowing 82–88; rugby 1–8; softball 249–290; tennis 304–319; track/outdoor 286–331; and water polo 27–34. While equestrian and rugby had the least teams in the group, the highest number of them played tennis.

To reveal and analyze the number of members that sponsor NCAA Division I women's teams, Table 2.3 includes data about them for seasons of the 2000–2001, 2010–2011, and 2015–2016 academic years. The table includes five sports that existed in the fall and 10 each in the winter and spring. Next are highlights of the data and its significance within and across periods.

Table 2.3. Women's Sports Teams, NCAA Divisions I–III, Selected Academic Years.

Sport	I			II			III		
	2000	**2010**	**2015**	**2000**	**2010**	**2015**	**2000**	**2010**	**2015**
Fall									
Archery	3	0	0	0	0	0	0	0	0
Cross Country	318	333	343	255	283	309	350	410	423
Field Hockey	76	79	78	25	26	31	147	159	165
Soccer	274	315	328	199	242	268	378	427	439
Volleyball	308	321	329	271	292	310	396	426	433
Winter									
Badminton	0	0	0	0	0	0	3	0	0
Basketball	318	335	344	288	302	323	414	435	442
Bowling	22	33	33	3	21	26	0	8	11
Fencing	26	23	24	3	3	4	17	15	15
Gymnastics	67	63	61	7	5	7	16	15	15
Ice Hockey	27	35	36	2	3	5	34	49	58
Rifle	31	22	8	2	4	1	12	8	0
Skiing	14	12	12	10	7	7	24	16	15
Squash	8	10	11	0	0	0	22	19	19
Swimming	185	195	196	67	86	95	227	243	253
Track/Indoor	279	305	324	112	152	191	202	237	280
Spring									
Beach Volleyball	0	0	48	0	0	7	0	0	4
Equestrian	9	18	19	7	5	4	31	23	11
Golf	206	248	261	85	160	197	146	167	206
Lacrosse	71	89	110	26	62	101	141	206	274
Rowing	82	85	88	14	17	16	42	40	41
Rugby	0	2	8	0	1	2	0	2	2
Softball	249	283	290	250	279	301	378	407	415
Tennis	312	314	317	217	230	233	362	377	377
Track/Outdoor	286	312	331	160	188	241	250	278	311
Triathlon	0	0	0	0	0	3	0	0	1
Water Polo	27	33	32	8	8	10	15	19	17

Note: NCAA is the National Athletic Association. Academic Years were actually 2000–2001, 2010–2011, and 2015–2016. Swimming includes diving and synchronized swimming.

Source: "NCAA Sports Sponsorship and Participation Rates Report 1981–1982 to 2014–2015." http://www.ncaa.org cited 13 March 2017 and "Sports Sponsorship, Participation and Demographics Search." http://www.ncaa.org cited 8 March 2017.

In the fall season, the number of women's sports teams increased from 979 to 1,078 or 10 percent. Except for archery, there was a total of 69 or approximately 7 percent more clubs in cross county, field hockey, soccer, and volleyball in 2010 than 2000. Although field hockey declined by one team after 2010 and archery did not return as a sport, the trend in growth continued into 2015 for cross county, soccer, and volleyball.

During the 17-year period, cross country grew larger by 7 percent, soccer 19 percent, and volleyball 6 percent. In other words, these sports became increasingly competitive and popular activities among colleges and universities, and also reasons to recruit and sign contracts with competent and outstanding women SAs who graduated from high school. Compared to men's fall sports in NCAA Division I, women had fewer of them overall each year but their growth rate was three times higher from 2010 to 2015. While only men's teams existed in football and women's in field hockey, the latter group of athletes dominated the numbers in cross country, soccer, and volleyball. Consequently, schools became increasingly equitable, diversified, and busy in their types of sports programs during these years.

During the winter season, women's sports programs increased by 56 or 5 percent from 2000 to 2010 and then by 16 or 2 percent after 2010. While basketball, ice hockey, squash, and swimming advanced throughout the 17-year period, ultimately there were fewer teams in fencing, gymnastics, rifle and skiing. Meanwhile, some of the other women's sports either decreased or increased in number but then changed again after 2010. As denoted in Table 2.3, the two largest and smallest in the winter group were, respectively, basketball and indoor track, besides badminton, squash and skiing.

With respect to other results in their winter seasons, women had seven more teams than men in 2000, 95 more in 2010, and 116 more in 2015. Among the most popular sports in both groups of Division I, basketball ranked first, track second, and swimming third while the least in number included rifle, skiing, and squash. Since 2000, women's sports have increased faster than men's because of such things as Title IX, differences in their operating costs and funding, and diversifying sports programs within schools.

Relative to women's spring seasons in NCAA Division I, their total number of clubs rose by 142 or 11 percent from 2000 to 2010 and then by

120 or 8 percent after 2010. Within the first period (2000–2010), all sports increased in size except for beach volleyball and triathlon. And, except for a small decline in water polo and no change in triathlon, they increased again during 2010–2015 including beach volleyball from zero to 48. Among schools in the Division, spring rather than fall or winter, has been the ideal season for them to significantly increase their women's athletic programs.

After comparing results for the spring season in Division I as reflected in Tables 2.2 and 2.3, women's teams exceeded men's by 30 in 2000, 178 in 2010, and 277 in 2015. To that end, colleges and universities have been successful in recruiting and signing enough female and male athletes during the early 2000s to satisfy NCAA standards and likewise financing the operations of teams with plenty of players such as golf, tennis, and track plus women's softball.

Division II

According to NCAA documents about Division II, the number of women's teams varied by season during 2000–2015. From most-to-least per sport, these included archery 0–3, cross country 3–25, field hockey 25–30, soccer 199–267, and volleyball 259–309 in the fall; basketball 276–321, bowling 3–25, fencing 3–4, gymnastics 5–7, ice hockey 1–4, rifle 1–5, skiing 6–10, swimming 67–98, and indoor track 108–189 in the winter; and beach volleyball 1–7, equestrian 4–7, golf 85–195, lacrosse 26–100, rowing 14–18, rugby 1–2, softball 250–299, tennis 217–240, outdoor track 154–236, triathlon 0–3, and water polo 7–12 in the spring. Thus, this was the distribution of teams across academic years.

In the fall seasons of this Division, the number of women's sports teams increased from 750 in 2000 to 843 or 12 percent through 2010, and then five academic years later to 918 or 8 percent. During each period, there was growth in cross country, field hockey, soccer, and volleyball. Ranked from most to least populated on college and university campuses in the fall among women athletes, volleyball placed first and field hockey fourth.

For each of these years in Division II, women's teams exceeded the number of men's by 167 in 2000, 209 in 2010, and 216 in 2015. Except for men's football, rowing and rugby, there were also more women clubs in each of the other sports including field hockey. As such, this reflects differences in the types of games played between schools in higher education from September to November across America.

In winter seasons of this Division, at least nine women sports were active each academic year from 2000 to 2015. As a group, they expanded from 494 in 2000 to 583 in 2010 or 18 percent and then to 519 or 13 percent by 2015. Basketball, indoor track, and swimming — which had the most total teams — were followed numerically by bowling, skiing, and then gymnastics, fencing, ice hockey, and rifle. The women's sports that declined, however, were rifle and skiing while badminton and squash did not exist in Division II.

During winters, there were more men's than women's teams as of 2000 but not in 2010 and 2015. While those in basketball were equal numerically in 2000 and 2010 and nearly the same in 2015, women's bowling, swimming, and indoor track each experienced greater growth than men's. Meanwhile, the two group's other sports within the division only changed marginally. In retrospect, the number of women's teams in Division II became increasingly larger in winters because of emphasis on equity, being schools' newest programs, and athletes' motivation to play sports and win games.

Between 2000 and 2015 in the division, a maximum of 11 women's sports had games in the spring. From 767, they increased by 183 or 23 percent from 2000 to 2010 and then by 158 or 16 percent in the next five academic years. Softball, tennis, and outdoor track contained the most teams in the group while the fewest included equestrian, rugby, triathlon, and water polo. The only sports whose teams fell within the 17-year period were equestrian (twice) and rowing (once). Similar to the fall and winter seasons, women's teams in Division II basically expanded throughout the period and provided an opportunity for athletes to excel in games while getting their education.

Men's sports teams — which had increased by 184 or 23 percent in the spring — did not expand in number and percent as did women's. Besides men's baseball, Division II schools allocated more resources to support and promote such other spring sports as golf, softball, tennis, and outdoor track. This, in turn, mostly benefited college and university women athletes and their coaches, and eventually competitive female high school players in these sports.

Division III

According to NCAA reports published on Division III, the number of women's teams varied by season during 2000–2015. From most to least per sport, these included , cross country 350–425, field hockey 147–165, soccer 378–439, and volleyball 396–434 in the fall; badminton 0–4, basketball 412–443, bowling 0–11, fencing 14–17, gymnastics 14–16, ice hockey 34–58, rifle 3–12, skiing 14–24, swimming 227–255, and indoor track 201–273 in the winter; and beach volleyball 0–2, equestrian 21–31, golf 143–200, lacrosse 141–273, rowing 40–43, rugby 1–3, softball 378–415, tennis 355–380, outdoor track 249–313, triathlon 0–1, and water polo 15–21 in the spring.

During fall seasons, the four women sports combined had increased their number of teams from 1,271 to 1,422 or 11 percent (2000–2010) and then to 1,460 or 2 percent (2010–2015). These included cross country, field hockey, soccer, and volleyball. For cultural, economic, and sport-specific reasons, the most growth occurred in cross country and soccer and least in field hockey and volleyball. Thus, these were significant changes for schools in this division and their female SAs.

In comparison to number of women's teams in fall seasons of the other two divisions, Division III's growth rate of 14 percent from 2000 to 2015 ranked second to Division II's but ahead of the rates in Division I. Also, Division III had the most sports teams in 2000, 2010, and 2015. Consequently, the four women's sports were popular among athletes and across all divisions in the NCAA during these multiyear seasons.

Within the 17-year period in winters of Division III schools, five women's sports teams each declined and increased during 2000 to 2010. But then basketball, bowling, ice hockey, swimming, and indoor track continued to expand during the next five academic years. While rifle and skiing teams trended downward, others such as fencing, gymnastics, and squash did not change from 2010 to 2015. Thus, there were mixed results in winter seasons among the group of female sports in this NCAA division.

Across all winter sports, Division III had more women's teams than the other divisions in 2010 and 2015 but not in 2000. In 2015–2016, for example, it ranked first among the group in number of basketball, ice hockey, skiing, squash, and swimming teams while Division I had the most in bowling, fencing, gymnastics, rifle, and indoor track. This, in turn, denotes the distribution of teams in winter sports among three NCAA divisions from academic years 2000–2001 to 2015–2016.

During spring seasons in Division III, the number of women's teams increased from 1,365 to 1,519 or 11 percent from 2000 to 2010 and then by 140 or 9 percent in the next five academic years. Golf, lacrosse, softball, and outdoor track expanded throughout the period, but not beach volleyball, equestrian, rowing, rugby, tennis, triathlon, and water polo. Among both groups of sports, softball and then tennis and outdoor track contained the most squads in the division, while the least included beach volleyball, rugby, and triathlon.

Comparing the three NCAA divisions in spring seasons, Division III had the most teams in 2000, 2010, and 2015. By sport in 2015–2016, for example, Division I was first in number of beach volleyball, equestrian, golf, rowing, rugby, outdoor track, and water polo clubs, Division II in triathlon, and Division III in lacrosse, softball, and tennis. Based on differences in costs to operate these sports and consistently be competitive in them, more schools in the future will likely downsize one or more of their programs from Division I to II and/or II to III rather than upgrade them from Division III to II and/or II to I.

In a 300-page report published in 2016, an NCAA assistant research director provided some interesting but also significant facts and other information about the number and type of men and women sports teams in American colleges and universities. Based on this chapter's contents and its purpose, scope and theme, the following are some highlights and observations regarding the data in the researchers' report.[9]

- The statistics published by the NCAA in the report — and used in this chapter — were derived from historical data supplied by its member

---

[9] *Idem*, Erin Irick, "Report: National Collegiate Athletic Association." The specific reports are: "NCAA Sports Sponsorship 1981–82 to 2015–16: Average Number of Teams Per Institution." http://www.ncaa.org cited 28 March 2017; "NCAA Sports Sponsorship 1981–82 to 2015–16: Divisions I, II and III Women's Teams Overall Average Squad Size." http://www.ncaa.org cited 28 March 2017; "NCAA Sports Sponsorship 1981–82 to 2015–16: Divisions I, II and III Men's Teams Overall Average Squad Size." http://www. ncaa.org cited 28 March 2017.

institutions. In fact, there were no audits or periodic follow-ups to completely verify the information provided by the institutions. While this information provided some facts and exposed certain trends in sponsorships from academic years 1981–1982 through 2015–2016, the data was not flawless or entirely accurate. For sports in which the NCAA did not offer a championship, the numbers could have been even less precise. Institutions, for example, are allowed to count a limited number of non-NCAA sports toward their membership minimums, but they may or may not report sponsorship figures for those teams. Moreover, no effort was made to determine the reason(s) for the addition or discontinuation of any team in the added and dropped sports sections.

In compiling the data, every effort was made to exclude those institutions and subsequently the teams associated with those institutions that added and/or dropped NCAA membership in any particular year. Therefore, only those teams at schools already members of the NCAA in a specific year were included in the added/dropped teams data.

- Due to increases in the number of NCAA member institutions, sponsorship numbers may not accurately reflect expansion or contraction of opportunities at the institutional level. An increase may simply be caused by the number of new institutions that joined the NCAA and sponsor teams for those sports. Other factors also may affect sports sponsorship rates at the collegiate level. For example, changes in high school and college student populations, fluctuations in schools' budgets, any changes in the value of private institution endowments, insurance costs, the popularity of any sport or sports, and gender-equity matters each can have an effect on sponsorships.

NCAA rules also may have a limited effect on participation and sponsorship patterns. To illustrate, the 1993–1994 academic year marked the first time institutions could not field teams at a lower divisional level than the rest of their program. As a result, many Division I institutions that fielded Division III football teams raised their team from Division III to I-AA while other institutions may have dropped the sport entirely.

- In 2015–2016, there were 133 men's and 146 women's teams added at NCAA member institutions. Since academic year 1988–1989, there have been 4,045 men's and 5,610 women's teams added with each specific academic year having more increases in women's than men's teams. In each division separately — with only a few exceptions — the general trend continued of adding more women's teams than men's each year.

  Also, in 2015–2016, the sports with the highest number of women's teams added were indoor and outdoor track and field, with 21 more indoor teams and 23 outdoor programs in each, followed by lacrosse with an additional 17 teams and golf with 14. And, the women's sport added the most since 1988–1989 has been golf with 704 new programs in the NCAA. In contrast, the sports with the highest number of men's teams added in 2015–2016 was outdoor and then indoor track and field each with 24 new programs. The men's sport that has been added the most since 1988–1989 has been indoor track and field with 524 new NCAA teams.

- In 2015–2016, 35 men's and 44 women's teams dropped at NCAA member institutions. Since the late 1980s, there have been 3,016 men's and 2,185 women's teams dropped with each specific academic year having more men's than women's teams terminated — except in the 2010–2011 academic year when 10 more women's than men's teams were dropped, and in 2012–2013, when one more women's team disbanded.

  Again, in 2015–2016, the sport with the highest number of women's teams dropped was tennis with 10, followed by swimming and diving each with eight. The women's sports that have been eliminated the most since 1988–1989 have been cross country and golf with 244 and 255 programs, respectively, and then indoor track and field with 240. The sport with the highest number of men's teams dropped in 2015–2016 was swimming/diving with six teams eliminated, followed by tennis and outdoor track and field. The men's sport dropped the most since the late 1980s has been indoor track and field with 322 teams discontinuing their programs in the NCAA.

- Besides that type of data, the NCAA report contained other detailed information about schools' sports teams and their history. For example, during the 2000–2001 to 2015–2016 academic years, there were changes in the average number of teams per institution. They averaged 18.8 in 2007–2008 to 19.2 in 2015–2016 within Division I; 13.2 in 2001–02 to 15.4 in 2015–2016 within Division II; and 16.3 in 2005–2006 to 18.0 in 2015–2016 within Division III.

On average, men's teams ranged from 7.8 to 8.2 players and women's from 8.5 to 9.4. Furthermore, since 2000–2001, women's average squad size has varied by sport. For example, bowling, golf, and rifle each averaged less than 10 athletes; basketball, cross country, and fencing each between 10 and 19; field hockey, ice hockey, lacrosse, soccer, and swimming/diving each in the 20s; equestrian and indoor and outdoor track each from the 20s to 30s; and rowing in the 40s to 50s. For men's sports, the average squad size has been largest in football and smallest in rifle. Other sports with less than 20 athletes include basketball, squash and volleyball, and with more than 20 are baseball, water polo, and wrestling.[10]

NATIONAL ASSOCIATION OF INTERCOLLEGIATE ATHLETICS

With its home office in Kansas City, Missouri, the National Association of Intercollegiate Athletics (NAIA) is a governing body of small athletics programs dedicated to character-driven intercollegiate athletics. Beginning with the tipoff of a men's basketball tournament in Kansas City in 1937, the organization continues to administer programs and championships in proper balance with the overall college educational experience.[11]

Every NAIA institution (school) must sponsor a minimum of six championship sports no later than the beginning of the fourth full academic year of active membership. Single gender institutions must sponsor

---

[10] For this national organization, see "History of the NAIA," http://www.naia.org cited 27 March 2017.

[11] "NAIA Colleges and Universities." http://www.http://www.playnaia.org cited 27 March 2017.

a minimum of three championship sports no later than the beginning of the fourth full academic year of active membership. Affiliated conferences, however, often have more strict sponsorship requirements. Institutions in the process of building sports programs have the option of sponsoring an intercollegiate sport and opting out of championships on a year-by-year basis. This affords the institution scheduling advantages and requires application of rules for participating SAs in that sport.

The NAIA has three levels of competition. An "emerging" sport requires 15 or more institutions sponsoring as varsity and declared; an "invitational" sport has 25 or more institutions sponsoring as varsity and declared for a postseason with the approval of the National Administrative Council (NAC); and a "championship" sport has 40 or more institutions sponsoring as varsity with a minimum of two invitationals' and approval of the NAC.

As of the 2015–2016 academic year, the NAIA included 250 member schools, 21 conferences, and 25 national championships. The organization featured sports programs in the following seasons: football and men and women cross country and soccer in the fall; Division I and II men and women basketball, men and women swimming and indoor track, and wrestling and competitive cheer and dance in the winter; and baseball, softball, and men and women golf, tennis, and outdoor track and field in the spring. In addition, men's bowling and women's wrestling are emerging sports, and men's and women's lacrosse and women's wrestling are invitational sports.[12]

From academic years 2008–2009 to 2014–2015 in the NAIA, schools' men's teams increased from 1,254 to 1,321 or 5 percent. The most popular sports in seasons were cross country and soccer in the fall, basketball and football in winters, and baseball and golf in the spring. Among the group of 26 sports during the period, 10 or 38 percent of them declined in number of teams. These included such well-known sports as soccer, basketball, football, and baseball. Based on the data in Table A2.3 of the

---

[12] "National Junior College Athletic Association." http://www.njcaa.org cited 19 March 2017; "NJCAA Participation Figures-Men's Division." http://www.njcaa.org cited 18 March 2017; "NJCAA Participation Figures-Women's Division." http://www.njcaa.org cited 18 March 2017.

Appendix and other information, men's sports teams have expanded annually by less than 1 percent in the NAIA because of schools' limited budgets, small growth in student populations, and investments in academics rather than sports programs.

Within the NAIA, the number of women's athletic teams also increased by 5 percent from 2008–2009 to 2014–2015. Of 25 sports in the group, 10 decreased during the period while the other 15 added more teams including archery and cross country in the fall season, bowling and outdoor track and field in winters, and golf and outdoor track and field in the spring.

According to Table A2.4 in the Appendix, such important women sports as soccer, volleyball, basketball, and softball each had fewer teams than in 2008–2009. As of 2014–2015, there were zero squads in rifle and table tennis. To achieve equity among the two groups, the difference between number of men's and women's sports teams changed by only three from 2008 compared to 2014.

NATIONAL JUNIOR COLLEGE ATHLETIC ASSOCIATION

Established in 1938 after the NCAA rejected a petition from 13 two-year colleges in California to grant their teams and athletes permission to compete at the track and field championships, the National Junior College Athletic Association (NJCAA) fosters a national program of athletic participation in an environment that supports equitable opportunities consistent with the educational objectives of member, two-year community, and junior colleges. Since it detracts from the organization's goal of promoting healthy and fair competition, the NJCAA prohibits unlawful discrimination based on sex, race, color, national origin, ancestry, disability, religion, creed, sexual orientation, age, or any other characteristic protected by applicable law in its governance, programs, regulations, and employment practices.[12]

Due to the growth and popularity of several sports, competitive divisions were launched by the organization during the early 1990s. In order for a sport to be granted divisional status, member college participation in the sport must meet the divisional structure guidelines published in the

NJCAA bylaws. Member colleges are permitted to participate in any division of a sponsored sport of the association and also across multiple divisions in various sports if in the best interest of the institution.

Every two years, member colleges must declare the sports to be sponsored and in which division to participate. During the two-year commitment period, member colleges are locked into the divisions. Competing within a specific division of an NJCAA-sponsored sport comes with policies and guidelines published in the organization's bylaws.

Serving as the national governing body for two-year college athletics in the U.S., the NJCAA is the nation's second-largest national intercollegiate sports organization following the NCAA. Each year, more than 58,000 SAs from over 500 member colleges compete in at least 28 different sports. In addition, the NJCAA hosts 48 national championship events each year.

Each institution belonging to the NJCAA chooses to compete on the Divisions I, II, or III level in designated sports. Division I colleges may offer full athletic scholarships — a maximum of tuition, fees, room and board, course-related books, up to $250 in course-required supplies, and transportation costs one time per academic year to and from the college by direct route. Division II colleges are limited to awarding tuition, fees, course-related books, and up to $250 in course-required supplies. Division III institutions may provide no athletically related financial assistance. However, NJCAA colleges that do not offer athletic aid may choose to participate at the Division I or II level.

SPORTS PROGRAMS

Men's Division

Since 2006, the NJCAA's programs included four men's sports in the fall season, six in the winter, and five in the spring. The total number of teams ranged from a low of 1,681 in 2006 to a high of 1,854 in 2012. During a 10-year period (2006–2015), the group initially increased for three years, declined in 2009, increased from 2010 to 2012, and then dropped in 2013, 2014, and 2015. By season, the number of fall teams ranged from 371 in 2006 to 469 in 2013; winter teams from 558 in 2006 to 608 in 2012; and spring teams from 727 in 2015 to 800 in 2008 (Table 2.4).

Table 2.4.   NJCAA Men's Teams, by Sport and Season, 2006–07 to 2015–16 Academic Years.

Sport	2006	2007	2008	2009	2010	2011	2012	2013	2014	2015
Fall										
Cross Country	103	107	113	116	116	125	130	139	129	131
Football	64	66	70	69	70	72	68	68	64	66
Half Marathon	18	17	26	24	28	33	26	32	12	10
Soccer	186	194	219	221	224	226	229	230	217	219
Winter										
Basketball	419	428	438	434	440	437	445	442	439	434
Bowling	22	20	22	23	25	27	27	26	22	23
Ice Hockey	9	9	10	9	11	11	11	10	8	6
Swimming	19	16	18	20	21	22	21	17	14	12
T&F/Indoor	50	51	60	57	53	55	59	59	50	43
Wrestling	39	41	44	44	45	47	45	42	43	42
Spring										
Baseball	385	387	398	400	398	396	397	394	391	389
Golf	197	198	216	216	211	208	207	203	178	174
Lacrosse	23	24	27	28	27	30	29	31	31	29
Tennis	77	73	80	77	74	78	76	76	70	61
T&F/Outdoor	70	74	79	78	79	79	84	83	77	74

Note: Abbreviations include the National Junior College Athletic Association (NJCAA) and Track & Field (T&F). Academic Years are actually 2006–2007 to 2015–2016. Swimming includes diving.

Source: "NJCAA Participation Figures-Men's Division." http://www.njcaa.org cited 18 March 2017.

While each NJCAA men's sport changed during various years, some numerically declined as of 2015. These were the half marathon in the fall season; ice hockey, swimming, and indoor track and field in winter; and golf and tennis in the spring. Furthermore, such sports as football, bowling, wrestling, baseball, lacrosse, and outdoor track and field each increased by less than 10 teams during the period. Thus, the most growth in men's sports occurred in cross country, soccer, and basketball.

For economic and sport-specific reasons, there has been a downward trend in the number of men's teams per sport in recent years. For example,

6 or 40 percent of 15 NJCAA sports fell in 2012; 7 or 46 percent in 2013; 13 or 86 percent in 2014; and 11 or 73 percent in 2015. Apparently, some colleges and universities decided not to renew their membership, transferred one or more of their teams to the NCAA or NAIA, or simply dropped a sport because of increasing costs, change in strategy of their athletics department, and/or other factors.

Women's Division

Since 2006, schools in the NJCAA have included four women's sports in the fall and winter seasons and five in the spring. The total number of teams ranged from a low of 1,535 in 2006 to a high of 1,853 in 2013. During a 10-year period, they increased consecutively for eight years (2006–2013) and then decreased to 1,716 (2014) and again to 1,681 (2015). By season, the number of teams in the fall ranged from 528 in 2006 to 698 in 2013; in the winter from 454 in 2006 to 519 in 2012; and in the spring from 553 in 2006 to 651 in 2010 (Table 2.5).

While each NJCAA women's sport changed in different ways during various years, some numerically declined in 2006 compared to 2015. These were the half marathon in the fall, swimming in the winter, and golf and tennis in the spring. Furthermore, such sports as bowling, lacrosse, and outdoor track and field each increased by less than 10 teams during the period while those in indoor track and field remained at 46. Thus, the most successful women's sports of the association have been cross country, soccer, volleyball, basketball, and softball.

For economic and sport-specific reasons, there has been an uneven yet discouraging trend in number of women's teams per sport in recent years — except in 2013. For example, 5 or 38 percent of 13 NJCAA sports declined in 2010, 2011, and 2012; 12 or 92 percent in 2014; and 11 or 84 percent of the group in 2015. Evidently, some colleges and universities did not renew their membership in the association, shifted one or more of their teams to the NCAA or NAIA, or they simply eliminated a sport because of increasing costs to operate it, change in strategy of their athletics department, and/or other factors.

In comparing NJCAA sports for the 2015–2016 academic year, schools had the most women teams in basketball and then golf, volleyball, soccer and cross country, but fewest in the half marathon, swimming, and

Table 2.5. NJCAA Women's Teams, by Sport and Season, 2006–07 to 2015–16 Academic Years.

Sport	2006	2007	2008	2009	2010	2011	2012	2013	2014	2015
Fall										
Cross Country	97	103	122	128	129	135	139	152	137	133
Half Marathon	15	15	27	23	29	35	30	30	15	12
Soccer	145	148	183	186	194	196	200	200	189	184
Volleyball	271	292	298	303	311	309	316	316	308	314
Winter										
Basketball	376	382	396	397	404	404	414	406	400	389
Bowling	15	16	19	20	24	24	25	25	21	20
Swimming	17	16	19	21	20	22	21	17	14	12
T&F/Indoor	46	51	62	60	56	57	59	63	53	46
Spring										
Golf	59	64	89	93	92	87	83	86	55	54
Lacrosse	12	14	17	17	19	18	17	18	18	17
Softball	329	331	361	361	372	365	370	370	351	349
Tennis	85	88	92	89	87	86	83	85	75	75
T&F/Outdoor	68	67	83	82	81	83	87	85	80	76

Note: Abbreviations include the National Junior College Athletic Association (NJCAA) and Track & Field (T&F). Academic Years are actually 2006–2007 to 2015–2016.

Source: "NJCAA Participation Figures-Women's Division." http://www.njcaa.org cited 18 March 2017.

bowling. Besides all-male football, ice hockey, baseball and wrestling, men also led in such sports as soccer, basketball, bowling, golf, and lacrosse. In 2006, however, more men's teams existed than women's other than in tennis. Because of Title IX, equity goals, and redistribution of funds in schools' budgets, there have been many changes in the numbers and types of teams within the NJCAA. This, in turn, improved college sports by providing opportunities for different SAs to compete and win championships.

Chapter 3

STUDENT ATHLETE POPULATION

While normally enrolled as students in high schools, some male and female athletes — if eligible academically — played on one or different varsity sports teams. If they competed and successfully performed at scoring points in basketball or excelled with other skills during their junior and/or senior years while in school, colleges and/or universities (academic institutions) located in the United States (U.S.) and/or elsewhere recruited them before graduation.[1]

Upon signing a national letter of intent and then meeting eligibility requirements for admission into a college or university, outstanding high school athletes would likely be granted a scholarship and decide to attend a specific school in higher education based on various factors. Besides athletic history, other reasons include their academic major, type of scholarship, amount of financial aid offered to them to participate in a particular sport or sports, location and reputation of the institution, and personal and family preferences. After accepting a scholarship and then

---

[1] Three books on topics related to student athletes are: Dana Brooks and Ronald Althouse, *Diversity and Social Justice in College Sports: Sport Management and the Student Athlete* (Morgantown, WV: Fitness Information Technology, 2007); Algerian Hart and F. Erik Brooks, *The Student Athlete's Guide to College Success* (Westport, CT: Greenwood Publishing, 2016); Frank P. Jozsa Jr., *College Sports Inc.: How Commercialism Influences Intercollegiate Athletics* (New York, NY: Springer, 2013).

enrolling in College X or University Y, they become a student athlete (SA) in their class.

Depending on the assets, budgets, and resources of their school's athletic department, SAs have an opportunity to use the services of advisors, coaches, counsellors, mentors, and tutors while in a college or university and also receive other types of assistance to maintain at least a minimum grade point average (GPA) or number of credits each semester in order to qualify for and participate on a sports team during their freshman through senior years. A few of them will — while being an underclassman or graduate student — perform in a sport above expectations. After chosen by a team in a player draft, a fraction of them may sign a contract with a professional franchise to play in a major sports league based in America or abroad.

For decades, U.S. schools have submitted statistics and other types of information about their SAs to the National Collegiate Athletic Association (NCAA) currently based in Indianapolis, Indiana. After collecting and organizing the data, the NCAA also publishes various articles, reports, and studies of schools that sponsor sports programs in Divisions I, II, and III. These documents, in part, include tables containing such information as the fraction of men and women SAs on college and university sports teams during various academic years, demographic data including their age, gender and race, the distribution of male and female SAs by type of sport, and perhaps types of financial aid and scholarships awarded to these players.

In addition to these NCAA publications, the University of Central Florida's Institute for Diversity and Ethics in Sports uses NCAA data and other information from surveys and the literature as a way to create report cards and publish different articles and studies about topics such as SAs' gender, graduation rates, and their racial profiles by school, sport, and year.[2]

In this chapter, the first section reveals in tables the number of men and women SAs and their participation on teams in NCAA sports for

---

[2]For information about the organization and its role in college sports, see "National Collegiate Athletic Association." http://www.britannica.com cited 28 March 2017 and "National Collegiate Athletic Association: History." http://www.thefreedictionary.com cited 28 March 2017.

different academic years followed by the second section, which discusses the distribution of athletes in Divisions I, II, and III sports programs. After that information, other tables denote SAs' gender and race by sport during their schools' 2015–2016 academic year. Finally, there is data about SAs in sports programs of the National Association of Intercollegiate Athletics (NAIA) and National Junior College Athletic Association (NJCAA). Because of these tables of data, the book's audiences learn about the development, growth, and population of SAs in different college and university sports programs across the U.S. and also any trends in their participation rate during various seasons.

NCAA

As reflected on its website ncaa.org, the NCAA did not request and annually publish data and other facts about SAs in sports programs of U.S. colleges and universities prior to 1981. Collected and reported in only five-year intervals, this was insufficient information for college and university officials who used it to make decisions regarding their sports programs including benefits and costs, number and type of scholarships, and other things. Then, from the 1981–1982 to 1999–2000 academic years, the NCAA became more thorough in its research and thereby obtained additional information from schools about men and women SAs and eventually reported and distributed that data to the public.

Sports Period I

A variety of factors affect the roles of male and female SAs in schools and their participation at the collegiate level. Some of these, for example, are changes in high school and college and university student populations, budget priorities, fluctuation in the value of private and public institution endowments, insurance expenses, and the popularity of amateur sport or sports, gender-equity matters, and regulations and rules. Also contributing to SAs participation are institutions being an NCAA member, current schools changing their divisional classification, and which sport or sports are designated as championships. The following are statistics and some other data and information that highlight SAs in schools' sports programs from the 1981–1982 to 1999–2000 academic years.[3]

First, the number of men or male SAs in NCAA Division I, II, and III schools as a group increased from 167,055 in the 1981–1982 academic year to 208,481 in 1999–2000 for a growth rate of almost 25 percent. During the period, the number of women or female athletes also increased but from 64,390 to 146,617 or approximately 128 percent. In total, that was an addition of 123,653 SAs or 53 percent more of them. These changes occurred for several reasons including the enactment, implementation, and enforcement of Title IX, schools' investments in their sports programs and athletes, and the contribution, encouragement, and support of the NCAA.

By division, the changes in numbers and percentages were as follows for men and women SAs combined for the 19 academic years in colleges and universities: 100,203 to 145,640 or 45 percent growth in Division I; 49,706 to 74,374 or 49 percent growth in Division II; and 81,536 to 135,085 or 65 percent growth in Division III. Interestingly, the largest change in SAs' participation happened within smaller colleges and universities whose athletes typically do not receive full athletic scholarships, rather than in large and more prominent and wealthy schools that award scholarships and provide other benefits to their players particularly in football and men's basketball programs.

Second, regarding specific changes in sports participation in these academic years of colleges and universities, the biggest positive and negative of them happened, respectively, in 1982–1983 at 10 percent and then in 1987–1988 at more than –4 percent. Furthermore, almost the exact overall results in academic years occurred in Division III schools but not those in Divisions I and II.

Among the two groups of SAs, men's highest and lowest changes overall in participation were approximately 6 percent in 1984–1985 and –6 percent in 1987–1988, and women's at 9 percent in 1998–1999 and about –3 percent in 1986–1987. More specifically, results were the same in 1987–1988 for men and in 1998–1999 for women in Division I, in

---

[3] The data appears in Erin Irick, "Report: National Collegiate Athletic Association." http://www.ncaa.publications.org cited 23 March 2017.

1986–1987 for women in Division II, and also in 1987–1988 for men in Division III and in 1986–1987 for women in Division III. For various reasons including their schools' budgets and strategies regarding sports, SAs highest and lowest participation varied to some extent across these academic years.

Third, the overall average number of SAs per institution (school) ranged from a low of approximately 316 in the 1994–1995 academic year to a high of 372 in 1985–1986. While men SAs varied from 199 in 1994–1995 to 254 in 1984–1985, women's averaged from 98 in 1981–1982 to 144 in 1998–1999 and 1999–2000. During the period, therefore, the former group's averages tended to decline after the early 1980s, while those of women SAs steadily increased and always ranked highest between the two groups of players.

In NCAA divisions, the overall low–high averages of SAs per institution were 388–463 in Division I, 227–303 in Division II, and 286–325 in Division III. Among these groups, men's averages were highest in either 1984–1985 or 1985–1986 but also lowest in 1981–1982 in Division I and in 1994–1995 in Divisions II and III. Alternatively, women's were different than men's by being lowest in the early 1980s and highest in the late 1990s. As discussed before, these trends also existed in the number of men and women SAs who participated in sports programs from 1981–1982 to 1999–2000.

Fourth, besides that type of data, the NCAA also reported the number of men and women SAs by sport for the fall, winter, and spring seasons of the 1981–1999 academic years. Across all divisions, most men athletes participated in cross country and soccer in the fall, basketball, and indoor track in the winter, and baseball and outdoor track in the spring. During these seasons, respectively, fewer of them were active in such sports as archery and volleyball, bowling and rifle, and equestrian and sailing. Thus, men's football, basketball, and baseball teams were traditionally among the most popular sports during the period.

Fifth, men's sports had different growth rates in the participation of SAs from 1981–1982 to 1999–2000. For example, while volleyball increased 18 percent, cross country 20 percent, and soccer 40 percent in the fall season, rowing shrunk by 19 percent and archery 86 percent. In winter sports, some of the largest and smallest percentage gains were, respectively, in indoor track (27 percent), basketball (37 percent) and football (58 percent), and fencing (–58 percent), gymnastics (–73 percent), and both equestrian and badminton (–100 percent). During spring seasons, baseball, lacrosse, and sailing each increased in SAs participation by at least 50 percent among men while equestrian and water polo each had negative percentages. As denoted later in this chapter, these and other team sports continued to experience changes in growth among men SAs.

Sixth, regarding women SAs in NCAA Divisions I–III and their sports during seasons, they primarily participated in soccer and volleyball in the fall, basketball and indoor track in the winter, and outdoor track and softball in the spring. For females, the least popular sports included archery and field hockey in September–November, badminton and squash in December–March, and equestrian and water polo in April–June. Similar to men SAs, freshman to senior women athletes also competed on schools' sports teams to win the most games or matches in regular seasons and then qualify for conference titles and championships.

Seventh, among women SAs and their participation during 1981–1982 to 1999–2000, their growth rates in fall seasons were positive or highest in volleyball (56 percent), cross country (154 percent) and soccer (880 percent) but negative or lowest in field hockey (–10 percent) and archery (–50 percent). In winters, such sports as bowling, rifle, and indoor track each increased more than 100 percent while badminton, fencing, and gymnastics decreased in number of SAs. Then in spring seasons, sports with some of the largest changes were softball (103 percent), water polo (122 percent), golf (193 percent), and rowing (387 percent) while none of the group had negative growth.

Based on these and other changes, only five women sports had smaller participation numbers from 1981–1982 to 1999–2000 versus 12 for men. Evidently, schools reallocated some of their resources and shifted funds from men to women teams in several sports because of equity issues and other reasons.

Eighth, as of 1999–2000, 208,481 men or 58 percent of total SAs were men and 146,617 or 42 percent of women each participated in sports programs of U.S. colleges and universities. More specifically, the group of players included 145,640 athletes or 41 percent in Division I, 74,374 or 21 percent in Division II, and 135,085 or 38 percent in Division III.

Ninth, after schools combined women's synchronized swimming with their swimming/diving program, men and women SAs each played in 24 team sports in the 1999–2000 academic year. For each group, the three largest of them were men's football, baseball, and outdoor track followed by women's soccer and then outdoor and indoor track. Thus, one or more of these sports dominated fall, winter, and spring seasons that year at colleges and universities.

Tenth, as of 1999–2000, schools' smallest sports programs included men's archery, bowling, and gymnastics and also women's archery, badminton, and bowling. Others with less than 1,000 male athletes were fencing, gymnastics, rifle, sailing, skiing, squash and water polo, and fewer than 1,000 women athletes were equestrian, fencing, rifle, skiing, squash, and water polo. In part, this denotes the distribution of men and women who played minor sports of schools in higher education at the end of the twentieth century.

These highlights conclude the activities and changes in Sport Period I regarding the numbers and percentages of men and women SAs who participated in NCAA Divisions I, II, and III sports programs during fall, winter, and spring seasons in colleges and universities across America. For more specific information about schools' sports and their SAs during the 1980s and 1990s, see this chapter's Notes.

To continue, the next section contains similar data and other information but different results and in greater detail concerning SAs who performed on teams in various fall, winter, and spring sports during one or more academic years from 2000–2001 to 2015–2016. From researching these topics, tables are provided in the chapter and also Appendix, to use as references.

Sports Period II

During the initial 16 academic years of the 2000s, the NCAA became more a part of schools' sports programs, which in turn, affected the participation of their SAs. In 2000–2001, for example, women's ice hockey and water polo were removed from the list of emerging sports and the NCAA sponsored a national collegiate championship in those sports. Then in 2001–2002, Division III established women's ice hockey as a divisional championship while schools in Divisions I and II participated in a national collegiate championship. Also in women's rowing, the national collegiate championship was reclassified and divisional champions established in Divisions I–III.[4]

In 2002–2003, rugby was added as an emerging sport for women in each division and, in 2004, women's bowling was removed from the list of emerging sports and the NCAA sponsored a national collegiate championship in that sport. Five years later, women's archery, badminton, synchronized swimming, and team handball were removed from the list of emerging sports in the three divisions due to lack of sponsorships. Then in 2010, sand volleyball was added to the list of emerging sports for women in Divisions I and II.

With respect to data obtained from the NCAA, Tables 3.1–3.3 in this chapter and A3.1–A3.3 in the Appendix reflect recent trends in the population of SAs in U.S. colleges and universities. Then, Tables 3.4 and 3.5 plus some in the Appendix denote the number of men and women who participated in sports programs of schools in the NAIA during the 2008–2009 to 2014–2015 academic years, and Tables 3.6 and 3.7 in the NJCAA for 2006–2007 to 2015–2016.

Table 3.1 contains the number of men and women SAs who participated in 31 sports within Divisions I, II, and III during three academic years. In 2000–2001, 220,781 or 58 percent of the group were male athletes and, 15 years later, females totaled 214,089 or 43 percent of all players. In other words, men SAs increased by more than 57,600 during the period while the number of women expanded by 56,400. As a result, the ratio of men-to-women SAs remained about the same from the 2000–2001 to 2015–2016 academic year despite efforts by the NCAA and school officials to update the percentages and make them equal or approximately equal between the two groups of athletes.

With respect to participation by all SAs as of the 2015–2016 academic year across the fall, winter, and spring seasons, team sports with more men plus women were cross country, golf, ice hockey, lacrosse, rugby, soccer, swimming, tennis, indoor and outdoor track, volleyball, and water

---

[4]The primary source for this topic and others is "NCAA Emerging Sports Timeline." http://www.ncaa.org cited 21 March 2017.

Table 3.1.   Men and Women SAs, NCAA Divisions I–III, by Academic Years.

Sport	2000–2001		2010–2011		2015–2016	
	Men	**Women**	**Men**	**Women**	**Men**	**Women**
Archery	11	46	0	0	0	0
Badminton	0	33	0	0	0	0
Baseball	26,195	0	31,264	0	34,555	0
Basketball	20,194	14,799	17,500	15,708	18,684	16,590
Beach Volleyball	0	0	0	0	0	909
Bowling	16	213	39	565	4	599
Cross Country	11,165	12,335	13,976	15,319	14,412	15,958
Equestrian	135	1,187	11	1,490	15	1,357
Fencing	899	683	605	655	647	721
Field Hockey	0	5,348	0	5,729	0	6,032
Football	58,315	0	66,887	0	73,660	0
Golf	7,987	3,529	8,436	4,565	8,676	5,293
Gymnastics	367	1,414	318	1,463	320	1,502
Ice Hockey	3,846	1,380	3,944	2,049	4,102	2,289
Lacrosse	6,767	5,256	10,424	8,068	13,466	11,375
Rifle	499	284	208	181	163	194
Rowing	1,958	6,348	2,269	6,974	2,343	7,469
Rugby	NA	NA	64	197	164	372
Sailing	361	0	520	0	458	0
Skiing	607	572	470	485	417	436
Soccer	18,597	19,141	22,573	24,671	24,803	27,358
Softball	0	15,506	0	18,188	0	19,679
Squash	446	433	495	401	488	406
Swimming	7,529	10,500	9,213	12,118	9,455	12,400
Tennis	7,655	8,600	8,050	8,908	8,092	8,933
Track/Indoor	17,970	16,718	22,750	23,413	25,220	26,880
Track/Outdoor	20,928	18,925	26,118	25,295	28,341	29,062
Triathlon	0	0	0	0	4	21
Volleyball	1,183	13,358	1,456	15,597	1,899	17,118

(*Continued*)

Table 3.1.   (*Continued*)

Sport	2000–2001		2010–2011		2015–2016	
	Men	**Women**	**Men**	**Women**	**Men**	**Women**
Water Polo	911	1,056	1,018	1,193	1,014	1,136
Wrestling	6,240	0	6,736	0	7,075	0

Note: Besides National Collegiate Athletic Association (NCAA), Not Applicable (NA) means the NCAA did not track data of the sport that year. NCAA Divisions are I, II, and III. Swimming includes synchronized swimming.

Source: "Sport Sponsorship, Participation, and Demographics Search." http://web1.ncaa.org cited 8 March 2017.

polo. While outdoor track, soccer, and indoor track had the largest number of athletes and ranked from first to third within this group, the fewest played lacrosse, rugby, and water polo.

Consequently, schools had expanded these sports for both men and women SAs to compete in games and for other students and fans to attend and enjoy them as audiences. In contrast, sports with fewer SAs from the beginning to end of the period (2000–2001 to 2015–2016) included archery, rifle, and skiing. Because of increasing costs to operate them, lack of demand from SAs, not being available to play them in most high schools, and other reasons, participation in these three sports will continue to decline in colleges and universities.

As of the 2015–2016 academic year, another topic to highlight and focus on in Table 3.1 is NCAA team sports that realized an increase or decrease in participation from 2000 to 2001 but not among both men and women SAs. These were basketball, bowling, equestrian, fencing, gymnastics, and squash. Being only 6 or 19 percent of all team sports, the other 81 percent of them changed in different ways regarding participation by SAs of both sexes. These differences are discussed later in sections of the chapter.

Excluding such single-gender sports as badminton, baseball, beach volleyball, field hockey, football, ailing, softball, and wrestling but including changes in SAs participation from 2000–2001 to 2010–2011 and then 2010–2011 to 2015–2016, there are mixed results with respect to trends among seasons for each sport. In fall seasons, for example, there were increasingly more SAs across the 16 academic years in cross country, rowing, soccer, and volleyball while archery ceased to exist sometime before 2010–2011.

During winter seasons, the total number of men plus women SAs who had competed in such sports as basketball, fencing, and gymnastics declined but then changed and increased in 2015–2016. In addition, different results occurred for other NCAA winter sports like bowling, ice hockey, swimming, and indoor track. Because of their popularity among both groups of SAs and also non-athlete students and fans, these continued to expand throughout the periods.

In spring seasons, more SAs increasingly participated in golf, lacrosse, tennis, outdoor track, and water polo during each of the three academic years. But there were variations — increases or decreases — during at least one or two of these periods among the numbers of SAs who performed in equestrian and triathlon competitions. In other words, the majority of NCAA sports had different growth rates with respect to total SAs participating in them especially those with both men and women.

To summarize the overall trends in Table 3.1, the number of SAs participating in these 31 sports during seasons increased by 70,131 or almost 19 percent from 2000–2001 to 2010–2011 and then by 44,000 or approximately 10 percent from 2010–2011 to 2015–2016. Across the entire period — but excluding athletes in single-gender sports — there were 114,121 additional men plus women SAs who had specifically competed in cross country, soccer, and volleyball during fall seasons, in basketball, swimming, and indoor track during winters, and in lacrosse, tennis, and outdoor track in the spring months of academic years.

In the next section of this chapter, the key topic shifts from analyzing the total population of SAs to the number and distribution of men and then women athletes that performed during the 2000–2001, 2010–2011, and 2015–2016 academic years on teams in sports of NCAA Divisions I, II, and III. Although specific and more involved in some ways than other contents, this section reveals differences and similarities between male and female SAs and their role in fall, winter, and spring sports programs of colleges and universities. Following this section is a discussion of data — contained in four tables of the Appendix — that reveal the race of men and women SAs who played sports in NCAA divisions during the 2015–2016 academic year.

MEN SAs

In Table 3.2 is the number and distribution of men SAs by type of sport in each of three seasons of schools' academic years within divisions of the NCAA. The table consists of 27 team sports including 7 or approximately 26 percent of them in the fall, 11 or about 41 percent in the winter, and 9 or exactly 33 percent in the spring.

Division I

According to data in columns two to four of the table, the number of men SAs increased by 6,057 or 7 percent from academic years 2000 (2000–2001) to 2010 (2010–2011) and then by 3,929 or 4 percent to 2015 (2015–2016). With respect to the entire period, their participation changed from 86,567 to 96,553 or 11 percent.[5]

During fall seasons — which represented 41–42 percent of the group in Division I — there were more male SAs in five sports in 2010 than 2000 — and except for archery and volleyball — also in 2015 than 2010. Throughout the period, the most populated and probably popular sport was football followed by soccer, cross country, rowing, volleyball, rugby, and archery. While football and rowing each had growth in male SAs slightly above 16 percent, cross country's expanded by 10 percent, soccer's 9 percent, and volleyball's less than one percent. For various reasons, archery and rugby did not exist from 2000 to 2015.

In December–March (roughly winter season) from 2000–2001 to 2010–2011, NCAA Division I men's sports teams consisted of an additional 1,339 — or about 6 percent more — SAs. While the number of these athletes in basketball, squash, swimming, and indoor track each increased, there were fewer of them in six others while bowling had zero, being not a sanctioned sport.

---

[5]For more details and data, see "Division I." http://www.ncaa.org cited 23 March 2017.

Table 3.2. Men SAs, by Sports and Seasons, NCAA Divisions, Selected Academic Years.

	Divisions								
	I			II			III		
Sports	2000	2010	2015	2000	2010	2015	2000	2010	2015
Fall									
Archery	11	0	0	0	0	0	0	0	0
Cross Country	4,331	4,844	4,799	2,576	3,356	3,679	4,258	5,776	5,934
Football	24,408	26,087	28,380	13,879	17,921	19,484	20,028	23,879	25,796
Rowing	1,184	1,241	1,378	140	65	52	634	963	913
Rugby	NA	0	70	NA	0	44	NA	64	50
Soccer	5,346	5,719	5,877	4,190	5,357	6,635	9,061	11,497	12,291
Volleyball	392	467	394	262	270	467	529	719	1,038
Winter									
Basketball	4,493	5,199	5,472	4,435	5,000	5,450	6,723	7,301	7,762
Bowling	0	0	0	16	39	0	0	0	4
Fencing	387	373	389	126	36	28	386	196	230
Gymnastics	326	297	304	9	0	0	32	21	16
Ice Hockey	1,653	1,596	1,633	196	180	185	1,997	2,168	2,284
Rifle	278	135	126	13	23	21	208	50	16
Skiing	180	167	152	103	76	71	324	227	194
Squash	158	174	199	0	0	0	288	321	289
Swimming	3,621	3,837	3,721	946	1,379	1,500	2,962	3,997	4,234
Track/ Indoor	8,946	9,792	10,094	3,146	4,628	5,826	5,878	8,330	9,300
Wrestling	2,754	2,565	2,501	1,177	1,780	1,946	2,309	2,391	2,628
Spring									
Baseball	9,491	10,046	10,430	7,169	9,248	10,660	9,535	11,970	13,465
Equestrian	0	0	2	50	0	0	85	11	13
Golf	3,164	2,951	2,941	1,918	2,328	2,470	2,905	3,157	3,265
Lacrosse	2,305	2,740	3,139	870	1,572	2,504	3,592	6,112	7,803

(*Continued*)

Table 3.2.   (*Continued*)

Sports	Divisions								
	I			II			III		
	2000	2010	2015	2000	2010	2015	2000	2010	2015
Sailing	132	196	268	5	18	14	224	306	176
Tennis	2,780	2,657	2,644	1,620	1,744	1,749	3,255	3,649	3,691
Track/ Outdoor	9,693	10,944	11,066	4,065	5,853	7,189	7,170	9,321	10,077
Triathlon	0	0	0	0	0	0	0	0	4
Water Polo	534	597	574	107	126	147	270	295	293

Note: Provisional National Collegiate Athletic Association (NCAA) member schools are included in the sport. Data includes all conferences. Academic Years are actually 2000–2001, 2010–2011, and 2015–2016. Not Applicable (NA) means the NCAA did not track data of the sport that year. Swimming includes diving.

Source: "Sport Sponsorship, Participation, and Demographics Search." http://web1.ncaa.org cited 8 March 2017 and Frank P. Jozsa Jr., *College Sports Inc.: How Commercialism Influences Intercollegiate Athletics* (New York, NY: Springer, 2013).

Although the largest positive changes occurred in basketball and indoor track, sports with a reduction in SAs included, for example, fencing and gymnastics. Then from 2010–2011 to 2015–2016, more male athletes continued to join teams in such sports as basketball, squash, swimming, and indoor track but fewer of them had participated in rifle, skiing, and wrestling. Across the entire period, most sports had uneven growth because of less and then more or less SAs. Proportionately, most male athletes competed in indoor track, basketball, swimming, and wrestling.

Among men SAs on teams in spring seasons, they increased by 2,032 or 7 percent from 2000 to 2010 and then by 933 or 3 percent to 2015. Continually baseball, lacrosse, sailing, and outdoor track had more athletes while those playing golf and tennis steadily dropped in number. Water polo, meanwhile, had more and then fewer players. Also, the number of SAs in outdoor track led the group followed by those in baseball, golf, tennis, lacrosse, and sailing. Interestingly, equestrian had two men riding their horses in events with triathlon having zero athletes.

In summarizing men SAs on sports teams within Division I, the number of them increased by 11 percent from the 2000–2001 to 2015–2016 academic year. Of the total per season across years and among the sports, 41 percent of these athletes participated in the fall, 26 percent in the winter, and 33 percent in the spring. The most popular team sports for men players were football, baseball, and then indoor track while the fewest of them — besides bowling and triathlon — participated in archery, equestrian, rugby, and rifle. During the period, 17 or approximately 55 percent of the sports involved more male SAs but, in 2015–2016, there were zero who played games or matches in archery, bowling, and triathlon.

Division II

From the 2000–2001 to 2010–2011 academic year in sports of schools in this NCAA division, the total number of men SAs on teams increased by 14,017 or approximately 29 percent and then by 9,086 or 14 percent as of 2015–2016. As a result, there was greater growth — although fewer male SAs in Division II sports — than those who participated in Division I.[6]

As denoted in Table 3.2 for each of three seasons in Division II, the majority of sports included more men SAs as of 2015. In the fall, for example, only rowing had fewer athletes than in 2000 while cross country, football, rugby, soccer, and volleyball each included more of them. During the period, the number of male SAs increased from 21,047 to 30,361 or 44 percent particularly in football programs. In fact, this sport generates most revenue for colleges and universities and their athletic departments.

In winter seasons as of the division's 2015–2016 academic year, the number of male SAs increased by 4,860 or 47 percent throughout the period. This, in turn, contributed to the growth of five sports including basketball, rifle, swimming, indoor track, and wrestling. Besides bowling, fencing, and gymnastics, fewer athletes participated in ice hockey and skiing. Interestingly, bowling, gymnastics, and squash each had zero men SAs as of 2015. Compared to those in Division I, the growth of SAs in winter sports was much greater in this division percentagewise, but not numerically,

---

[6]There are links to student athletes and their participation in "Division II." http://www.ncaa.org cited 23 March 2017.

although similar in basketball. Given the trends in Table 3.2, fencing and perhaps skiing will cease to exist as a Division II winter sport before 2020.

Regarding spring seasons in sports of Division II, there was an increase of 5,121 male SAs or 32 percent more from the 2000–2001 to 2010–2011 academic year and an additional 3,808 or 18 percent in the next five years. Except for equestrian, the number of men athletes in the other sports expanded especially in baseball, lacrosse, and outdoor track. In Division I, however, golf and tennis declined among men's spring sports, and furthermore Division II had significantly more SAs involved in baseball as of 2015. Because of differences in growth and other factors, the number of male athletes in sports programs of these divisions fell from 39,549 in 2000 to 26,432 in 2015.

To conclude an analysis of NCAA Division II sports from 2000 to 2015, the growth of men SAs was relatively higher in percent than in Division I. Within the former division, the most populated sports among male athletes were football and soccer in the fall, basketball and indoor track in winters, and baseball and outdoor track in spring seasons. Overall, five sports had zero participation while football ranked first, baseball second, outdoor track third, soccer fourth, and basketball fifth. Consequently, during the period of academic years, there was impressive growth in male SAs who played in sports programs of schools in Division II.

Division III

From 2000–2001 to 2010–2011 in this division, 20,068 or 24 percent more male SAs played on sports teams and by 2015–2016, there was an additional 9,045 of them or 8 percent. Although less growth occurred percentagewise than in Division II, Division III's increase in these athletes surpassed the number of those in Division I in 2010 and even more than in 2015.[7]

Except for archery and rugby in sports of the fall season, the others in Division III included more male players as of 2015. While SAs in volleyball almost doubled since 2000, cross country in addition to football,

---

[7]For the history and philosophy of this NCAA division, see "Division III." http://www.ncaa.org cited 23 March 2017.

rowing, and soccer each expanded by at least 25 percent. During September–November of 16 academic years in this division, the total number of male SAs increased by 11,512 or 33 percent. By far, football and soccer combined had more than 82 percent of the male athletes on teams in fall sports of Division III.

During winter seasons in Division III from 2000–2001 to 2015–2016, an additional 5,800 male SAs participated in the group of 11 sports. While there were fewer athletes in fencing, gymnastics, rifle, and skiing at the end of the period, more of them existed in basketball, bowling, ice hockey, squash, swimming, indoor track, and wrestling. Similar to those in Divisions I and II, basketball and indoor track had the most male athletes in winter seasons with the smallest number of them participating in bowling, gymnastics, and rifle.

By 2010, Division III ranked ahead of the two other NCAA divisions in male SAs being players on teams in winter sports programs. Among schools within these divisions, this change was caused by differences in costs to operate sports and improve their competitiveness from November to March during one or more academic years and also due to budget restrictions and other factors including growth in student populations, and perhaps downsizing any athletic programs from Division II to Division III.

In spring months of Division III sports during the 2000–2015 academic years, the number of male SAs increased by 11,751 or 43 percent. Except for equestrian and sailing, additional athletes joined teams in the other seven sports. While those in lacrosse more than doubled, there were at least 3,900 more SAs involved in baseball, almost 3,000 in outdoor track, hundreds in golf and tennis, but less than 25 more in water polo. Between 2010 and 2015, at least four men athletes competed in triathlons that typically required them to swim, bike, run, and/or perform other tasks at different distances in their schools' races.

Compared to sports programs in the other NCAA divisions, those in Division III contained the largest number of male SAs from 2010–2011 to 2015–2016. During fall seasons, for example, the division's sports had more men participating on teams in cross country, soccer, and volleyball, but not in archery, football, rowing, and rugby. In winters, meanwhile, Division III led others in men athletes playing football, ice hockey, skiing, squash, and swimming but not in other sports. Regarding only spring seasons, Division III ranked first relative to other divisions in males competing in baseball, equestrian, golf, lacrosse, tennis, and triathlon.

As of the 2000–2001 academic year, Table 3.2 reports data that reveals different changes within and among sports programs in three NCAA divisions with respect to participation by male SAs on teams. While the data denotes growth in number of players across the majority of sports, it also indicates their population during fall, winter, and spring seasons. Whether trends in the numbers continue after 2016–2017 depends on many things. Importantly, these include schools' athletic budgets and decisions about operating their sports programs efficiently and more equitably.

WOMEN SAs

In Table 3.3 is the number and distribution of women (female) SAs by type of sport in each of three seasons and academic years within divisions of the NCAA. The table consists of 27 team sports including five or approximately 18 percent of them in the fall and 11 each or about 41 percent in the winter and also spring.

Division I

From the schools' 2000–2001 to 2010–2011 academic year, the number of women SAs in teams increased by 13,802 or 21 percent and then another 5,166 or approximately 7 percent in 2015–16. In fall seasons, more athletes joined five sports during the period while archery ceased operating sometime before 2010. For some reason, the only sport that had more and then marginally fewer female players was cross country but not field hockey, soccer, and volleyball. From 2010 to 2015, an additional 4,372 women SAs or 24 percent became members of teams in these sports. This represented about 23 percent in total growth in the numbers of them throughout the period.

In schools' winter seasons — which included 11 sports — an additional 4,287 females became SAs from 2000 to 2010 and in the next five academic years, another 857 began to play in games. Respectively, for each period of academic years, this was an increase in growth of female

Table 3.3. Women SAs, Sports and Seasons, NCAA Divisions, Selected Academic Years.

Sports	I			II			III		
	2000	2010	2015	2000	2010	2015	2000	2010	2015
Fall									
Archery	46	0	0	0	0	0	0	0	0
Cross Country	4,865	6,097	5,947	2,780	3,430	3,897	4,690	5,810	6,114
Field Hockey	1,687	1,769	1,795	603	589	741	3,058	3,371	3,496
Soccer	6,905	8,473	9,144	4,298	6,003	7,336	7,938	10,195	10,878
Volleyball	4,250	4,833	5,239	3,604	4,404	4,968	5,504	6,360	6,911
Winter									
Badminton	0	0	0	0	0	0	33	0	0
Basketball	4,706	4,820	4,990	4,090	4,482	4,920	6,003	6,406	6,680
Bowling	189	292	283	24	203	223	0	70	93
Fencing	408	373	403	39	43	54	236	239	264
Gymnastics	1,079	1,095	1,058	98	101	130	237	267	314
Ice Hockey	643	824	855	47	71	98	690	1,154	1,336
Rifle	211	136	164	13	19	15	60	26	15
Skiing	204	205	168	109	88	81	259	192	187
Squash	125	135	151	0	0	0	308	266	255
Swimming	4,608	5,492	5,523	1,286	1,662	1,853	4,606	4,964	5,024
Track/Indoor	9,095	12,183	12,817	2,755	4,414	5,921	4,868	6,816	8,142
Spring									
Beach Volleyball	0	0	758	0	0	121	0	0	30
Equestrian	424	729	701	180	141	102	583	620	554
Golf	1,813	2,099	2,176	621	1,236	1,561	1,095	1,230	1,556
Lacrosse	1,846	2,433	3,344	562	1,418	2,320	2,848	4,217	5,711
Rowing	4,485	5,195	5,653	519	503	498	1,344	1,276	1,318
Rugby	NA	50	213	NA	55	87	NA	92	72

(Continued)

Table 3.3.   (*Continued*)

Sports	Divisions								
	I			**II**			**III**		
	2000	**2010**	**2015**	**2000**	**2010**	**2015**	**2000**	**2010**	**2015**
Softball	4,781	5,633	6,042	4,375	5,355	5,991	6,350	7,200	7,646
Tennis	2,933	2,907	2,910	1,866	2,026	2,067	3,801	3,975	3,954
Track/Outdoor	9,238	12,467	13,136	3,712	5,203	7,104	5,975	7,625	8,808
Triathlon	0	0	0	0	0	16	0	0	5
Water Polo	626	729	665	175	146	208	255	318	263

Note: SAs of provisional National Collegiate Athletic Association (NCAA) member schools are included in the sport. Data includes all conferences. Academic Years are actually 2000–2001, 2010–2011, and 2015–2016. Not Applicable (NA) means the NCAA did not track data of the sport that year. Swimming includes diving and synchronized swimming.

Source: "Sport Sponsorship, Participation, and Demographics Search." http://web1.ncaa.org cited 8 March 2017 and Frank P. Jozsa Jr., *College Sports Inc.: How Commercialism Influences Intercollegiate Athletics* (New York, NY: Springer, 2013).

athletes of 20 percent and then by 3 percent. While the number of fencing, gymnastics, rifle, and skiing SAs declined, there were more in the other six sports but especially in basketball, swimming, and indoor track. Proportionately, for example, bowling had experienced 43 percent growth and ice hockey 32 percent while basketball, being the third most populated sport in the group, increased only 6 percent.

While there were more men SAs than women in 2000, this changed as of 2010 when the latter group of athletes exceeded the former by more than 1,400 and then 1,800 in 2015. This occurred for several reasons including the enforcement of Title IX, increase in number of undergraduate women students, more resources devoted to schools' winter sports programs, additional financial aid for athletes, and growth of winter sports within high schools and among colleges and universities.

Based on the data for three academic years of Division I in Table 3.3, the largest improvement in women SAs took place in seasons of spring sports. Excluding tennis, which fell by 23, the number of female athletes increased by more than 6,000 or 23 percent from 2000 to 2010 and then by another 3,356 or 10 percent to 2015. Percentagewise, several of these sports grew at least 40 percent including those in beach volleyball, equestrian, lacrosse, rugby, and outdoor track. In contrast, such team sports as golf, rowing, softball, and water polo also added female players.

In comparison to winter seasons in Division I, the number of women athletes surpassed men by the spring of 2010 and to a greater extent in 2015. Female SAs received advantages because schools increasingly sponsored softball, rugby, and more equestrian teams. Meanwhile, men's golf and tennis declined and relatively small numbers of male SAs participated in their sailing and water polo teams. Thus, spring sports have become more popular and entertaining among women athletes and also for other undergraduate students in colleges and universities.

To summarize the role of women who participated in NCAA Division I sports programs, these athletes have become more prominent among schools in higher education. From 2000 to 2010 and then through 2015, their numbers increased with more of them involved in spring than fall and winter seasons. Outdoor and indoor track, softball, and soccer teams are most populated with females while the least in the group of sports include bowling, rifle, skiing, squash, and rugby. If trends continue, female SAs will dominate winter and spring sports in the future but not those in the fall because of football and its appeal to alumni, students in colleges and universities, fans in communities across the U.S., and schools who receive revenue from the sport.

Division II

During the early 2000s within this NCAA division, the number of sports teams expanded in numerous colleges and universities and so did females in their impact and influence as SAs. In fall seasons, for example, women athletes increased by more than 3,100 or 27 percent from the 2000 to 2010 academic years and then by 2015, added another 2,516 or 17 percent to the total. Since 2000, they became more competitive and thus involved in cross country, field hockey, soccer, and volleyball. Excluding football, their participation exceeded men's in total and percentagewise. Although fewer than in Division I during fall seasons, the number of women SAs rose by more than 5,600 in order to try and win games in schools' sports programs.

Among nine winter sports that were active from academic years 2000 to 2010, female SAs increased by 2,622 or approximately 31 percent in NCAA Division II athletic programs. Then five years later, schools added another 2,212 or almost 20 percent. This, in turn, exceeded the growth rate of men athletes in spring sports within Division I colleges and universities.

While badminton and squash each had zero Division II teams during winters of these years, the participation of women in eight sports increased but nevertheless declined in skiing. The most impressive growth in female SAs occurred in bowling, ice hockey, and indoor track followed by basketball, swimming, and indoor track. Interestingly, skiing also trended downward among Division I and III women athletes. Comparing their populations, Division II had significantly less participants than the other NCAA groups because of fewer teams and number of sports in winter seasons.

There were significant increases in the number of women SAs among schools in Division II spring sports programs. From academic years 2000 to 2010, 4,073 or approximately 34 percent more female athletes participated on teams and then five years later, another 3,992 or 25 percent competed in various sports. Besides reductions in equestrian and rowing, the other nine sports experienced growth each period, especially golf, lacrosse, softball, tennis, and outdoor track. Meanwhile, beach volleyball and triathlon also expanded from zero women SAs after the 2010–2011 academic year.

On a percentage basis, the increase among women athletes in Division II spring sports was greater than those in Divisions I and III. That was because of tremendous growth in golf, lacrosse, softball, and outdoor track. These changes in participation also occurred due to more generous and valuable scholarships being awarded to high school SAs, increases in budgets of colleges and universities, and a growing interest in athletics by such groups as alumni, other students, and fans within local communities and metropolitan areas.

To summarize the participation of female SAs in NCAA Division II sports, they increased both numerically and percentagewise from the 2000 to 2010 academic years and then during 2010 to 2015. They mostly played on soccer and volleyball teams in the fall, indoor track, and basketball in winters, and outdoor track and softball in spring seasons.

Although fewer of them participated than those in Divisions I and III each season, females on teams in Division II declined from 2000 to 2015 only in skiing, equestrian, and rowing. Indeed, this represents impressive growth for the group. However, because of increasingly higher costs to operate athletic programs in Division II — especially football and men's basketball — some schools may ultimately decide to transfer these and their other expensive sports to Division III.

Division III

During the 2000 to 2010 academic years in this NCAA division, the number of women SAs increased from 60,735 to 72,689 or 19 percent and then five years later, another 6,937 or approximately 9 percent of them joined teams. With respect to 2000–2010, this was slower growth in female athletes percentagewise than in Divisions I and II but ahead of Division I's increase from 2010 to 2015.

In fall seasons of NCAA Division III, female athletes increased by a total of 4,519 or 21 percent from 2000 to 2010 and then through 2015 by another 1,663 or 6 percent. Similar to those in Divisions I and II, fall sports added more women SAs. In 2015, the former division had the most players on teams in cross country, field hockey, soccer, and volleyball. Of these sports, soccer had the greatest growth at 37 percent and also the most athletes at 10,878. As of 2000, 2010, and 2015, these exceeded changes in Divisions I and II. Indeed, this was an important period for women who participated in schools' Division III sports programs.

During the fall of 16 academic years (2000–2015), the number of male SAs increased by 11,512 or 33 percent in Division III sports while women's participation expanded by 6,182 or 29 percent. However, female sports had fewer athletes each year than men's from September to November. In other words, there were 13,293 fewer females than males in 2000, 17,162 less in 2010, and 18,623 fewer in 2015.

Thus, the totals between the two groups of SAs increased during the period despite equity standards of the NCAA and also schools with teams involved in Division III sports. Certainly, a primary reason for differences in growth of participation among women and men athletes in fall seasons was because of more football teams and their players. In addition, men's volleyball, cross country, rowing, and soccer each expanded at least 25 percent.

Regarding schools' winter seasons as members of Division III sports, the number of female SAs increased by 3,133 or 18 percent from 2000 to 2010 and then by another 1,910 or 9 percent during 2010–2015. While seven sports included more women athletes on teams from 2000 to 2015, there were less of them in badminton, rifle, skiing, and squash. Besides basketball, swimming, and indoor track, they also played on teams in bowling, fencing, gymnastics, and ice hockey. Numerically during March to May, more women SAs participated in Division III sports programs than those in Division II but not Division I.

In winters of the 2000–2001 to 2015–2016 academic years, the number of male SAs in Division III sports increased by 4,860 or 47 percent while women's teams — during the period — had 5,043 or 29 percent more athletes. Compared to a decline in men's participation in bowling, fencing, gymnastics, rifle, and skiing, women had fewer athletes only in rifle, skiing, and squash.

Per academic year, there were 3,840 fewer female SAs than males in 2000, 4,600 less in 2010, and 4,647 fewer in 2015. The differences in participation between the two groups of athletes were primarily because of the number of their teams in basketball, ice hockey, swimming, indoor track, and wrestling. Before 2025, the gap between sexes will substantially close as women increasingly participate in winter sports within schools of Division III.

With respect to spring seasons in Division III, 4,302 or 19 percent more women participated on sports squads from the 2000–2001 to 2010–2011 academic years and, five years later, another 3,364 or 34 percent of them joined teams. While the number of these female athletes declined in equestrian rowing and rugby, more played beach volleyball, golf, lacrosse, and five other spring sports. More specifically, the women SAs in lacrosse expanded by 100 percent, outdoor track 47 percent, golf 42 percent, and softball 20 percent.

In spring months of Division III sports during the 2000–2015 academic years, the number of male SAs increased by 11,751 or 43 percent while women's changes were, respectively, 7,666 or 34 percent. Except for equestrian and sailing, additional male athletes joined seven other sports including lacrosse — which more than doubled — and also baseball, outdoor track, golf, tennis, and water polo. In comparison to them, women's participation in tennis and water polo each increased less than 5 percent. As in the fall and spring seasons of the division, those who became athletes in the two groups increased during the period. The differences between men and women were 4,785 in 2000, 8,268 in 2010, and 8,870 in 2015. Based on these results, there was less equity between sexes.

To summarize women SAs and their participation on NCAA Division III sports teams from 2000–2001 to 2015–2016, they increased both numerically and percentagewise throughout the period. These athletes focused most on joining clubs in cross country, soccer, and volleyball in fall seasons, and basketball, swimming, and indoor track in winters, and lacrosse, softball, and outdoor track in the spring. Although female SAs were outnumbered increasingly by men within the division, their participation in schools' sports programs has improved which, in turn, benefits them, their colleges and universities, and the NCAA.

In the next section, there is recent data regarding the race of SAs on teams in sports of three NCAA divisions as of their schools' 2015–2016 academic year. The numbers of them by race — which include white, black, Hispanic, and other groups — are distributed among men (males) and women (females) athletes of various sports within all divisions in Table A3.1, and also each division in Tables A3.2–A3.4 of the Appendix. Following are the highlights and important results of the data.

SAs Race

Divisions I–III

Based on the data in Table A3.1 for schools' 2015–2016 academic year, the total number of SAs by race was 66 percent white, 16 percent black, 5 percent Hispanic, and 13 percent other races. For a specific group of them, 175,051 or 54 percent of white athletes were males and their primary sports included football, baseball, outdoor and indoor track, and soccer. Besides the three all-female sports of beach volleyball, field hockey, and softball, less than 25 of them played in such activities as bowling, equestrian, and triathlon. The 151,504 white women athletes mostly competed on soccer, outdoor and indoor track, softball, and volleyball teams. However, relatively few of them performed on squads in rifle, rugby, squash, and triathlon. Of the 29 sports in the table, there were more white males than females in eight or approximately 27 percent of the group.[8]

Among 78,550 black SAs, 70 percent were males and the other 30 percent females. While the former group of athletes mostly played football and then basketball, outdoor and indoor track, and soccer, less than 15 each performed in such sports as rifle, sailing, skiing, squash, and water polo. Meanwhile, the 23,900 black women SAs primarily joined outdoor and indoor track, basketball, volleyball, and soccer teams, but not many on those in equestrian, ice hockey, rifle, squash, and water polo.

Regarding all sports involving black athletes, females were a majority in 12 or 41 percent of them, and also equal or about equal with the number of males in cross country, skiing, squash, and water polo. With respect to their race on a percentage basis, white athletes had a more equitable distribution of sexes in schools' sports programs than blacks during their 2015–2016 academic year.

Among those in Table A3.1, there were 25,875 Hispanic SAs with 15,032 or 58 percent being males and the other proportion females. The former group mostly participated on soccer and then football, baseball, and outdoor and indoor track teams while women primarily played on those in soccer, softball, outdoor and indoor track, and cross country. For each subset of athletes, respectively, relatively fewer men were involved on squads in equestrian, rifle, skiing, and triathlon and, regarding females, a small number of them existed in rifle, skiing, squash, and triathlon.

Besides beach volleyball, field hockey, and softball, women athletes dominated the population of Hispanic men in 13 or 50 percent of the sports but not, for example, in cross country, golf, skiing, tennis, and outdoor and indoor track. Although there were more male black athletes in several team sports, results were similar among the distribution of

---

[8]The data in Table A3.1 is contained in NCAA report "Sport Sponsorship, Participation, and Demographics Search." http://web1.ncaa.org cited 8 March 2017.

Hispanic and white SAs. Across males and females in all sports, black SAs had a larger imbalance of them compared to the other groups.

For the 61,229 SAs of other races besides white, black, and Hispanic, 55 percent were males and 27,482 females. The former group of athletes participated mostly on teams in football, soccer, outdoor and indoor track, and tennis while the largest number of females competed in outdoor track, soccer, indoor track, tennis, and basketball. Other than baseball, football, sailing and wrestling, there were considerably more men athletes who played on teams in such sports as basketball, cross country, golf, ice hockey, lacrosse, skiing, and squash. Of the 29 NCAA sports in Table A3.1, women were most prominent in 15 or approximately 52 percent of them. From an equity perspective, the distribution of SAs in other races ranked below whites but ahead of blacks and Hispanics.

Division I

In this division, the proportions among groups of SAs were 59 percent white, 21 percent black, 5 percent Hispanic, and 15 percent other races in schools' 2015–2016 academic year. Regarding each group's distribution of men/women athletes, respectively, they equaled 50/50 percent, 66/34 percent, 53/47 percent, and 51/49 percent. From a gender perspective in Division I, white players had the most equitable distribution of SAs followed by other races and then Hispanics and blacks. These results also occurred across other NCAA divisions (Table A3.2).

While white men participated primarily in football, baseball, outdoor and indoor track, and soccer of Division I sports, a large number of white women athletes competed on cross county and swimming teams besides those in outdoor and indoor track and also soccer. Of the 28 sports in the division, men SAs had the largest population in 8 or only 28 percent of them. Yet, their proportion equaled women's overall, in part, due to 11,240 of them in football, 8,222 in baseball, and 1,867 in wrestling.

Football and then basketball, outdoor and indoor track, and soccer teams were black men's most important sports, and for women SAs, they participated in four of them, but volleyball rather than football. Although zero black athletes in the division had representation in sailing or skiing, only a few African–American men competed in rifle, squash, volleyball, and water polo and, similarly, black women competed in equestrian, ice hockey, rifle, squash, and water polo. Because of different factors including number of scholarships and types of sports and their popularity, the number of men to women black SAs almost equaled 2-to-1.

Among Hispanic athletes in schools of NCAA Division I, men mostly played on football, baseball, soccer, and outdoor and indoor track teams, and women on those in softball and cross country plus soccer, softball, and track rather than any in football, baseball, sailing, and wrestling. Sexes combined, only a few participated in bowling, equestrian, ice hockey, rifle, skiing, and squash. With the least number of SAs among races at 8,656, Hispanic athletes tended to compete mostly on teams in major and popular sports within colleges and universities.

Regarding other races in Table A3.2, SAs consisted of 14,201 men and 13,880 women. Besides football, more than 975 men each played on track, tennis, and soccer teams, and so did women except they participated in rowing rather than football. Despite being only 15 percent of all races, the total number of these athletes was more than Hispanics, but less compared to white or black SAs.

Division II

Among 120,433 athletes in this division during schools' 2015–2016 academic year, 61 percent were white, 19 percent black, 7 percent Hispanic, and 13 percent other races. The distribution of men/women by race, respectively, resulted in 54/46 percent, 73/27 percent, 57/43 percent, and 59/41 percent. In comparison, other divisions had similar distributions by race (Table A3.3).

The most populated sports for white men SAs in NCAA Division II included baseball and then football, outdoor and indoor track, and soccer. Rather than football and baseball, white women athletes competed in volleyball and softball besides track and soccer. Both groups, however, had relatively small numbers of players in fencing, ice hockey, rifle, and rugby. In 20 or 71 percent of the sports, more women than men participated particularly in beach volleyball, bowling, equestrian, field hockey, gymnastics, softball, and triathlon.

Regarding black SAs, there were 16,984 men and 6,415 women in Division II sports during schools' 2015–2016 academic year. Men mostly played on football, basketball, track, and baseball teams while women won and lost against opponents in basketball, track, volleyball, and cross country. Interestingly, zero athletes in the division participated in equestrian, ice hockey, sailing, skiing, and triathlon. Since some of these sports are not popular and also expensive to operate, most midsized and small colleges and universities had no incentives to fund or support them.

Based on data in Table A3.3 of the Appendix, such team sports as soccer, baseball, football, outdoor track, and cross country appealed to Hispanic men athletes and except for baseball and football, women SAs participated in softball and indoor track besides cross country, soccer, and outdoor track. With respect to all sports, Hispanic men had more athletes than women in 10 or 5 percent of them but similar numbers in fencing, golf, lacrosse, rugby, and swimming, and also 19 each in water polo.

Regarding participation in sports among other races in Division II, men athletes totaled 9,124 and women 6,379. While the former group primarily played on soccer, football, baseball, tennis, and outdoor track teams, women mostly populated clubs in soccer, track, tennis, and basketball. They also had more competitors than men in 13 or 46 percent of the sports. Because of schools' budget problems and sport-specific reasons, few SAs of other races existed in beach volleyball, bowling, equestrian, gymnastics, rifle and sailing, and none of them in the triathlon.

Division III

According to information in Table A3.4 of the Appendix, the distribution of 191,473 SAs in Division III sports included 77 percent white, 9 percent black, 5 percent Hispanic, and 9 percent other races. For ratios of men/women athletes by group, these were, respectively, 56/44 percent, 73/27 percent, 63/37 percent, and 58/42 percent. Thus, black men and white women had the highest proportions of players on teams in schools' 2015–2016 academic year.[9]

---

[9] *Idem,* "Sport Sponsorship, Participation, and Demographics Search."

Within races of Division III, the 82,311 white men SAs competed mostly in football, baseball, soccer, outdoor track, and lacrosse while the largest number of white women participated on soccer, track, softball, and volleyball teams. In addition, females also contributed more athletes than men to 14 or 50 percent of the sports. Combined, the fewest white SAs were involved in beach volleyball, rifle, rugby, and triathlon. Across races among men and women, whites had the most equitable distribution in this division during schools' 2015–2016 academic year.

Of 17,921 total black SAs in Table A3.4, men primarily performed on football teams and then in basketball, track, and soccer. Women, meanwhile, competed primarily in basketball followed by track, volleyball, and soccer. Only a few of each group, however, participated in fencing, gymnastics, rugby, squash, and water polo, and none of them choose triathlon as a sport. Compared to those in other races, black men had the highest proportion of SAs at 73 percent and women the lowest at 27 percent. This result, in turn, reflects their abilities, experiences, and interests in becoming college or university athletes.

With the second highest proportion of SAs among races in NCAA Division III during the 2015–2016 academic year, Hispanic men primarily played on soccer teams and then those in football, baseball, and track. Rather than football and baseball, Hispanic women athletes trained and competed to be successful in soccer and also softball, outdoor track, cross country, and volleyball. Furthermore, they had more athletes than men in 13 or 46 percent of the sports. Of least importance as sports for both genders were equestrian, rifle, rugby, skiing, squash, and triathlon.

Given their total of 18,073, other races had the second largest population of SAs in sports of Division III. While men athletes were primarily on teams in football, soccer, track, and baseball, the largest groups of women players enjoyed cross country, soccer, swimming, track, and volleyball. Only a few athletes participated in beach volleyball, bowling, rifle, skiing, and triathlon, but more than 2,100 each in football and soccer programs. In 14 or 50 percent of sports in the division, the number of men SAs exceeded women, in part, because of their schools' decision to join the NCAA and provide funds for athletes' equipment, games, uniforms, and other things.

This concludes the section on the race of SAs and their role within college and university sports programs of NCAA Divisions I, II, and III during the 2015–2016 academic year. Next is some interesting data about the population of athletes and their schools' affiliation with two other national sports organizations. Although not as specific as information about the NCAA and its divisions, the data reveals the types of sports programs sponsored by colleges and universities and the number of men and women who participated in them during various periods.

NAIA

Three years after being named National College Basketball by Dr. James Naismith, the organization was known as the National Association of Intercollegiate Basketball beginning in 1940. Twelve years later, its named changed to NAIA and thus introduced championships in men's golf, tennis, and outdoor track and field. Throughout the next several decades, the NAIA administered sports programs and championships in proper balance with the overall college educational experience. This section reveals the number and distribution of men and women SAs who participated in each NAIA sport during seven academic years.[10]

According to data in Table 3.4, the number of men SAs was 33,353 each academic year during 2008–2014. Across the sports, they ranged from 1,389 in 2008 to 1,605 in 2011. While football averaged 8,291 athletes, baseball 6,835 and soccer 5,501, there were less than 100 each on average in such sports as rowing, ice hockey, skiing, equestrian, and sailing.

With respect to only academic years 2008 and 2014, the average number of athletes increased by 5,518 or 17 percent. In 2012, the number of SAs decreased for some reason but then significantly increased in 2013 and 2014. After 2011, athletes in several sports temporarily declined including those in cross country, football, baseball, and indoor and outdoor track and field.

---

[10] See "Men Student Athlete Participation," http://www.naia.org cited 26 April 2017 and "Women Student Athlete Participation," http://www.naia.org cited 26 April 2017.

Table 3.4.   Men SAs, by NAIA Sport, 2008 to 2014 Academic Years.

Sport	2008	2009	2010	2011	2012	2013	2014
Fall							
Archery	0	0	0	0	10	14	17
Cross Country	733	950	980	950	885	1,044	1,030
Rowing	40	54	43	42	53	48	53
Soccer	5,262	5,513	5,490	5,528	5,551	5,520	5,646
Volleyball	336	335	337	293	333	374	407
Winter							
Basketball	4,451	4,511	4,539	4,471	4,428	4,333	4,596
Bowling	195	315	379	387	491	519	540
Football	8,066	8,061	7,988	8,409	7,948	8,316	9,251
Gymnastics	0	0	0	0	0	23	14
Ice Hockey	80	125	49	54	127	149	204
Rifle	54	69	0	0	0	0	0
Rodeo	141	157	172	157	122	103	100
Table Tennis	7	15	0	0	0	0	0
Skiing	36	29	21	23	26	19	24
Swimming	285	320	271	327	286	323	379
T&F/Indoor	416	619	630	545	477	647	834
Weightlifting	0	10	0	0	0	0	0
Wrestling	779	886	976	1,073	1,154	1,254	1,377
Spring							
Baseball	6,537	6,971	6,913	6,935	6,762	6,642	7,090
Equestrian	9	10	3	4	10	16	21
Golf	1,645	1,748	1,822	1,737	1,644	1,696	1,761
Lacrosse	151	213	332	315	348	450	535
Sailing	22	22	30	33	28	23	16
Tennis	870	925	955	1,006	974	1,041	1,079
T&F/Outdoor	715	1,007	1,189	1,100	1,018	1,224	1,459
Water Polo	103	93	59	54	31	29	45

Note: NAIA is National Association of Intercollegiate Athletics. There were no NAIA teams in the sport during academic years with zero men SAs. Swimming includes diving. T&F is Track and Field.

Source: "Men Student Athlete Participation." http://www.naia.org cited 26 April 2017.

Each year, NAIA winter sports had the largest participation of men SAs and also in the spring and fall. In 2014, for example, there were 17,292 in the winter followed by 12,006 in the spring and earlier 7,153 in the fall. By sport, respectively, they averaged 1,729, 1,500, and 1,430 athletes. As denoted in the table by season, men athletes mostly played on teams in soccer and cross country in the fall, football, and basketball in winters, and baseball and golf in the spring.

Regarding participation by men SAs on teams as of 2014, some sports have declined since 2008 while the majority of others added more athletes. Rodeo, skiing, sailing, and water polo each had relatively fewer athletes during the period compared to such large and more populated sports as football, which increased by 1,185 or 14 percent, baseball by 553 or 8 percent, and soccer by 384 or 7 percent.

Percentagewise, sports like bowling, ice hockey, indoor and outdoor track and field, and lacrosse more than doubled. Overall, there has been above-average growth in schools' sports programs in the NAIA and number of men on teams that play games to win conference titles and championships.

Based on information in Table 3.5, women students have also become more involved athletically by participating on teams in NAIA sports from 2008 to 2014. During each year of the period, they averaged 22,188 as players or 1,170 per sport. Soccer ranked first with 4,676 women SAs per year, basketball second at 3,885, and softball third at 3,862. The next most populated women sport was volleyball followed by outdoor track and field and then lacrosse and cross country.

The only year with fewer female athletes than previously was in 2012. That year, the number of women SAs in such sports as cross country, basketball, swimming, softball, indoor and outdoor track and field, and water polo decreased despite more in several others like bowling, equestrian, golf, and lacrosse. Because the number of men athletes also declined in 2012 especially in football and golf, some schools reduced their budgets and eliminated teams in various male and female NAIA sports.

Among women SAs, more of them participated on teams in fall seasons than those in winter and spring. In 2014, for example, soccer and volleyball combined included approximately 8,600 female athletes while

Table 3.5.   Women SAs, by NAIA Sport, 2008 to 2014 Academic Years.

Sport	2008	2009	2010	2011	2012	2013	2014
Fall							
Archery	0	0	0	0	10	27	26
Cross Country	708	883	928	949	916	1,021	1,039
Field Hockey	54	34	32	35	36	37	46
Soccer	4,431	4,714	4,672	4,706	4,705	4,718	4,788
Volleyball	3,534	3,653	3,745	3,794	3,759	3,794	3,844
Winter							
Basketball	3,871	4,017	3,964	3,917	3,863	3,789	3,780
Bowling	152	229	303	345	384	435	474
Gymnastics	0	0	0	23	0	18	13
Ice Hockey	31	27	24	23	17	23	41
Rifle	12	19	0	0	0	0	0
Rodeo	102	146	136	139	95	95	111
Skiing	32	31	20	25	25	21	22
Swimming	230	265	164	231	107	114	141
Table Tennis	6	5	0	0	0	0	0
T&F/Indoor	305	493	538	468	427	622	771
Wrestling	143	154	136	174	178	171	268
Spring							
Beach Volleyball	0	0	0	215	387	573	700
Equestrian	238	254	110	130	169	201	205
Golf	809	860	902	960	992	1,046	1,076
Lacrosse	123	144	201	252	300	306	461
Rowing	35	40	46	35	27	19	27
Sailing	3	3	10	12	6	7	3
Softball	3,608	3,884	3,812	3,958	3,843	3,923	4,009
Tennis	973	990	992	987	946	946	992
T&F/Outdoor	578	826	1,010	987	902	1,063	1,299
Water Polo	86	87	58	52	23	15	37

Note: NAIA is National Association of Intercollegiate Athletics. There were no NAIA teams in the sport during academic years with zero women SAs. Swimming includes diving and synchronized swimming. T&F is Track and Field.

Source: "Women Student Athlete Participation." http://www.naia.org cited 26 April 2017.

5,621 played in winter sports and another 8,809 in the spring with about 5,300 of the latter group on teams in softball and outdoor track and field. Men SAs, meanwhile, had a relatively larger number in winter than fall or spring because of football, basketball, and wrestling.

After comparing their participation in 2008 to 2014, the number of women athletes declined in field hockey, basketball, rifle, table tennis, skiing, swimming, equestrian, rowing, and water polo — and except for sailing with three each both years — they otherwise increased in other sports. In contrast to that group, female participation more than doubled in bowling and indoor and outdoor track and field, and among the largest NAIA sports, by 401 or 11 percent in softball, 357 or 9 percent in soccer, and 310 or 8 percent in volleyball.

During the seven-year academic period in the NAIA, men SAs on teams increased by 5,518 or 17 percent and women by 4,109 or 20 percent. While both groups improved their participation athletically, schools' athletic departments provided additional opportunities and financial support for females to compete on teams in each season. Thus, sports became more important, popular, and prominent among students in higher education.

NJCAA

The movement to form a unique sports association dedicated to America's two-year colleges happened in 1937 when several track and field coaches and administrators gathered in Fresno, California. A year later, the NCAA rejected a petition from 13 two-year colleges in California to grant their teams and athletes permission to compete at the NCAA track and field championships.[11]

Following the NCAA's rejection, these colleges' officials gathered again in Fresno during the spring of 1938 to organize and form an

---

[11] The NJCAA's founding member schools included Bakersfield College, Chaffey College, Compton College, Fullerton Junior College, Glendale Junior College, Los Angeles City College, Pasadena Junior College, Riverside Junior College, Sacramento Junior College, San Bernardino Valley College, San Mateo Junior College, Santa Monica City College, and Visalia Junior College. See "NJCAA History," http://www.njcaa.org cited 18 March 2017.

association that promoted and supervised a national athletics program exclusively for junior and community colleges. In May, the first constitution of the NJCAA was accepted by its charter members and the organization held its first national championship event in mid-1939.

On its website, the NJCAA lists several sports programs for schools and their athletes. These include baseball, football, ice hockey, swimming/diving, and wrestling for men and 11 other team sports for men and women. The following data — within two tables — reveals the number of men and then women SAs by sport for 10 academic years. The major changes in these numbers are examined to denote their impact on sports in higher education.[12]

As depicted in Table 3.6, the number of men SAs in all NJCAA sports ranged from 31,806 in 2006 — academic year 2006–2007 — to 36,544 in 2011 — academic year 2011–2012. More specifically, during seasons of the organization's 10-year period, the number of male athletes who participated in sports increased five times since 2006 but also declined in 2010, 2012, 2014, and 2015. These occurred, in part, because of changes in the financial status and mission of colleges, decisions by school officials to join and/or withdraw their sport(s) from the NJCAA, growth and decline in number of members, and other factors.

Regarding fall seasons, the lowest number of men SAs was 9,502 in 2006 and highest at 11,338 in 2015. Throughout the period, soccer averaged the most athletes at 4,917 followed by football at 4,749, cross country at 1,023, and the half marathon at 103. Furthermore, the number of SAs in each of these sports decreased in one or more years including soccer twice, football three times, cross country four times, and the half marathon five times. Based on these results, soccer has been the most successful in the group with respect to the average and total growth of athletes in the sport while the half marathon steadily declined from 2011 to 2014 and also included the fewest male SAs from 2006 to 2015.

---

[12] Review the data for this organization at "NJCAA Participation Figures-Men's Division," http://www.njcaa.org cited 18 March 2017, and "NJCAA Participation Figures-Women's Division," http://www.njcaa.org cited 18 March 2017.

Table 3.6. Men SAs, by NJCAA Sport and Season, 2006 to 2015 Academic Years.

Sport	2006	2007	2008	2009	2010	2011	2012	2013	2014	2015
Fall										
Cross Country	884	955	947	1,027	1,045	1,102	1,055	1,089	1,085	1,044
Football	4,398	4,582	4,664	5,031	4,942	5,021	4,735	4,618	4,704	4,800
Half Marathon	98	110	104	107	146	118	114	101	66	69
Soccer	4,122	4,428	4,624	5,024	5,111	5,064	4,976	5,109	5,295	5,425
Winter										
Basketball	6,076	6,292	6,494	6,787	6,642	6,877	6,864	6,899	6,821	6,565
Bowling	164	149	142	136	167	158	175	186	164	161
Ice Hockey	237	241	238	197	205	236	214	211	212	170
Swimming	204	166	192	225	229	253	233	166	173	148
T&F/Indoor	884	889	1,027	1,031	951	1,019	1,079	1,125	1,082	917
Wrestling	805	797	862	943	914	962	983	939	947	845
Spring										
Baseball	10,057	10,179	10,430	10,950	11,047	11,276	11,111	11,347	11,228	11,202
Golf	1,619	1,638	1,703	1,734	1,678	1,724	1,645	1,532	1,395	1,405
Lacrosse	558	613	681	691	679	685	770	750	767	715
Tennis	636	639	679	692	622	639	612	599	567	549
T&F/Outdoor	1,127	1,242	1,416	1,496	1,398	1,410	1,407	1,437	1,452	1,300

Note: NJCAA is the National Junior College Athletic Association. Academic Years are actually 2006–2007 to 2015–2016. T&F is Track and Field. Swimming includes diving.

Source: "NJCAA Participation Figures-Men's Division." http://www.njcaa.org cited 18 March 2017.

With respect to winter seasons in the NJCAA's six sports, the fewest male athletes played in 2006 and most in 2012. During the period, basketball had the highest average of SAs at 6,631 and then indoor track and field at 1,000, wrestling at 899, ice hockey at 216, swimming at 198, and bowling at 160. For various reasons such as schools and changes in their budgets and programs during academic years, the number of male athletes declined in each sport in some years including indoor track and field three times and basketball, swimming, and wrestling each four times, ice hockey five times, and bowling six times. Because it was entertaining and popular among students and fans and also contributed to schools' revenue, basketball had the most men SAs in winter seasons followed by indoor track and field and then wrestling. Alternatively, bowling had the fewest athletes and thus ranked sixth in the group.

Among five spring sports, the number of male SAs ranged from 13,997 in 2006 to 15,734 in 2011. On average, baseball had the highest number of players at 10,882 each year and then golf at 1,607, outdoor track and field at 1,368, lacrosse at 690, and finally tennis at 623. During some years, there were fewer SAs in these sports than before including baseball, lacrosse, and outdoor track and field each three times, golf four times, and tennis five times. According to the data, about 31 percent of men SAs participated in baseball during spring seasons but only 2 percent in tennis. This denotes the distribution of athletes in schools' sports from March to early June.

The variation in women SAs by academic years in NJCAA sports is depicted in Table 3.7. According to the data, the number of female athletes ranged from 18,417 in 2006 to 22,573 in 2014. Because of numerous teams in men's football, wrestling, and baseball and despite plenty in women's softball, these results were considerably less than male athletes' low-to-high numbers of 31,806–to–36,108. Moreover, the difference was 138,500 or 13,850 per year between number of men and women who participated in these sports during seasons of the period.

In fall season of the NJCAA, the least and most number of women athletes competed, respectively, at 6,288 in 2006 and at 8,443 in 2014. Per year, they averaged 3,609 in volleyball, 3,214 in soccer, 797 in cross country, and 73 in the half marathon. While the number of female SAs declined only once each in soccer and volleyball, they fell three times in cross country and four times in the half marathon. Given these results during seasons, the most populated and perhaps successful sport among female women athletes was volleyball and then soccer, cross country, and the half marathon.

During winters of NJCAA sports, 5,388 women SAs played on teams in 2006 and 6,321 in 2011. From 2006 to 2015, basketball averaged 5,110 of these athletes per year, indoor track and field 633, swimming 158, and bowling 44. While the number of them in bowling dropped in three of the 10 years, women SAs participation also declined four times each in

Table 3.7.   Women SAs, by NJCAA Sport and Season, 2006 to 2015 Academic Year.

Sport	2006	2007	2008	2009	2010	2011	2012	2013	2014	2015
Fall										
Cross Country	573	658	741	812	858	849	838	892	858	897
Half Marathon	73	66	75	82	104	79	75	89	81	60
Soccer	2,427	2,508	2,931	3,210	3,325	3,436	3,492	3,598	3,654	3,562
Volleyball	3,215	3,432	3,458	3,589	3,613	3,585	3,701	3,744	3,850	3,910
Winter										
Basketball	4,673	4,801	4,880	5,198	5,264	5,435	5,346	5,260	5,229	5,021
Bowling	94	83	83	84	85	80	100	112	114	105
Swimming	148	131	177	199	180	188	157	140	140	126
T&F/Indoor	473	475	616	655	643	618	646	764	749	692
Spring										
Golf	246	256	285	311	290	272	281	266	266	289
Lacrosse	197	234	279	286	286	298	273	277	299	301
Softball	5,035	5,088	5,263	5,652	5,692	5,566	5,640	5,616	5,787	5,708
Tennis	621	674	676	713	651	621	576	607	573	565
T&F/Outdoor	642	665	822	867	876	835	883	973	973	921

Note: NJCAA is the National Junior College Athletic Association. Academic Years are actually 2006–2007 to 2015–2016. T&F is Track and Field. Swimming includes diving.

Source: "NJCAA Participation Figures-Women's Division." http://www.njcaa.org cited 18 March 2017.

basketball and outdoor track and field, and five times in swimming. Thus, basketball has been the dominant NJCAA sport for female athletes in winter seasons, with bowling being least important.

Regarding five sports in the spring, the fewest and largest number of women SAs performed, respectively, in 2006 and 2014. While softball averaged the most female athletes at 5,504 per year during the periods, lacrosse had only 273. Although participation in the latter sport declined from 2011 to 2012, it also fell twice in outdoor track and field, three times each in golf and softball, and five times in tennis. Nevertheless, softball had the most women SAs throughout the period in spring seasons.

From 2007 to 2008 and again in 2008 to 2009, the participation of women athletes increased in all NJCAA sports. Even so, from 2010 to 2011 and again in 2014 to 2015, 9 or 69 percent of NJCAA sports were less populated among female SAs. Similar results occurred for men athletes from 2014 to 2015 but not in other years. For various reasons, the organization's women sports have been more volatile than men's, in part, because of differences in the number of member colleges and universities who sponsored sports teams in the fall, winter, and spring seasons.

Chapter 4

STUDENT ATHLETES ACADEMIC PERFORMANCES

After competing in one or more team sports during their high school career, some male and female athletes were good enough to be recruited and then eventually accept an athletic scholarship to a college or university. Their decision to attend a particular school in higher education depends on several factors including their type of scholarship and sport, the schools' location, reputation and success, friends and family preferences, coaches' experiences, plans, and historical win–loss records in regular seasons and tournaments, and other personal and sport-specific reasons.

To be admitted into a program of study, student athletes (SAs) must meet the academic requirements of a college or university. In Divisions I and II, the National Collegiate Athletic Association (NCAA) sets initial eligibility standards that consider such things as grade point average (GPA), standardized test scores, and core courses completed in high school and grades in them. Division III schools, meanwhile, hold SAs to challenging but similar overall standards based on the college or university (institution or school) in which they enroll.[1]

---

[1] For more data and information about the organization and its history, policies, requirements, and rules, see "National Collegiate Athletic Association." http://www.britannica.com cited 28 March 2017 and "National Collegiate Athletic Association: History." http://www.thefreedictionary.com cited 28 March 2017. Two books on the NCAA and various college sports topics are Joe Crowley, *In the Arena: The NCAA's First Century*

Schools in higher education are accountable for the academic achievement and progress of their athletes. In Division I, for example, only teams that make a threshold score can participate in championships while those that underperform academically may be penalized including their practices, games and seasons, suspension of their coaches, and reduction in financial aid and/or scholarships. Beginning in the 2019 (2019–2020) academic year, Division I schools' share of NCAA revenue will be linked to academic achievement. While the NCAA distributes funds to schools whose SAs need assistance in the classroom, this will be the first year the amount of money depends on their teams' academic success.

Colleges and universities expect their SAs on teams to commit to academics and pursuit of a degree, and they also require them to meet yearly standards to be eligible to compete. Their athletes' success is continuously tracked using such different measures as grades in their classes, minimum credit hours per team, and overall progress toward earning a degree. In Divisions I, II, and III, schools must confirm the academic eligibility of their SAs to satisfy the NCAA. Those declared ineligible, however, must complete the reinstatement process to compete again.

In the next section are tables indicating different but important academic results of men (male) and women (female) SAs on teams in, respectively, NCAA Divisions I, II, and III sports for selected years or other time periods. Although historic, the data and its interpretation are interesting, relevant, and unique to this chapter's contents because the information denotes athletes' progress, status, and success — or lack thereof — in attempting and completing mostly undergraduate classes individually and as a group at colleges and universities in communities across the United States (U.S.).

DIVISION I

Academic Progress Report

As requirements, schools in this NCAA division normally field teams in at least seven sports each for men and women or six for men and eight

---

(Indianapolis, IN: National Collegiate Athletic Association, 2006), and John Fizel and Rodney D. Fort, *Economics of College Sports: Studies in Sports Economics* (Westport, CT: Praeger, 2004).

for women, with no less than two team sports for each gender. In addition, they must meet minimum financial aid awards for their athletics program and establish maximum financial aid to be awarded for each sport. For those other than football and basketball, schools must play 100 percent of the minimum number of games and/or matches against Division I opponents — while anything over the minimum number of them has to be 50 percent in Division I.

Implemented by the NCAA in 2003 as part of an ambitious academic reform effort in Division I, the Academic Progress Rate (APR) holds schools accountable for the academic progress of their SAs through a team-based metric that accounts for the eligibility and retention of each player for each academic period. The APR actually emerged when Division I presidents and chancellors sought a more timely assessment of academic success at their colleges and universities. At the time, the best measure was a graduation rate calculated under a federally- mandated methodology — which was based on a six-year window and did not take transfers of athletes into account.[2]

Besides developing an APR, schools' presidents also adopted a new graduation rate methodology — titled the Graduation Success Rate (GSR) — that more accurately reflected SA transfer patterns and other factors affecting their graduation. The APR system, meanwhile, includes rewards for superior academic performance and penalizes teams that do not achieve certain benchmarks. Data for it is collected annually from schools by the NCAA, and results are announced each spring. The Division I Committee on Academics (CoA) oversees the APR as part of its responsibilities with the Academic Performance Program. The CoA, which sets policies and recommends legislative changes to the Division I Board of Directors, has the final say on academic changes in Division I.

More specifically, the APR holds institutions accountable for the academic progress of their SAs through a team-based metric that accounts for the eligibility and retention of them each academic term. It is calculated as follows: each SA receiving athletically-related financial aid earns one point for attending school and one point for being academically eligible. A team's total points are divided by the number possible and then

---

[2]Two references are "Division I Academic Progress Report." http://www.ncaa.org cited 6 March 2017 and "Division I Academics," http://www.ncaa.org cited 6 March 2017.

multiplied by 1,000 to equal its APR score. In addition to a team's current-year APR, its rolling four-year APR is also used to determine accountability of schools by the NCAA.

While a score of 930 on the APR is the minimum academic threshold of which a team can be eligible for the postseason, 1,000 means every SA remained eligible and returned to school. Points are deducted for ineligible athletes or those not retained in the sports program. According to Table 4.1 — which contains results by sport and its season for six academic years — men SAs averaged 970 for the period in 12 NCAA team sports. Although ice hockey ranked first, swimming second, and golf and tennis each tied for third, the lowest APRs included track and field and wrestling each tied for ninth, basketball at eleventh, and football twelfth.[3]

There are different ways to read and interpret data in the table. By academic year, for example, the average APRs increased from 966 in both 2009–2010 and 2010–2011 to 976 in 2014–2015. This indicated progress across all sports regarding SAs and their eligibility and retention to qualify for and participate on teams in athletic programs of schools in Division I. In fact, there were no APRs below the minimum threshold. The two major revenue sports — football and men's basketball — had incrementally higher scores almost every year because schools invested additional resources to provide advisors, counseling, and other educational assets and programs to help their SAs succeed in their classes each semester.

Based on the three seasons in Table 4.1, men's highest average APR per team was in five spring sports at 972 and lowest in three fall sports at 966. While the groups' scores increased each academic year from 2010–2011 to 2014–2015 and relative to the fall and winter seasons, they fell in 2010–2011 but then remained constant in 2014–2015 during spring seasons. Thus, schools need to primarily focus on improving APRs of football SAs in fall sports in addition to basketball players in winters and track and field athletes in the spring.

Among APRs of all men's sports during these six academic years in Division I, five scores dropped in 2010–2011 but none in 2011–1202 and only two each in 2012–2013 and 2013–2014. Throughout the period, ice

---

[3]The data is in "Average APRs by Sport for Men's Teams." http://www.ncaa.org cited 16 March 2017.

Table 4.1. Men SAs' Average APRs by Sport, NCAA Division I, Selected Academic Years.

Sport	2009–2010	2010–2011	2011–2012	2012–2013	2013–2014	2014–2015
Fall						
Cross Country	973	975	975	977	976	978
Football	945	947	952	958	962	965
Soccer	969	966	970	971	976	974
Winter						
Basketball	948	951	958	963	965	965
Ice Hockey	982	982	985	985	986	988
Swimming	975	976	979	981	980	979
Wrestling	960	957	965	965	971	978
Spring						
Baseball	963	963	965	970	973	971
Golf	971	970	975	981	986	983
Lacrosse	973	972	979	977	979	982
Tennis	976	973	978	978	979	981
Track & Field	961	961	968	967	971	969

Note: Abbreviated is Academic Progress Report (APR) and National Collegiate Athletic Association (NCAA).The symbol & represents the word and. These are single-year APRs in sports with 50 or more teams. Data was based on $N = 5{,}722$ squads that participated in these sports for six academic years. The sample is 12 sports.

Source: "Average APRs by Sport for Men's Teams." http://www.ncaa.org cited 16 March 2017.

hockey finished first or tied for first in APR each year while football placed 12th except in 2014–2015 when tied with basketball. Such differences between sports existed due to various reasons. These included study habits of players, and time required for them to practice and train for their games, and also because they missed classes due to travel commitments. Besides football and basketball athletes, these problems also affected males on teams in track and field, wrestling, and baseball.

To reveal and truly analyze the academic performance and progress of male athletes in schools within Division I sports programs, such things as changes in their GPA, degree of difficulty in major and minor programs of study, and other specific factors need to be reported in some way and then used to measure progress while in school. Otherwise, the current APR will continue to be a key statistic calculated and published by the NCAA.

Compared to male teams' performances, Table 4.2 denotes the results for female SAs during six academic years in Division I sports. Overall, their average APR of 983 was 1.3 percent higher than men's. Among women teams by sport, gymnastics ranked first at 990, lacrosse second at

Table 4.2.　Women SAs' Average APRs by Sport, NCAA Division I, Selected Academic Years.

Sport	2009–2010	2010–2011	2011–2012	2012–2013	2013–2014	2014–2015
Fall						
Cross Country	981	983	984	983	988	988
Field Hockey	990	990	987	984	989	989
Soccer	978	980	982	983	986	986
Volleyball	977	978	980	983	985	986
Winter						
Basketball	969	971	974	974	980	981
Gymnastics	990	987	987	993	991	992
Swimming	987	985	988	987	991	991
Spring						
Golf	985	983	986	987	990	991
Lacrosse	986	989	988	992	992	992
Rowing	985	986	986	988	989	988
Softball	976	977	977	980	982	984
Tennis	974	985	983	984	985	986
Track & Field	974	975	980	979	983	981

Note: Abbreviated is Academic Progress Report (APR) and National Collegiate Athletic Association (NCAA). The symbol & represents the word and. These are single-year APRs in sports with 50 or more teams. Data was based on N=5,722 squads that participated in these sports for six academic years. The sample is 13 sports.

Source: "Average APRs by Sport for Women's Teams." http://www.ncaa.org cited 16 March 2017.

989, and field hockey and swimming each at 988. Alternatively, the lowest average scores were in basketball at 974, track and field at 978, and softball at 979. Similar to male athletes, female basketball players also struggled academically based on their APR results.[4]

From one academic year to another throughout the period in the table, the average APRs of such women team sports as basketball, soccer, softball, and volleyball either increased or did not change. The others, meanwhile, declined at least once. However, average scores increased each year or from 980 in 2009–2010 to 987 in 2013–2014 and remained there the next year.

There are other interesting features of women's average APRs. As of 2014–2015, for example, they were 983 each in fall and spring seasons and 984 in winters across the 13 sports. Therefore, the results did not change much, i.e., from 980 in 2009–2010 to 987 in 2014–2015 or less than 1 percent. In other words, men's and women's APRs increased by a relatively small number of points and also percentagewise despite expensive investments by Division I schools to help their SAs progress academically in their major courses of study and eventually graduate with an undergraduate degree.

During seasons within academic years, female athletes achieved better results in cross country and field hockey than soccer and volleyball played from September to November; in gymnastics and swimming than basketball during winters; and in golf and lacrosse than the four other sports in the spring. Based on the data in Table 4.2, women basketball and track and field teams had inferior results and thus, they need the most improvements educationally. Simply put, colleges and universities should provide more advisors, counselors, mentors, and additional resources to raise APRs of female teams in these two sports.

From the 2009–2010 to 2014–2015 academic years, the gap between women's and men's average APRs decreased from 14 to 11 percentage points. This indicates that SAs in both groups progressed in their academic performances throughout the period. But more specifically, women athletes in these sports are significantly closer than men to 1,000 points or

---

[4] See the "Average APRs by Sport for Women's Teams." http://www.ncaa.org cited 16 March 2017.

being 100 percent eligible and returning to school to complete requirement and earn a bachelor's degree.

Across all sports, several things were important in the APRs of male and female SAs. Whether they sought degrees in science, technology, engineering, or mathematics in comparison to less rigorous disciplines, for example, influenced many athletes' academic progress from 2009 to 2015. Furthermore, each school had core requirements for students to complete a degree. And, some SAs choose challenging electives while others enrolled in easy classes primarily to increase their GPA. In the end, these were factors causing the variation of APR scores for both genders.

Various reports from the NCAA and studies by academic and professional researchers and scholars reveal more detailed information and also historical data about the academic performances of SAs. Some topics include, for example, athletes' average eligibility and retention rates and their comparative advantages and disadvantages in competing in intercollegiate athletics; accuracy of SAs actual graduation rates; NCAA academic performance metrics; problems with football and men's basketball programs; penalizing teams for lack of academic progress; and ranking colleges who care about their athletes' classes and graduation.[5]

GRADUATION SUCCESS RATE

Because the ultimate goal of the college and university experience is graduation of their SAs in four years, the NCAA has devoted resources to learn more about graduation rates. These schools are required by NCAA legislation and federal law — for example, Student Right-to-Know Act of 1990 — to report all students' graduation rates while institutions offering

---

[5] This book's Bibliography contains several scholarly articles about student athletes' controversies and problems from such sources as *The Chronicle of Higher* Education, *Journal of College Student Development*, *Journal of College and Character*, *Diverse Issues in Higher Education*, *Journal of Blacks in Higher Education*, and *Journal of College Admission*. Other references are "Average Eligibility Rate by Sport for Men's Teams." ncaa.org cited 16 March 2017; "Average Retention Rate by Sport for Men's Teams." ncaa.org cited 1 March 2017; "Average Eligibility Rate by Sport for Women's Teams." ncaa.org cited 16 March 2017 and "Average Retention Rate by Sport for Women's Teams." ncaa.org cited 16 March2017.

financial aid to players must also report these for their SAs. In fact, the NCAA acquires SAs' graduation rate data from the Department of Education's Integrated Post-Secondary Data System Graduation Rate Survey (IPEDS-GRS).[6]

The graduation rate directly based on IPEDS-GRS — which is the methodology the U.S. Department of Education requires — is the proportion of first-year, full-time SAs who entered a school on aid based on athletics and graduated from that institution within six years. This federal rate does not account for students who transferred from their original institution and graduated elsewhere. These are considered non-graduates at both the college they left and the one from which they eventually graduated.

This section of the chapter provides some unique but interesting results for men and women SAs who played on teams in NCAA Division I sports programs within a 10-academic year period. It reveals, by sport and season, these athletes' GSR which, in turn, denotes to what extent they succeeded in obtaining their degree despite numerous hours spent practicing and training for — and also performing on teams in — games for their college or university.

In Table 4.3 are GSRs for men SAs in 17 team sports, by season, during 10 academic years. Expressed as percentages, this data reveals to what extent and when male athletes graduated from a college or university after participating in Division I sports for one or more seasons.

During the period of academic years in the table, the average GSR for the group of men SAs was 80 percent. By sport, gymnastics ranked first at 88 percent with fencing, lacrosse, and water polo tied for second each at 87 percent. The worst scores, however, included football at 69 percent, basketball at 70 percent, and wrestling at 73 percent. Among years, the lowest and highest GSRs were, respectively, 77 percent in 2009 and 86 percent in 2016. Although scores fell in 2009 and 2012, they increased from 2013 to 2016. Based on their distribution from 69 to 88 percent with a mean of 80, these results were below average to average before 2013 but then above average in later academic years.

---

[6]Read, for example, Gary Brown, "NCAA Graduation Rates: A Quarter-Century of Tracking Academic Success." http://www.ncaa.org cited 1 April 2017.

Table 4.3. GSR Trends, NCAA Men's Sports, Division I, Selected Academic Years.

Sport	2007	2008	2009	2010	2011	2012	2013	2014	2015	2016
Fall										
Cross Country/Track	73	75	74	72	78	77	73	80	82	81
Soccer	75	80	77	77	82	79	83	80	84	83
Volleyball	84	80	67	72	87	78	90	83	89	89
Winter										
Basketball	63	65	65	66	67	74	72	73	76	80
Fencing	84	81	81	100	89	89	85	89	90	90
Football	65	64	65	66	70	69	70	73	75	75
Gymnastics	84	86	85	89	92	88	92	88	90	94
Ice Hockey	79	80	79	81	88	82	86	92	88	91
Rifle	82	77	80	82	83	70	90	86	88	87
Skiing	76	88	85	77	90	88	83	80	86	96
Swimming	84	86	81	84	87	83	83	87	86	87
Wrestling	73	70	71	73	74	73	75	75	77	76
Spring										
Baseball	67	71	69	69	77	75	75	78	79	81
Golf	80	79	80	83	82	82	83	86	85	88
Lacrosse	90	90	83	88	89	85	87	90	88	83
Tennis	81	84	86	80	88	86	82	86	91	93
Water Polo	87	91	85	80	87	81	93	87	86	94

Note: NCAA is National Collegiate Athletic Association. Data is percentages. Football is an average of teams in the Football Bowl Subdivision and Football Championship Subdivision. GSR Trends are in percentages. For these academic years, each sample is 17 sports.

Source: "Graduation Success Rate Trends for Division I Men's Sports." http://www.ncaa.org cited 13 April 2017.

Besides the lowest and highest scores for men SAs, athletes on baseball and cross country/track teams underperformed academically while those who played ice hockey, tennis, skiing, and swimming did better than some others in the group such as any in golf, rifle, soccer, and volleyball. In 2016, however, the majority of GSRs improved particularly in water polo while those in football and volleyball remained unchanged. Since 2013, there has been an upward trend in graduation scores of men athletes, which indicates academic success.

Among seasons across all academic years in Table 4.3, the average GSRs of male SAs were higher in spring sports than those in the fall and winter because lacrosse, tennis, and water polo teams had relatively good to very good scores while cross country/track and also basketball, football, and wrestling ranked below-average to average. Furthermore, GSRs declined in 2009 and 2012 by larger margins in fall and winter seasons than scores in the spring. Several factors caused these differences to occur including the number and GPA of seniors eligible to graduate in each sport, teams' academic performances during previous years, and the distribution of athletes by age, race, and socio–economic background.

To compare GSRs between genders, the data for women SAs on teams in 18 NCAA sports appears in Table 4.4. From the 2007 to 2016 academic years, their average success rate was 89 or 11 percent higher than men's. While those in gymnastics, lacrosse, and skiing each tied for first at 94 percent, the three worst in the group included bowling, rifle, and basketball. For some reason, the GSRs of women's bowling teams significantly increased in 2011 and 2014 as did rifle in 2011 and 2013 while basketball improved by almost 10 percent in the period.

For other highlights of data in the table, women's teams in such sports as crew, fencing, field hockey, ice hockey, and swimming each averaged above 90 percent but bowling was below 80. However, if trends in GSRs continue after 2016, bowling's average — which exceeded 87 percent from 2014 to 2016 — will eventually be greater than those in several other sports. Regarding all 18 of them and their SAs graduation rates, they averaged 93 percent as of 2016 with rifle lowest at 87 and skiing highest at 100. Thus, women's teams achieved excellent academic results especially since 2014.

By season, the average GSRs of women teams in Division I was highest in the spring at 90 percent and lowest in winters at 87. While scores declined only once during April to June of 2009, they fell twice in fall seasons and three times in winters. In 2008, for example, ice hockey decreased by nine points and then two and four years later, respectively, four sports decreased in the fall season and at least that many in the winter. However, GSRs surged in some other years because of such things as number and size of teams, better and more productive academic advisors and tutors, and schools' investments in resources to educate their female athletes.

Although women play on basketball teams, they do not participate in baseball, football, or wrestling. Since the latter sports typically require a

Table 4.4.   GSR Trends, NCAA Women's Sports, Division I, Selected Academic Years.

Sport	2007	2008	2009	2010	2011	2012	2013	2014	2015	2016
Fall										
Cross Country/Track	84	85	85	82	86	84	84	86	88	90
Field Hockey	93	93	94	92	95	93	91	97	96	95
Soccer	89	89	88	87	91	88	88	91	92	92
Volleyball	88	88	89	86	90	89	89	92	92	93
Winter										
Basketball	81	85	82	84	85	83	84	86	88	89
Bowling	68	78	86	63	81	61	63	83	90	89
Fencing	89	87	100	88	94	93	93	92	89	96
Gymnastics	94	92	92	91	91	96	94	95	98	97
Ice Hockey	96	87	89	89	94	95	94	95	99	94
Rifle	80	80	82	73	83	70	90	86	88	87
Skiing	100	96	95	90	92	91	91	97	90	100
Spring										
Crew	91	91	92	92	91	94	93	93	94	95
Golf	88	86	89	87	88	91	91	90	93	95
Lacrosse	94	95	92	93	94	96	94	94	96	95
Softball	86	87	85	85	86	85	85	88	91	90
Swimming	91	90	91	90	91	92	91	93	94	94
Tennis	89	90	88	89	90	92	88	95	94	93
Water Polo	81	91	91	91	91	88	96	91	91	90

Note: NCAA is National Collegiate Athletic Association. Data is percentages. The sample is 18 sports.

Source: "Graduation Success Rate Trends for Division I Women's Sports." http://www.ncaa.org cited 13 April 2017.

lot of SAs' time and efforts to practice, train, and prepare for games and tournaments, their male athletes have less opportunity to study for their classes and score passing grades on quizzes, examinations, and term papers in them. Also, football earns the most revenue among Division I schools which, in turn, demands players to perform well and defeat opponents to win games in regular seasons and then qualify for bowls in postseasons. As such, SAs in football must focus too much on sports rather than academics and that negatively affects their graduation rates.

During November 2017, the NCAA's GSR report showed progress because 77 percent of black athletes received diplomas from 2014 to 2017 and 87 percent of all college athletes graduated. Men's basketball had a record-high of 82 percent and women's 92 percent. In addition, players on FBS teams finished at 78 percent including 78 percent in men's basketball, 73 percent in football, and 90 percent in women's basketball. Among black athletes, the overall rate has improved more than 20 percentage points since 2002.[7]

This concludes the analysis of APRs and GSRs of men and women SAs and their teams in Division I sports during various academic years of schools. For the most part, the data reveals differences and trends between them while the author provided reasons for why females have better results than males from an academic perspective in American colleges and universities.

ELIGIBILITY RATES

To interpret data in NCAA reports, eligibility and retention rates are percentages on a 1,000-point scale. An eligibility rate of 987 in a sport, for example, means that SAs on teams earned 98.7 percent of their possible eligibility points. Athletes can earn one each eligibility and retention point per school term. Furthermore, they earn points by being eligible and retained, in school, respectively, in the following term.

A male or female SA — eligible after the fall semester who returns to participate in the spring — is also eligible the following fall, and then returns to a team, earns four points. However, someone who is eligible after the fall but does not return would earn only one or two points. The sum of eligibility and retention points possible and earned determines scores on the NCAA's APR.

According to an NCAA report on eligibility rates of men SAs on schools' teams in Division I sports from the 2009–2010 to 2014–2015

---

[7] "Average Eligibility Rates by Sport for Men's Teams." http://www.ncaa.org cited 16 March 2017.

academic years, their average score was 971 across 12 sports. While ice hockey ranked first at 988, tennis second at 982, and lacrosse third at 980, the three lowest rates included football at 946, track and field at 954, and wrestling at 963. Besides these six sports, baseball and also golf, soccer, and swimming were above-average but not basketball and cross country. Thus, the men's average score exceeded the minimum eligibility rate of 930 for the period.[8]

Because the rates of teams in men's basketball, cross country, and football never declined during any year and only once each in baseball, ice hockey, soccer, swimming, track and field, and wrestling, and twice each in golf, lacrosse and tennis, there was progress by SAs being eligible to play in games for their schools. Throughout the six academic years, the ranges in rates were football's 931, 933, and 942 to ice hockey's 990, 991, and 992. Although football improved from 931 in 2009–2010 to 962 in 2014–2015, the sport had the lowest rate in the latter year, and then basketball, cross county, and wrestling.

From the second to sixth academic years of the report, zero rates dropped in 2011–2012, one in 2013–2014, two in 2012–2013, three in 2014–2015, and 6 or 50 percent of the groups' in 2010–2011. Based on this distribution, athletic departments in Division I schools became more conscientious about their SAs' eligibility requirements after 2010–2011 and thus invested resources in fall, winter, and spring sports programs to get their athletes educated especially in football and men's basketball.

During the period, Division I women teams' eligibility rate averaged 985 or approximately 1–2 percent higher than men's. Of females' 13 sports, field hockey ranked first at 993, lacrosse second at 991, and golf and gymnastics each tied for third at 990. Meanwhile, those with the lowest rates were track and field's 973, basketball's and softball's 980, and cross country's 983. Besides the former group of sports, others with above-average scores included rowing, soccer, swimming, and tennis but not volleyball.[9]

In these years of the division, rates did not decline in women's basketball, cross country, lacrosse, soccer, softball, tennis, and volleyball,

---

[8] "Average Eligibility Rates by Sport for Women's Teams." http://www.ncaa.org cited 16 March 2017.

[9] "Average Retention Rates by Sport for Men's Teams." http://www.ncaa.org cited 16 March 2017.

only once each in golf, gymnastics, rowing and swimming, and twice each in field hockey and track and field. Throughout the period, rates in the majority of these sports also did not decline as much as men's.

Within the period, eligibility scores in women's field hockey, golf, rowing, and swimming dropped in 2010–2011 but then in only one sport during each of the next four years including field hockey in 2011–2012, track and field in 2012–2013 and 2014–2015, and gymnastics in 2013–2014. These were impressive results for schools and their athletic departments regarding the NCAA's academic requirements in female sports.

For both men and women teams, basketball and a few other sports in Division I had below-average eligibility rates. Undoubtedly, such factors as too much time and energy spent by SAs to practice and train and also travel to and from games — rather than studying for their classes and preparing for examinations — contributed in some way to their inferior academic results. To improve them, schools need to allocate more resources to raise rates and ensure their athletes in each sport be eligible for regular-season games and postseason tournaments.

RETENTION RATES

Division I

Regarding another issue about higher education and SAs on teams, the retention rate averaged 964 (or 96.4 percent) for NCAA Division I men's sports from the 2009–2010 to 2014–2015 academic years. Cross country and ice hockey each tied for first place at 977 followed by swimming at 976 and then golf at 972. The three lowest among the group were basketball at 940, baseball at 952, and football at 953. Besides them, soccer and wrestling also scored below 964 but not golf, lacrosse, tennis, and track and field.[10]

Across 12 sports in the six academic-year period, football's retention rates did not decline while those in basketball, golf, ice hockey, lacrosse, swimming, and wrestling each dropped once and twice in baseball, cross country, soccer and tennis, and also three times in track and field. Since

---

[10] "Average Retention Rates by Sport for Women's Teams." http://www.ncaa.org cited 16 March 2017.

football generates the most revenue for schools in the division, it is important for schools to retain their SAs to play games in each season.

For other scores about eligibility, the rates in baseball and cross country each dropped in 2011–2012, three sports in both 2012–2013 and 2013–2014, four in 2010–2011, and five in 2014–2015. Based on these results, there is no clear-cut positive or negative trend in the data although 8 or 66 percent of the sports declined after 2012–2013 but not football, lacrosse, tennis, and wrestling.

In 2009–2010 compared to 2014–2015, the retention rates of nine male sports increased while cross country remained at 976, swimming at 975, and track and field at 970. Of the group, basketball improved by 17 percentage points, wrestling by 15, and golf by 12. Thus, most schools were able to retain their SAs in Division I sports programs.

With respect to 13 women's sports in the division across six academic years (2009–2014), their retention rate averaged 979 or 15 percentage points higher than men's. Among the group, gymnastics had the highest rate at 988 followed by lacrosse at 986 and then swimming at 985. Alternatively, the lowest scores were basketball at 965, softball at 974, and soccer at 975. Besides those in the former group, five other women sports ranked above 979 but not tennis and volleyball.[11]

During the period, the retention rates in women's basketball, lacrosse, soccer, softball, and volleyball never dropped while those in golf, gymnastics, rowing, swimming, and tennis each fell once, cross country and track and field each twice, and field hockey three times. Except for gymnastics' seven percentage point decrease in 2010–2011, the other changes in scores were relatively small.

From 2012–2013 to 2014–2015, rates in women's cross country, field hockey, and track and field each fell twice, indicating problems for schools to retain their SAs. But in 8 or 61 percent of the sports, their rates increased especially in basketball. Although rowing's remained at 985, the sport is above-average among the group.

Similar to those in eligibility, women teams generally have higher retention rates than men in the majority of NCAA sports. In fact, there

---

[11] References for this NCAA division include "Division II." http://www.ncaa.org cited 23 March 2017 and "Division II Academic Philosophy." http://www.ncaa.org cited 6 March 2017.

was a 16 percentage-point difference between genders in 2009–2010 and 14 in 2014. Despite more resources devoted to retaining men SAs particularly in Division I basketball and football programs, women continue to remain in school and participate in sports. Although average retention rates in women's basketball, soccer, and softball are at the bottom of the distribution, they have improved since 2009–2010 and likely will after 2014–2015.

In the next section, there is data and other information about topics regarding SAs and their academic performances in schools within NCAA Division II sports. It is interesting, special, and unique to research, study, and learn about since these colleges and universities typically have fewer students and less resources for athletes, and also their athletic departments operate sports programs with smaller budgets than those in Division I.

Division II

As of 1972, the NCAA's smaller schools were grouped together in the College Division. Then in 1973, the division split in two when the NCAA began using numeric designations to identify its types of sports. The organization's members — colleges and universities — wanting to offer athletic scholarships — or compete against those who did — became Division II while those choosing not to offer athletic scholarships established Division III. A large minority of Division II institutions (schools) has less than 5,000 students and only a few consist of more than 15,000. The division has a diverse membership including some in Puerto Rico, and also expanded its capacity enough to welcome an international member.[12]

Division II institutions must sponsor at least five each sports for men and women — or four men and six women — with two team sports for each gender and play seasons represented by each of them. There are number of games and participant minimums for each sport and scheduling criteria with football and men's and women's basketball teams each playing at least 50 percent of their games against Division

---

[12] "Division II Academic Success Rate." http://www.ncaa.org cited 6 March 2017.

II or Football Bowl Subdivision (FBS) or Football Championship Subdivision (FCS) opponents.

For sports other than football and basketball, there are no scheduling requirements. Besides no attendance requirements for football or arena size in basketball, there are maximum financial aid awards for each sport, a separate limit on financial aid awards in men's sports, and teams usually feature a number of local or in-state SAs. Many of them pay for their expenses through a combination of scholarships, grants, student loans, and employment earnings. Like other academic departments on campus, Division II athletics programs are financed based on the school's budget and from traditional rivalries with regional institutions who dominate their sports schedules.

ACADEMIC SUCCESS RATE

In 2006, NCAA Division II established an Academic Success Rate (ASR) — which unlike the federal graduation rate (FGR) — measures graduation outcomes for SAs not receiving athletically-related financial aid. In addition, the ASR includes transfer athletes and midyear enrollees in the cohort, whereas the FGR does not. Because of those additional criteria, the Division II cohort includes nearly twice as many SAs as the federal study.[13]

When the GSR was developed for Division I, the member schools in Divisions II and III wondered whether a similar methodology could apply to them even though the characteristics of membership are different in each division. For example, Division I SAs are more likely than their Division II counterparts to receive a full athletics grant-in-aid. In Division II, grants are based on a partial-scholarship model whereby many athletes receive a portion of athletics-based aid but few get a "full ride". Division II also has a greater number of SAs who participate in sports without receiving any athletics-based aid at all.

For schools in Division II, their ASR is similar to the GSR. However, it also includes freshmen who did not receive athletics aid but did participate in athletics. As the GSR does in Division I, the ASR reveals SAs'

---

[13] "ASR Trends for Division II Men's Sports." http://www.ncaa.org cited 16 March 2017.

graduation rates that are much higher than those established by the federal methodology.

From year-to-year, ASRs are usually not as high as graduation rates of SAs in Divisions I and III. But on average, they are higher than graduation rates of the school's general student body. An important reason for differences between divisions is that the academic missions of many Division II institutions cater to non-traditional students and families who have no history of being associated with higher education. To demonstrate the positive effect that athletics participation has on academic performance of athletes at this division's schools, the gap in graduation rates between Division II SAs and the general student body is typically wider than those in Division I but not Division III.

Table 4.5 contains ASRs (in percentages) of men SAs on teams in 16 Division II sports for eight academic years. Among the group, skiing ranked first at 88 percent followed by rifle at 85 percent and fencing at 83 percent. Alternatively, the three lowest rates were football's 53, wrestling's 56, and basketball's 58. Based on an average ASR of 72 percent, 9 or 56 percent of the men's sports had higher rates while the other seven scored below it.[14]

With respect to individual sports within the group, none of them experienced an increase in their ASRs each year. While baseball and ice hockey each declined only in 2012, cross country/track in 2013, and soccer in 2015, fencing and wrestling each fell four times and the others declined in two or three years. For various reasons, the averages of 10 or approximately 62 percent of the sports dropped in 2012 but only volleyball and water polo did in 2014 and fencing, soccer, and wrestling in 2015.

Besides that information, there were other interesting results from the data in Table 4.5. Between 2010 and 2016, for example, the ASRs of such sports as football, cross country/track, and lacrosse actually but gradually decreased while those in soccer, basketball, and baseball did not change much at, respectively, 70–72, 58–60, and 69–71 percent. The sports with the greatest improvements in men's graduation rates since 2009 included fencing by 13 percentage points, ice hockey 8, water polo 7, and golf 6. Some reasons for these changes were because of

---

[14] "ASR Trends for Division II Women's Sports." http://www.ncaa.org cited 16 March 2017.

Table 4.5.   Men SAs' ASR Trends, by Sport, NCAA Division II, 2009–2016 Academic Years.

Sport	2009	2010	2011	2012	2013	2014	2015	2016
Fall								
Cross Country/Track	71	72	72	72	70	70	70	71
Soccer	68	70	71	72	72	72	71	72
Volleyball	68	66	71	72	71	70	70	71
Winter								
Basketball	58	59	60	58	58	58	58	58
Fencing	77	71	76	71	85	100	97	90
Football	53	54	54	54	53	53	53	51
Ice Hockey	75	78	78	77	77	79	81	83
Rifle	88	100	88	82	83	83	83	78
Skiing	85	88	87	86	88	89	89	93
Swimming	76	74	76	75	75	77	77	77
Wrestling	58	57	60	57	54	55	54	54
Spring								
Baseball	68	69	70	69	69	70	70	71
Golf	70	72	74	73	73	74	75	76
Lacrosse	75	77	76	76	74	74	74	70
Tennis	77	79	79	78	78	79	81	81
Water Polo	72	78	77	77	80	75	80	79

Note: Abbreviations are Academic Success Rate (ASR) and National Collegiate Athletic Association (NCAA). Data is four-class averages, in percent, by reporting year such as 2015 representing 2005–2008 cohorts and 2016 the 2006–2009 cohorts. The sample is 16 sports.

Source: "ASR Trends for Division II Men's Sports." http://www.ncaa.org cited 16 March 2017.

differences in the number and size of teams in each sport during years of the period, effectiveness of academic advisors, counselors, and tutors in helping to educate their school's male SAs, and investments in education programs.

By season, men SAs in spring sports had the highest average ASR at 74 percent but the lowest rates at 70 percent occurred for those who played on cross country/track, soccer, and/or volleyball teams in the fall. During winters, while basketball, football, and wrestling athletes had the worst academic results, male players in fencing, ice hockey, and skiing were more productive and did relatively better in the classroom. Given these outcomes, the former group of SAs had more problems attending classes, studying for exams, and learning from educational resources provided by their schools than those in the latter three sports. This, in turn, was the variation in athletes' scores across fall, winter, and spring seasons.

In sum, the average ASRs of male SAs on sports teams ranged from 71 percent each in 2009 and 2012 to 73 percent in 2011 and also in 2014 to 2016. Although the averages had fluctuated each year before 2014, the athletes' success rate percentages remained constant during the next three academic years.

Despite an increase in rates of 2 percentage points from 2009 to 2016, schools need to be more aggressive and commit to increase their academic support of men athletes especially those who participate on teams in basketball, wrestling, and football. Otherwise the ASRs of these SAs may decline which, in turn, will create problems for the schools and their athletic programs from the NCAA and also from sports conferences and perhaps national organizations that validate their educational programs.

Table 4.6 lists in columns the ASRs of women SAs on teams in 17 NCAA Division II sports of colleges and universities. During the period of academic years, their ASR averaged 84 or 12 percentage points higher than men's. While the range in females' ASRs varied from a low of 82 percent in 2009 to a high of 86 percent in 2016, they increased in 2010 and 2015 but also declined in 2012 and did not change in 2011, 2013, and 2014. Thus, women's ASRs expanded by 4 percentage points from the first to eighth year versus men's 2 percentage points.[15]

---

[15] Both the FGR and ASR measure SAs' graduation success within six years. However, the federal rate includes only first-time fall freshmen on athletics aid and only removes students who died, were disabled, or took an extended pause in their education to pursue military or church service. The ASR starts with the federal group, adds transfers and January enrollees, and then removes from all groups the exceptions listed above plus those athletes who left the institution while eligible to compete. Thus, the FGR and ASR are not equal because of different populations — ASR includes transfers, mid-year enrollees, and non-scholarship athletes — and also because of different calculation methods — ASR removes those who leave eligible.

Table 4.6.   Women SAs' ASR Trends, by Sport, Division II, 2009–2016 Academic Years.

Sport	2009	2010	2011	2012	2013	2014	2015	2016
Fall								
Cross County/Track	81	82	84	83	81	81	82	83
Field Hockey	91	92	92	93	94	95	94	94
Soccer	81	82	84	82	83	84	84	86
Volleyball	79	80	82	82	84	85	85	86
Winter								
Basketball	75	77	79	79	78	78	77	78
Bowling	63	91	88	85	79	79	82	79
Fencing	96	96	83	81	74	73	75	78
Gymnastics	80	89	86	85	87	89	93	93
Ice Hockey	80	82	82	83	84	83	85	87
Skiing	83	84	84	82	84	91	94	90
Swimming	85	87	88	87	85	86	87	89
Spring								
Crew	87	88	89	89	89	88	88	89
Golf	82	83	84	85	85	85	85	86
Lacrosse	89	90	90	90	90	91	91	91
Softball	80	81	82	81	81	81	82	82
Tennis	83	86	86	86	86	87	88	89
Water Polo	88	89	91	86	86	88	87	88

Note: Abbreviations are Academic Success Rate (ASR) and National Collegiate Athletic Association (NCAA). Data is four-class averages, in percent, by reporting year such as 2015 representing 2005–2008 cohorts and 2016 the 2006–2009 cohorts. The sample is 17 sports.

Source: "ASR Trends for Division II Women's Sports." http://www.ncaa.org cited 16 March 2017.

According to data in the table, women SAs who played field hockey had the highest-ranked average ASR at 93 percent followed by lacrosse's 90 and crew's 88. Besides those three sports, there were others with above-average results including gymnastics, skiing, swimming, tennis, and water polo. Alternatively, the lowest success rates of female athletes was 77 percent in basketball and then 80 in bowling and 81 in softball. Others that scored below-average were cross country/track, fencing, ice hockey, soccer, and volleyball. Consequently, this was the distribution of women's ASRs in Division II as of 2016.

Regarding each sport across the multiyear period, ASRs of women in golf, lacrosse, tennis, and volleyball did not decline in percentage points in contrast to all those of men's. Among specific years, all these sports had higher rates from 2009 to 2010 but one or more experienced lower percentages thereafter including three each in 2011 and 2014 to 2016, five in 2013, and nine in 2012. In contrast, the ASRs of 10 men's sports also fell in 2012. For various reasons, both groups' worst performances in success rates occurred that year but then recovered shortly thereafter.

Each sport in the division experienced proportional changes in their ASRs when comparing 2009 to 2016. While water polo's was 88 percent in the first and eighth years of the table, fencing's rate decreased from 96 to 78 percent. Others, meanwhile significantly increased, such as bowling by 16 percentage points, gymnastics 13, ice hockey and skiing and volleyball each seven, tennis six, soccer five, and swimming four. Those with the smallest increase in rates — other than water polo — included basketball at 3 percent and crew, cross country/track, lacrosse, and softball each at 2 percent. Interestingly, these were roughly similar to changes among those in men's sports despite a relatively large difference in their average ASRs.

Besides that information, other highlights existed among the data of 17 women sports in NCAA Division II. Regarding seasons, female SAs in spring sports had the highest average ASRs at 86 percent and then those in the fall at 85 and winter at 83. While lacrosse ranked first among the group in the spring, field hockey in the fall and gymnastics in winters, the worst rates were, respectively, softball, cross country/track, and basketball. Because of their commitment to be competitive, respected, and serious SAs, women's ASRs exceeded men's by 15 percentage points in fall season, 12 in the spring, and 11 in winters. There, of course, would be a much smaller gap between them without such all-male sports as baseball, football, and wrestling.

If trends continue after 2016, the gap in ASRs between women and men will likely increase rather than decrease or remain constant. From 2015 to 2016, for example, the average rate of male SAs declined while the ASR of females increased by one percentage point. Furthermore, such major sports as football, wrestling, and men's basketball did not appreciate in percentage points in recent years. In contrast, 10 or almost 60 percent of women's increased including highly-populated basketball, cross country/track, and soccer teams. Thus, schools may need to shift some of their resources among sports programs to keep more male athletes eligible and available to play in games.

FEDERAL GRADUATION RATE (FGR)

Adopted in 1990 and compiled by the U.S. Department of Education, the FGR is a different measurement than the ASR because it treats SAs who transfer as non-graduates of the original institution attended even if they graduated from another institution, and also does not include those in the graduation rate at the new institution from which they graduate. As a result, FGRs are lower than those of the ASR. Despite these differences, the NCAA publishes both groups of rates annually since they measure in some way athletes' graduation success within six years. Based on that information, this section identifies and discusses the trends in FGRs for men and women SAs on teams in Division II sports programs for eight reporting years.[16]

Men's FGRs

To determine players' academic success, Table 4.7 reveals four-class averages each of FGRs for men SAs on teams in 16 sports as calculated from 2009 to 2016. For the period, the average rate was 53 percent and ranged from a low of 50 percent in 2011 and also 2012 to a high of 56 percent in both 2015 and 2016. While the rate declined only in 2011 and remained constant in 2012 and 2016, it increased in other years.[17]

Across the period of years, rifle had the highest average FGR among male athletes at 69 percent followed by fencing at 66 and then swimming at 59. Alternatively, the three lowest averages by sport were football's

---

[16] "Federal Graduation Rate Trends for Division II Men's Sports." http://www.ncaa.org cited 16 March 2017.

[17] "Federal Graduation Rate Trends for Division II Women's Sports." http://www.ncaa.org cited 16 March 2017.

Table 4.7.   Men's FGR Trends, Division II, by Season, 2009–2016 Academic Years.

Sport	2009	2010	2011	2012	2013	2014	2015	2016
Fall								
Cross Country/Track	55	55	53	53	52	53	54	55
Soccer	50	51	52	52	53	53	52	53
Volleyball	42	40	40	46	54	54	56	54
Winter								
Basketball	46	46	46	44	44	45	45	46
Fencing	50	50	50	50	67	90	89	82
Football	43	43	43	42	41	41	41	40
Ice Hockey	51	51	50	50	53	57	64	66
Rifle	50	100	50	58	78	72	77	68
Skiing	47	46	42	43	52	59	57	58
Swimming	60	57	60	59	60	61	61	61
Wrestling	50	48	48	45	40	40	39	40
Spring								
Baseball	51	51	52	51	50	50	51	51
Golf	55	55	56	56	56	56	56	55
Lacrosse	59	57	56	57	54	53	54	51
Tennis	60	60	59	56	55	57	58	60
Water Polo	58	61	54	53	53	50	53	57

Note: Abbreviation is National Collegiate Athletic Association (NCAA). Data is four-class averages, in percent, by reporting year such as 2015 representing 2005–2008 cohorts and 2016 the 2006–2009 cohorts. The sample is 16 sports.

Source: "Federal Graduation Rate Trends for Division II Men's Sports." http://www.ncaa.org cited 16 March 2017.

41 percent, wrestling's 43, and basketball's 45. Besides those scores, others with above-average rates included golf, ice hockey, lacrosse, tennis, and water polo while baseball, skiing, soccer, and volleyball each finished below 53 percent. However, any SAs on cross country/track teams were average in FGRs. Overall, men's ranged from football's 41 percent to rifle's 69.

There were other interesting characteristics about the data in Table 4.7. First, while averages declined only one year in basketball (2012), golf

(2016), ice hockey (2011), and soccer (2015), they dropped twice each in baseball, cross country/track, fencing, swimming, and volleyball, three times each in football, rifle, skiing, tennis, and water polo, and four or five years each in lacrosse and wrestling. In other words, FGRs changed at least once in all men's sports within the division because of such things as differences in the number of SAs on teams, athletes' decisions to transfer from one school to another, and players' types of classes especially as juniors and seniors.

Second, rifle ranked first or second among male sports in most years while basketball was consistently either 13th or 14th and football at 14th, 15th, or 16th. In comparison to them, the other men's sports generally did not finish really high or very low in the group but placed somewhere between third and 12th or close to average. These included, for example, teams in cross country/track, soccer, and water polo.

Third, across the multiyear period, SAs in spring sports had the highest average FGR at 54 percent, and then those in the winters at 53 percent, and fall seasons at 51 percent. Nevertheless, average scores dropped in 2011, 2012, and 2013 during spring seasons, in 2011 and 2016 in winters, and only in 2010 among teams in the fall. Otherwise, the FGRs increased or remained constant in other years. Thus, SAs on teams in fall sports and not those in the winter or spring experienced less volatility or changes in graduation rates, in part, because of their commitment to graduate as senior students with an undergraduate degree within six academic years.

Fourth, FGRs declined or increased differently among the group of men's sports from 2010 to 2016. In 2014, for example, they fell in lacrosse, rifle, and water polo but either increased or did not change in the other 13 sports. But in 2011 and 2012, rates decreased in seven sports including tennis and water polo each twice. During other reporting years, the FGRs mostly increased or remained constant. From a federal perspective, this was the distribution of SAs' graduation rates among the 16 sports in Division II within the period.

Because of their different populations and methodologies, a large gap existed between men SAs' average FGR of 53 percent and ASR of 72 percent. Moreover, results were not similar among groups with the highest rates from one reporting year to another or by type of sport. While rifle, fencing, and swimming ranked first to third in FGRs, it was skiing, rifle, and fencing in ASRs. The lowest average rates in each method, however, were the same with basketball ranked 14th, wrestling 15th, and football 16th. Despite being interesting but also complex and unique statistics analyzed and applied by researchers and organizations like the NCAA, the FGR and ASR were actually accurate and more consistent in identifying men's team sports with the worst rates but not highest within Division II during the 2009 to 2016 period of academic years.

Women's FGRs

To continue discussing this topic, Table 4.8 reveals the trends in FGRs for SAs on women teams in 17 Division II sports for eight reporting years. Based on data in the table, the average graduation rate among females was 67 percent which, in comparison, exceeded male's by 15 percentage points.[18]

Among sports, the top three FGRs were in fencing at 97 percent followed by field hockey at 77 and lacrosse at 74. Alternatively, the lowest rates included softball and water polo each tied for 15th at 61 percent and basketball at 59. Besides those six team sports and tennis, the other 10 ranked above- or below-average within the group. While the former consisted only of swimming, the latter nine sports had average rates somewhere between 61 and 67 percent. Some tied, however, such as crew and gymnastics each at 62 percent, soccer and volleyball at 63, cross country/track and golf at 64, and ice hockey and skiing at 65. According to these results, women teams' FGRs were more concentrated or deviated less than men's with most percentages at or near the mean other than such outliers as fencing at the top of the distribution and basketball at the bottom of it.

Among reporting years from 2010 to 2016 inclusive, the average rates of female SAs increased in 2010, 2013, 2014, and 2016, decreased in 2011 and 2012, and did not change from 2014 to 2015. In addition, they ranged from 65 percent in 2012 to 69 percent in 2016, but with respect to the first and last year of the period, increased by only 3 percent. Based on this information, women's FGRs in their sports were always higher than men's with less volatility of them between years and across the period.

---

[18] *Idem*, see Note 5 in this section of the chapter.

But similar to those of males, female rates had very small but frequent percentage changes within Division II sports.

Other interesting but relevant facts are important to examine in Table 4.8. First, regarding changes in women's graduation rates of specific sports during the period, fencing was first each reporting year in scores with field

Table 4.8.   Women's FGR Trends, Division II, by Season, 2009–2016 Academic Years.

Sport	2009	2010	2011	2012	2013	2014	2015	2016
Fall								
Cross Country/Track	64	65	66	66	64	63	64	65
Field Hockey	80	77	79	75	77	78	78	76
Soccer	64	63	63	62	62	63	64	65
Volleyball	61	62	62	62	64	65	65	65
Winter								
Basketball	60	60	61	60	59	60	58	58
Bowling	69	83	76	59	61	62	63	61
Fencing	100	100	100	100	100	100	87	91
Gymnastics	63	62	53	51	58	66	71	74
Ice Hockey	65	64	59	60	65	66	70	74
Skiing	54	57	60	57	66	77	77	78
Swimming	73	74	74	72	69	70	70	72
Spring								
Crew	50	53	55	63	64	69	72	72
Golf	64	64	65	66	65	63	64	64
Lacrosse	79	76	76	74	72	74	72	71
Softball	63	63	62	61	61	61	61	62
Tennis	65	67	66	67	68	68	69	68
Water Polo	52	67	67	57	54	65	64	68

Note: Abbreviated is National Collegiate Athletic Association (NCAA). Data is four-class averages, in percent, by reporting year such as 2015 representing 2005–2008 cohorts and 2016 the 2006–2009 cohorts. The sample is 17 sports.

Source: "Federal Graduation Rate Trends for Division II Women's Sports." http://www.ncaa.org cited 16 March 2017.

hockey either second or third and lacrosse third for three times while basketball, softball, and/or water polo each ranked from 15th to 17th in the majority of years. Because of gradual improvements academically, FGRs of female skiing teams finished 15th or 16th in 2009, 2010, and 2012 but then third in 2014 and 2015 and also second in 2016.

Second, comparing FRGs in academic years 2009 to 2016, there were relatively large increases — besides skiing (from 54 to 78 percent) — in such women sports as crew, gymnastics, and water polo, while only small improvements in scores occurred in cross country/track, soccer, tennis, and volleyball. Alternatively, rates declined in basketball, bowling, fencing, field hockey, lacrosse, softball, and swimming but did not change in golf at 64 percent. As a result, this distribution denotes the variation in FRGs from the first compared to eighth reporting year of Division II female sports.

Third, with respect to changes in FRGs among all reporting years, only rates in cross country/track and golf declined on average in 2004–2007 relative to 10 sports in 2002–2005. During other four-year periods in Table 4.8, from three to six sports had smaller graduation rates of women athletes. But in men's sports within the division, the largest decline in average FRGs was seven each in 2001–2004 and 2002–2005 but only in lacrosse, rifle, and water polo during 2004 to 2007. Apparently, the SAs on sports teams in some schools failed to graduate on schedule because of grade problems and other issues.

Fourth, in each season throughout the multiyear period of Division II sports, the average FRGs of women athletes were highest in winter sports at 69 percent and then of those in the fall at 66 percent and in spring at 65 percent. Among each of these seasons, respectively, they ranged from 97 percent in fencing to 59 in basketball, 77 percent in field hockey to 63 each in soccer and volleyball, and 74 in lacrosse to 61 in softball. Because of different factors including their academic programs and educational resources while in school, the largest gap in graduation rates occurred among female SAs in cross country/track, field hockey, soccer, and volleyball.

Fifth, in the 2016 reporting year — or 2006–2009 period — the average FGRs increased in 13 women sports but also declined in bowling, field hockey, lacrosse, and tennis. Fencing's rate ranked first at 91 percent and basketball's 17th at 58 percent. In comparison to the 2010 reporting year — or 2000–2003 period — the graduation rates of women in 12 sports were higher led by fencing at 100 percent. But then field hockey, gymnastics, ice hockey, lacrosse, and soccer each had smaller percentages with crew being lowest at 50 percent. Within the two four-year periods, this depicts the difference in women FGRs reported in year 2010 relative to 2016.

This concludes the analysis of ASRs and FGRs of male and female SAs on teams in Division II sports during various academic years. For the most part, the data reveals differences and trends between them while the contents denoted reasons for why females had better results than males from an academic perspective in colleges and universities.

Reports of the NCAA and studies by researchers and scholars provide more information and also historical data about the academic performances of SAs in Division II sports. Some topics include, for example, their average eligibility and retention rates and also comparative advantage among classmates by being in intercollegiate athletics; accuracy and consistency of graduation rates; NCAA academic performance metrics; problems with football and men's basketball athletes; penalizing teams for academic problems; and ranking college programs.[19]

In the next section, there is data and other information about topics regarding SAs and their academic performances in schools within NCAA Division III sports. This subject is interesting, special, and unique to research, study, and learn about since these colleges and universities typically have fewer undergraduate students, less resources for athletes, and also their athletic departments operate sports programs with smaller budgets than those in Divisions I and II.

DIVISION III

Because academics, not sports, are always the primary focus of men and women SAs, this NCAA division minimizes conflicts between athletics and academics and keeps players on a path to graduate through shorter practices

---

[19] For the history and sports regarding this NCAA division and its schools and student athletes, see "Division III." http://www.ncaa.org cited 23 March 2017 and "Division III Academics." http://www.ncaa.org cited 6 March 2017.

and playing seasons, competing in less number of games per season, and avoiding redshirting and lengthy regional or national competitions that reduce time spent on their studies. Athletes are integrated on campus and treated like other members of the general student-body, which in turn, makes them accountable, committed, and responsible students. As denoted in this chapter, the NCAA has collected and reported graduation rates since the early 1990s for students — using the six-year federal methodology — and also for all SAs receiving athletically-related financial aid.[20]

Since 2010, Division III schools have voluntarily submitted data for officials to calculate an ASR — which is the percentage of non-scholarship SAs that either graduated or left school in good academic standing prior to graduation and also those that transferred into a school. Before 2010, there was no separate report on SAs in Division III schools because they did not award athletics grants-in-aid. While many Division III institutions and conferences tracked the academic success of their athletes, they used a variety of criteria such as number of graduates, grade-point average, and class rank. But now, the NCAA's reporting program produces data from a representative sample of schools and it consistently shows that Division III SAs graduate at higher rates than those in the student body.

Tracking the graduation success of men and women SAs in Division III sports is different than in the other NCAA divisions. That is because of the primary tenet of their philosophy, which calls for athletes to be treated the same as other students in every facet of their educational experience. As such, SAs in Division III do not receive athletics-based financial aid and are not subject to division-wide, initial-eligibility standards. Since the division's athletes do not receive athletics-based aid — which is an essential trigger in collecting graduation rates at Division I schools — those in Division III are not required to report rates specifically for their SAs although they still must fulfill the federal reporting requirement for the student body.

During the early 2000s, Division III schools had rapid membership growth yet withstood a vote by members to either create a new organization or subdivide the existing one. As a result, the division embarked on

---

[20] "Division III Men's Sports (Voluntary Schools)." http://www.ncaa.org cited 16 March 2017.

an identity initiative to define itself more than just "the division that does not grant athletics scholarships". In fact, part of that effort was to define what it stood for academically.

Until then, officials assumed that SAs in Division III schools did as well as their student peers in the classroom. But as the identity initiative gained momentum, college and university presidents and chancellors began to seek data upon which to make that claim. That was when the NCAA developed an ASR for the division's members.

The ASR for Division III schools is similar to the metric used for Division II institutions because it does not rely on SAs receiving athletics-based aid as a mechanism for being counted in the survey. As such, the ASR's accuracy and success is based on schools' ability, resources, and willingness to provide the information since it goes beyond their federal obligation.

In accordance with their philosophy, there is no legislative requirement for Division III schools to submit data on graduation rates. However, the division's Presidents Council was interested enough to collect the data and thus, encouraged their institutions to participate in a two-year pilot program to track the entering classes of academic years 2003 and 2004. Part of the premise was the belief that SAs were "out-graduating" their student-body peers as they might do in Divisions I and II and that Division III schools could reap the publicity benefit by proving it.

Men Athletes

Based on the data in Table 4.9, the two measures of graduation success for men SAs in Division III sports averaged, respectively, 84 percent for the ASR and 66 percent the FGR as of three reporting years. Across the 11 team sports in the division, the ASR — which does not rely on male athletes receiving athletics-based aid as the mechanism for being counted — was always much higher than the FGR because it includes different populations and calculation methods.[21]

---

[21] "Division III Women's Sports (Voluntary Schools)." http://www.ncaa.org cited 16 March 2017.

Table 4.9. Men SAs ASRs and FGRs by Sport, Division III, 2014–2016 Reporting Years.

Sport	2014		2015		2016	
	ASRs	FGRs	ASRs	FGRs	ASRs	FGRs
Fall						
Cross Country/Track	88	73	88	73	88	73
Soccer	84	66	83	64	83	65
Winter						
Basketball	81	61	81	60	80	60
Football	76	55	76	54	75	53
Ice Hockey	87	65	87	65	86	63
Swimming	88	76	88	76	87	76
Wrestling	82	60	81	61	82	63
Spring						
Baseball	84	64	84	64	86	66
Golf	86	66	86	67	88	70
Lacrosse	85	67	86	66	87	67
Tennis	92	77	91	76	91	76

Note: NCAA is the National Collegiate Athletic Association. The Academic Success Rates (ASRs) and Federal Graduation Rates (FGRs) are four-year averages. Based on reporting years 2014, 2015, and 2016, the entering cohorts were, respectively, 2004–2007, 2005–2008, and 2006–2009.

Source: "Average Federal Graduation Rates and ASRs for Division III Men's Sports (Voluntary Schools)." http://www.ncaa.org cited 21 April 2017.

To explain each statistic, the ASR ranked tennis first on average at 91 percent and then cross country/track and swimming each at 88 percent. But the lowest rates among the group were basketball and wrestling tied for ninth at 81 percent and football 11th at 76 percent. The FGR, meanwhile, had tennis and swimming tied for first and wrestling ninth, basketball 10th, and football 11th. Although their percentages did not equal each other, both types of rates had the same men's sports at the top and bottom of the distribution.

Among SAs in the 11 sports, the biggest gap between each of their average graduation rates was approximately 23 percentage points in ice hockey, 22 in football, and 20 each in wrestling, baseball, and golf. Alternatively, the smallest difference existed in swimming at 12 percentage points, and then cross country/track at 14, and tennis at 15. Because of the necessity to count transfer students and academic performances of other athletes, the ASRs and FGRs represent different groups of SAs.

From 2014 to 2015 for the ASR, three sports had lower rates but lacrosse increased from 85 to 86 percent while percentages of the other seven sports remained constant. In comparison, FGRs fell for five sports and increased from 60 to 61 percent in wrestling and 67 to 66 percent in golf, but did not change for four sports. Except for basketball, football, wrestling, golf, and lacrosse, both measurements were consistent in how they rated other sports in the two-year period.

During the 2015 to 2016 reporting years, the two methods had similar differences in men's graduation rates as in 2014–2015. While those in cross country/track and tennis did not change, dropped in football and ice hockey, and increased in wrestling, baseball, golf and lacrosse, the direction in rates varied in soccer, basketball, and swimming. This denotes that the ASR and FGR were consistent in determining percentages across the 11 male sports in the period.

By season, the ASRs averaged 81 percent in the fall and also 82 in winters and 86 in the spring. Respectively, FGRs were 60 percent and then 63 and 68. Even though one method was adopted by the NCAA in 1991 and the other during the early 2000s, they had the same trend across seasons for men SAs in these Division III sports from 2014 to 2016.

In 2014, the average ASRs were 86 percent each in fall and spring seasons but 82 in winters. During 2015 and 2016, however, rates were each 82 percent again in winters but higher in the fall and spring seasons. FGRs, meanwhile, were highest in the fall and lowest in winter in 2014, but then fall and spring rates were equal in 2014 and 2015 and above the 63 percent in winters. From one season to the next for men SAs at schools in Division III sports, graduation rates were consistent and thus changed by very small increments, as given in the data in Table 4.9.

Regarding the variation in each sport in 2014 and 2016, the ASRs equaled 88 percent in cross country/track and 82 percent in wrestling and also increased in baseball, golf, and lacrosse but otherwise declined in the other six sports. In these two reporting years, the FGR did not change in cross country/track, swimming and lacrosse yet increased in baseball, wrestling, and golf but declined in five others. As a result, there were differences between methods in measuring graduation rates among men SAs when comparing 2014 to 2016.

Women Athletes

Based on the data in Table 4.10 across three reporting years, the average graduation rates of women SAs in nine Division III sports were 93 percent according to the ASR and 77 percent when applying the FGR method. The three team sports with the highest rates were, respectively, by method, 97 percent in lacrosse, 96 in field hockey, and 95 in swimming versus 82 percent in lacrosse and then 81 in swimming and

Table 4.10.   Women SAs ASRs and FGRs by Sport, Division III, 2014–2016 Reporting Years.

Sport	2014		2015		2016	
	ASRs	FGRs	ASRs	FGRs	ASRs	FGRs
Fall						
Cross Country/Track	94	79	94	80	94	80
Field Hockey	95	79	96	79	97	81
Soccer	92	74	93	75	93	75
Volleyball	92	73	93	73	93	73
Winter						
Basketball	91	70	91	71	92	72
Swimming	95	80	94	81	95	82
Spring						
Lacrosse	96	83	97	81	97	81
Softball	92	75	93	76	92	75
Tennis	95	76	94	76	93	76

Note: NCAA is the National Collegiate Athletic Association. The Academic Success Rates (ASRs) and Federal Graduation Rates (FGRs) are four-year averages. Based on reporting years 2014, 2015, and 2016, the entering cohorts were, respectively, 2004–2007, 2005–2008, and 2006–2009.

Source: "Average Federal Graduation Rates and ASRs for Division III Women's Sports (Voluntary Schools)." http://www.ncaa.org cited 21 April 2017.

80 each in cross country/track and field hockey. Consequently, results were very similar in higher scores for the group of sports.

Among the three lowest rates each for the ASR and then FGR, they averaged 91 and 71 percent in basketball, 92 percent in softball and 73 percent in volleyball, and then 93 percent in both volleyball and soccer, and also 75 percent in soccer and softball. Thus, these Division III sports experienced the worst graduation rates among female athletes in reporting years' 2014–2016 as per data in Table 4.10.

From the 2014 to 2015 reporting year in Division III for women SAs, their ASRs increased in field hockey, soccer, volleyball, lacrosse, and softball but decreased in swimming and tennis. Furthermore, cross country/track remained at 94 percent and basketball at 91. In contrast, lacrosse was the only men's sport with a higher graduation rate during the one-year period. Besides ASRs, five women sports also had higher FGRs while lacrosse fell from 83 percent to 81 and three other rates did not change. For various reasons including their greater attendance and higher scores on quizzes and examinations in classes, women had more success than men percentagewise in graduating on schedule with an undergraduate degree.

In comparing women sports during the 2015 and then 2016 reporting years in the division, only ASRs in field hockey, basketball, and swimming improved while softball and tennis declined and four others each had the same percentages. Similarly, men's graduation rates were also mixed among schools in their sports. With respect to only FGRs, three women sports increased their graduation rates, five did not change, and softball declined from 76 percent to 75. Besides softball, the ASRs and FGRs of female SAs had approximately the same results in direction of rates for the other eight sports as of reporting year 2016.

Other interesting but relevant facts are evident based on the data in Table 4.10. First, in the three reporting years, respectively, women's ASRs averaged 93, 93, and 94 percent and their FGRs 76, 76, and 77 percent. For the two methods and same reporting years, men's ASRs were equal at 84 percent and then their FGRs at 66 percent. In other words, about the same differences existed between the two groups' graduation rates.

Second, women's ASRs were the same in fall and spring seasons of reporting years 2015 and 2016 and also FGRs in 2016 while their rates tended to be lower or equal in winters. Because the same results occurred in men's rates, this was due to types of sports in these seasons especially cross country-track in the fall, basketball in winters, and tennis in the spring.

Third, the gaps in average ASRs among Division III women sports was largest between field hockey and soccer/volleyball in fall seasons, swimming and basketball in winters, and lacrosse and softball in the spring. In FGRs, respectively, in these seasons, gaps were between cross country/track, field hockey and volleyball, swimming and basketball, and lacrosse and softball. Thus, the two methods provided similar results when comparing differences in sports' graduation rates across reporting years.

Fourth, with respect to reporting years' 2014 and 2016 among nine women sports in Division III, ASRs increased in field hockey, soccer, volleyball, basketball and lacrosse, decreased in tennis, and remained the same in cross country/track, swimming, and softball. In contrast to them, FGRs rose in cross country/track, field hockey, soccer, basketball, and swimming, fell in lacrosse, and did not change in volleyball, softball, and tennis. Based on the two methods of calculating rates, there were differences as to whether female athletes improved or did not improve academically in 2014 relative to 2016.

Fifth, for each reporting year, women's average ASRs exceeded men's by 9 percentage points in both 2014 and 2015 and also by 10 in 2016, and in FGRs females led males, respectively, by 10, 10, and 11. These results will likely continue in the future unless more schools in the division submit their athletes' graduation rates to the NCAA for each group, or the commitment by male SAs to graduate within six years significantly changes.

This completes the chapter and its contents about the academic performances of athletes in Divisions I, II, and III of the NCAA. It denotes, for example, which sports had the highest and lowest ASRs and FGRs in each division and also any differences in rates among male and female SAs in various reporting years. These results were analyzed in some way to explain their importance and trend given reports and other information from the NCAA and schools, and any studies by researchers and scholars.

Despite requests to acquire them, historical academic success and FGRs of SAs on teams in NAIA and NJCAA sports were not available in the literature either online or after contacting the two organizations. However, this book's Bibliography contains several articles, reports, and studies for data and information on other topics in higher education and team sports and any trends among colleges and universities in the U.S.

Chapter 5

ATHLETICS ENVIRONMENT

While enrolled as an underclassman or in a graduate program on a college or university campus somewhere in the United States (U.S.), various economic, financial, and social matters directly or indirectly influence the eligibility, lifestyle, retention, progress, and success of men (male) and women (female) student athletes (SAs) from both academic and sports perspectives. Besides classmates, coaches, and teammates, athletes also interact in different ways and have relations with administrators, faculty, and staff, and even with alumni and the local community. Compared to non-athletes, they have interesting but challenging and sometimes unique experiences in pursuing an education and then obtaining a degree while performing on one or more sports teams of their school.[1]

Based on personal knowledge and also readings that include articles, books, and Internet sources in the literature, Chapter 5 focuses on and discusses some topics and other important things that impact and perhaps change the efforts, viewpoints, and productivity of men and women SAs during their time enrolled in a college or university and perhaps thereafter

---

[1]Three books about student athletes are: Daniel Kissinger and Michael Miller, *College Student-Athletes: Challenges, Opportunities, and Policy Implications* (Charlotte, NC: Information Age Publishing, 2009); Carl Fertman, *Student-Athlete Success: Meeting The Challenges of College Life* (Burlington, MA: Jones & Bartlett Learning, 2008); Marc Isenberg and Richard Rhoads, *The Student Athlete Survival Guide* (Camden, ME: International Marine/Ragged Mountain Press, 2000).

as members of society. Thus, this chapter reveals the athletics environment and athletes in schools where they communicate with — and adjust to living among — other students during their late teens and then a few years before graduation.

COMMERCIALIZING COLLEGE SPORTS

For decades, many colleges and universities have increasingly 'commercialized' their men and women sports programs. Although these schools are non-profit educational organizations, they operate, at least financially, to generate more revenue than expenses in games of regular seasons and in any postseasons. To achieve that result, for example, may require decisions to establish ticket prices for seats and rent for suites; provide concessions before, during, and after games in their arena, ballpark, and/or stadium; advertise and promote the school's teams at home and away games; and control and manage other activities related to their sports programs. While this involves such officials as schools' administration, athletic department, faculty and staff, and owners of local businesses and other organizations, it also affects the education, lives, and future of SAs, especially those on teams in current fall, winter, and spring seasons.

After Chapter 2 — which includes sports programs of schools in Divisions I–III of the National Collegiate Athletic Association (NCAA) and the National Association of Intercollegiate Athletics (NAIA) and National Junior College Athletic Association (NJCAA) — Chapter 3 and then Chapter 4 contain the population and distribution of men and women SAs in schools associated with the three organizations and their academic performances. Based on information in these chapters and other literature, next is key financial data and its relationship to the role and status of athletes and their contribution to and participation on sports teams in colleges and universities.

Financial Data

As a result of schools' scheduling and operating sports programs in fall, winter, and spring seasons each academic year, a number of their athletic teams generate revenues for them but also incur expenses. Financially, the data in this section denotes how much colleges and universities collect and spend to play sports games or compete in matches or meets. As a result, the difference between revenues and expenses or net revenue is negative, positive, or zero.

If expenses exceed revenues, net revenue is negative. Thus, schools must subsidize their men and women sports with amounts from such things as student fees, ticket prices, money from the NCAA and television advertising, donations and gifts, and in other ways. If revenues exceed expenses from one or more sports, net revenue is positive and the surplus reallocated to other things by school officials. However, when revenues equal expenses, net revenue is zero dollars and the sport(s) breaks even financially.

Table 5.1, for example, lists the net revenues of men and women team sports in NCAA Divisions I and II and the distribution of these amounts in Fiscal Year 2014. Besides net revenues, the data also reflects the abilities, efforts, and success of SAs who performed in and won, lost, or tied games and also entertained such fans as other students and people in the community. What are some specific yet significant results contained in the table for each NCAA division?

First, with respect to Division I's Football Bowl Subdivision (FSB), men's basketball, football, and tennis were the only team sports with positive median net revenues in schools' Fiscal Year 2014. In contrast to that group, those with the largest negative amounts were men's baseball, ice hockey, and track and field, and also women's basketball, equestrian, and ice hockey. Because of money from the NCAA, student fees, and revenue from spectators who purchased tickets to attend basketball and football games and perhaps tennis matches and swimming meets, colleges and universities had to subsidize all or part of the operations of their other sports.

Second, such Division I sports combined as men and women gymnastics and lacrosse, soccer, swimming, track and field, volleyball, and water polo each had amounts greater than $1 million in negative revenue or losses from an accounting perspective. Since relatively few college teams and SAs participate in bowling and rifle, these sports had the smallest deficits. Although popular and prominent among athletes, even baseball, golf, and swimming had negative balances.

Table 5.1. Net Revenue, NCAA Divisions I and II, by Men and Women Sports, Fiscal Year 2014.

Sport	Division I		Division II	
	Men	**Women**	**Men**	**Women**
Baseball	(764)	NA	–	NA
Basketball	295	(1,898)	(4)	(<1)
Bowling	0	(62)	NA	NA
Crew	0	(950)	–	(92)
Equestrian	0	(1,025)	–	(<1)
Fencing	(207)	(261)	(<1)	<1
Field Hockey	NA	(724)	NA	–
Football	3,743	NA	(2)	NA
Golf	(294)	(316)	–	(<1)
Gymnastics	(376)	(815)	–	19
Ice Hockey	(1,066)	(1,423)	–	(32)
Lacrosse	(587)	(548)	(<1)	(2)
Rifle	(44)	(39)	–	–
Sand Volleyball	NA	(197)	NA	NA
Skiing	(358)	(476)	(2)	(6)
Soccer	(554)	(672)	–	(1)
Softball	NA	(717)	NA	(<1)
Swimming	(593)	(632)	–	(5)
Tennis	608	(379)	–	(<1)
Track and Field	(599)	(775)	(3)	(4)
Volleyball	(516)	(674)	–	(3)
Water Polo	(385)	(696)	–	4
Wrestling	(513)	NA	–	NA

Note: NCAA is the National Collegiate Athletic Association. Revenues are reported excluding all allocated revenues. Expenses are reported excluding third-party support. Track and Field includes cross country. Data excludes Other Sports. Amounts are median values in thousands of U.S. dollars. The symbol < means less than the amount and hyphen (–) as not determined or reported. NA is Not Applicable.

Source: "Total Generated Revenues and Expenses by Sport, Division I-Football Bowl Subdivision, Fiscal Year 2014," http://www.ncaa.org cited 30 April 2017, and "Total Generated Revenues and Expenses by Sport, Division II With Football, Fiscal Year 2014," http://www.ncaa.org cited 30 April 2017.

Third, based on the data in NCAA reports for Division I sports in Fiscal Year 2014, football generated more than $21.7 million in revenue followed by basketball's $5.7 million. For women's sports programs, the largest amounts were basketball's $271,000 and ice hockey's $201,000. In addition, men's bowling, crew, equestrian, and rifle were the only sports in the division with $0 in revenue while those four for women generated respectively $14,000, $106,000, $120,000, and $43,000. As with other sports, these were median values and not averages or total amounts.

Fourth, in Division I's Football Championship Subdivision (FCS), all men and women sports in Fiscal Year 2014 had negative or zero net revenues according to NCAA reports. In fact, their median values ranged from –$1,000 in men's fencing to –$138,000 in football. Regarding women's sports — which also had negative amounts — rifle had its net revenue at –$5,000 and gymnastics the worst at –$193,000.

Fifth, regarding Division II results as reported in the table, women's fencing, gymnastics, and water polo were the only team sports with positive net revenue. Conversely, the largest negative revenue occurred in women's crew, ice hockey, skiing, swimming, and then both track and field and men's basketball. Due to the number of teams and SAs on them, the majority of sports in the division had relatively smaller positive or negative median values than their counterparts in Division I.

Sixth, men's sports that generated the most revenues in Division II were ice hockey, football, and basketball while among women, these included ice hockey, basketball, and gymnastics. In contrast to them, the smallest amounts had been generated from games/matches/meets in men's fencing, water polo, and tennis, and also women's equestrian, tennis, and fencing. These groups denote, in part, which sports are most and least attended by fans on campuses of colleges and universities.

Seventh, Division II football and men's ice hockey had the largest median expenses in the two groups, with each amount greater than $1 million. Among other sports, men's golf, tennis, and water polo and also women's skiing, golf, and tennis had the lowest amounts. Such things as schools' payments for equipment, uniforms, transportation to and from away games, and insurance and other liabilities caused the former sports to be relatively expensive to operate while the latter six had less total costs for these items.

Eighth, excluding football from Division II, men's fencing and women's equestrian and gymnastics were the only team sports with positive net revenues. Alternatively, those with the largest negative median values included women's ice hockey at –$71,900 and men's rifle at –$38,800. Such sports as men's basketball, tennis, and volleyball and also women's soccer and volleyball each had less than –$1,000 for their median net revenue. Thus, amounts varied without football in the division and its effect on the allocation of resources to sports programs on campuses of colleges and universities.[2]

Besides those in Divisions I and II, Table A5.1 contains the median expenses of different sports in NCAA Division III for Fiscal Year 2014. Among men sports in the first group, football and then ice hockey and basketball cost the most to operate while among women, they were ice hockey first, basketball second, and gymnastics third. Alternatively, men's tennis, rifle and skiing — and at $34,000 each — women's golf, skiing, and tennis had the lowest median expenses.

Excluding football, however, amounts generally dropped across the distribution. For men, ice hockey had the highest median expenses followed by lacrosse and then a tie between baseball and basketball. And for women sports, ice hockey remained first and basketball second, but next was water polo instead of gymnastics. Furthermore, such sports as men's and women's skiing, swimming, and water polo each had greater expenses without football. According to data in the table, when schools have Division III football programs, their costs to operate other sports are also higher except for a few of them.

Based on information in Table 5.1, almost all Division I and II college and university athletic departments had required subsidies to financially operate their sports programs in Fiscal Year 2014. Simply put, they did not generate enough revenue from ticket sales at their games and other sources to exist in seasons. Based on amounts in the table plus those in Table A5.1, football had the largest net revenue in Division I sports and second most in Division II besides ice hockey, and the highest expenses

---

[2]There is more recent data in "Total Generated Revenues and Expenses By Sport, Division II With Football, Fiscal Year 2015–Median Values," http://www.ncaa.org cited 2 May 2017.

of the group in Division III. In addition, other prominent sports like men and women's golf, soccer, and swimming had negative net revenues and mixed results in their expenses.

EVENTS AND FACILITIES

For most intercollegiate sports, competition between teams includes games scheduled during regular seasons, and then if qualified, in postseason playoffs, series, and tournaments of their division and/or conference, and perhaps later both regionally and nationally. Three popular, special and well-attended events, for example, are baseball's College World Series, basketball's Division I men (and women) tournaments — nicknamed March Madness or Big Dance — and football's bowl system.

These are very important sports events commercially for several reasons. Besides promoting and giving publicity and recognition to schools and also generating revenue for them from ticket sales and television, they expose the competitiveness, leadership, and skill of SAs to officials of domestic and foreign professional and semi-professional franchises. The events also provide enjoyment, entertainment, and fun for fans, especially those who support in some way a specific sport or sports of a college or university.

Some critics, however, disagree and have problems with the business and economics of schools' sports events in seasons and postseasons and worry about SAs who participate in them. For example, there may be an incentive for colleges and universities to cheat and manipulate the academic performances of their athletes. This occurred, for many players, in a department at the University of North Carolina and some others in Division I. Furthermore, money from advertisements, game tickets, and television may corrupt higher education and cause coaches and SAs to deemphasize academics and not respect the non-financial long-term advantages and benefits of obtaining an undergraduate degree.

With respect to college and university sports facilities — besides arenas, ballparks, and stadiums — these schools' athletic teams and their SAs perform in home and away games or matches and meets in such venues as bowling alleys, gymnasiums, and swimming pools and also on golf courses, tennis courts, and track and fields at or near their campus.

This subject deals with such issues as the location, purpose, and size of the facility or facilities; whether construction and renovation or improvement of them should be funded from private and/or public sources; how to make decisions regarding original naming rights and periodically renewing them for more revenue; management, maintenance, and ownership of buildings and other types of facilities; and any current and future plans of schools to invest in and develop vacant and/or adjacent property in the area.

As a sample of topics in this section, the following references highlight different but important and critical aspects, implications, and viewpoints of commercialization with respect to colleges and their men and women sports programs[3]:

- In his book, *The Supreme Court and the NCAA: The Case for Less Commercialism and More Due Process in College Sports*, associate professor of law at Vermont Law School and former collegiate athlete Brian Porto examines two U.S. Supreme Court cases that paved the way for college sports to become the unwieldy and, at times, seemingly unmanageable enterprise that it is today. Recognizing that the amateur values of college sports have been seriously eroded in favor of commercialization and television contracts, Porto frames his argument for an educational exemption to antitrust laws around the landmark decisions in NCAA v. Board of Regents (1984) and NCAA v. Tarkanian (1988). In other words, he provides a rich and thorough analysis of the cases from the climate in college sports that precipitated such litigation to judicial procedural history and court testimony.

- According to former president of Indiana University and the NCAA Myles Brand, academic institutions strive to maximize the

---

[3] These readings include Joy Blanchard, "The Supreme Court and the NCAA: The Case for Less Commercialism and More Due Process in College Sports," *Review of Higher Education* (Spring 2013): 406–408; Myles Brand, "Show Colleges the Money, University Sports in Need of Some Commercialism," *Chicago Tribune* (6 April 2005): 1–2; Robert Schneider, "Developing the Moral Integrity of College Sport Through Commercialism," *Physical Culture and Sport* (2010): 30; Dan Thomasson, "Greed is True College Bowl Champion; Money is Motivation," *Beaumont Enterprise* (5 January 2011): A.7.

opportunities to participate in sports among the student body. Thus, they reallocate athletics department revenues to support SAs that do not produce any appreciable revenue including many men's and almost all women's sports. Most colleges and universities fall short of providing the number and quality of experiences that their athletes really want and perhaps need. Frankly, intercollegiate athletics could use more commercial dollars to help meet SAs' interests. Additional commercial revenue could also help close the gap between the current value of a scholarship and the full cost of attendance (COA). In part, the confusion about commercialism in college sports likely results from the differences in sensitivities to direct advertising among professional and college sports audiences.

- In an article published in 2010 and relevant to the role of colleges, Robert Schneider contends that identifying a professional 'fit' between a sport organization and commercial entity is imperative. The use of common sense, experience, and understanding human nature are useful when attempting to determine how particular commercialism efforts may consciously or subconsciously develop or reduce the moral integrity of sport. Beyond sport, the influences and risks of commercialism can be understood by observing its effect on non-sport organizations. Threats to the moral integrity of sport arise when entering into revenue-generating commercial agreements. Sport's overreliance on revenue from a commercial entity is a factor that can potentially cause deviation from a sport organization's morally based mission. Excessive expansion and lavish funding of sport organizations can contribute to overreliance on revenue from commercial entities. Personal greed can also play a role in detracting from the moral integrity of the mission.

- Amidst all the hurrah of college bowl seasons, nothing is more important to remember than the underlying reason behind these events, which are supposed to highlight the nation's best SAs. That reason is money. The bottom line, according to newspaper columnist Dan Thomasson, is really all that counts in an improbable, dishonest exercise in anti-competitive commercialism called the Bowl Championship Series, foisted off on Americans as the true determiner of America's number one football team. Although not a part of the cabal that controls this infamous business, Texas Christen University in 2011 fought its way through to finally dispel that notion dragging with it the Boise States' and Utah' that have been so absurdly denied the same opportunity over the years.

- In Chapter 7 of my book *College Sports Inc.: How Commercialism Influences Intercollegiate Athletics*, a few important but relevant conclusions were (a) due to fiscal problems in municipal, state, and the federal government, there will be less enthusiasm by administration officials, faculty, and trustees to expand major sports programs and the number of teams sponsored by colleges and universities in NCAA Divisions I, II, and III; (b) athletic directors at big-time sports schools have plenty of opportunities to obtain funds from alumni, boosters, businesses, and civic organizations in the private sector; and (c) baseball's College World Series, basketball's March Madness, and football's bowls will continue to provide commercial appeal especially to retailers and other businesses, local and national television networks, and cities in metropolitan areas that host them.[4]

STUDENT ATHLETES

Based on their high school education, are all or most SAs committed and actually prepared to succeed in college? In 2014, a University of Kansas (UK) study, for example, suggested a simpler, more universal but radical way to motivate these students. Give them a reason to come to school — even if that has nothing to do with academics. Some researchers at UK analyzed high-school testing, graduation, and attendance data and found that the state's athletes attended school more often than non-athletes. They also had a higher graduation rate — 98 percent of athletes in the class of 2012 compared with 90 percent of non-athletes. The higher graduation could be, in part, because teachers had lower standards for SAs, in other words, passing them without doing all assignments and other work. But then, state test data challenged that theory since athletes also scored

---

[4]Frank P. Jozsa Jr., *College Sports Inc.: How Commercialism Influences Intercollegiate Athletics* (New York, NY: Springer, 2013).

higher on the state's assessments than non-athletes in all subject areas. Obviously, these male and female SAs learned something in their classes.

The athletes' relatively strong performance on the state tests was remarkable when considering their performance on American College Testing (ACT) examinations. In fact, they scored lower than non-athletes on the ACT English and reading subsections despite scoring higher in those areas on the state test. This suggested that, at least in language arts, athletes are not inherently smarter than non-athletes. They were, however, more successful in classes at their school. According to the lead researcher of the study, this may be related to the requirements that Kansas puts on its athletes in which they must pass five credit units per semester to be eligible to play. Most high schools in the state also requested their students attend classes daily to be allowed to participate in practices or play in a game that day.[5]

EDUCATION STANDARDS

NCAA Division I

After they finish their classwork and graduate from high school, some SAs — with or without a scholarship — will enroll in a program at an NCAA Division I college or university and choose a major field of study. To be eligible to compete in sports during their years at a school in this division, they must meet the following requirements: complete 16 core courses including four years of English, three of mathematics (Algebra 1 or higher), two of natural/physical science, an additional year of English, mathematics or natural/physical science, two years of social science, four additional years of English, mathematics, natural/physical science, social science, foreign language, comparative religion or philosophy, and complete 10 core courses including seven in English, mathematics, or natural/physical science before the seventh semester.[6]

---

[5] For more information about the study, see Eleanor Barkhorn, "Athletes Are More Likely to Finish High School Than Non-Athletes," http://www.theatlantic.com cited 2 May 2017.

[6] "Play Division I Sports," http://www.ncaa.org cited 3 May 2017.

Once they begin their seventh semester at a school, SAs may not repeat or replace any of the 10 courses to improve their core-course grade-point-average (GPA) and must earn at least a 2.3 GPA in the core courses and achieve a Scholastic Application Test (SAT) combined score or ACT sum score matching the core-course GPA on the Division I sliding scale, which balances the test score and core-course GPA. If athletes have a relatively low test score, they need a higher core-course GPA to become eligible. And if they have a low core-course GPA, athletes need a higher test score for eligibility.

NCAA Division II

To be eligible and compete in NCAA sports during their first year at a Division II school, SAs must meet academic requirements for their core courses, GPA, and test scores. However, these requirements will change for any men and women athletes who enroll full-time at a Division II school after August 1, 2018.[7]

If enrolled before August 1, 2018, SAs must graduate from high school and meet the following requirements: complete 16 core courses including three years of English, two each of mathematics (Algebra I or higher) and also of natural or physical science (including one year of lab science if the high school offered it), three additional courses of English, mathematics or natural or physical science, two of social science, and four more of English, mathematics, natural or physical science, social science, foreign language, comparative religion, or philosophy. Finally, they must earn at least a 2.0 GPA in their core courses and an SAT combined score of 820 or an ACT sum score of 68.

After August 1, 2018, SAs must graduate from high school and meet each of the following requirements: complete 16 core courses including three years of English, two of mathematics (Algebra I or higher) and also of natural or physical science (including one year of lab science if the high school offered it), three additional years of English, mathematics, or natural or physical science, two years of social science, and four additional years of English, mathematics, natural or physical science, social science,

---

[7] "Play Division II Sports," http://www.ncaa.org cited 3 May 2017.

foreign language, comparative religion, or philosophy. Furthermore, they must earn at least a 2.2 GPA in their core courses and an SAT combined score or ACT sum score matching the core-course GPA on the Division II sliding scale — which balances the test score and core-course GPA. If an athlete has a low test score, he or she needs a higher core-course GPA to become eligible. And if SAs have a low core-course GPA, they need a higher test score for eligibility.

NCAA Division III

To compete in this division, men and women SAs do not need to register with the NCAA, which has no academic requirements for DIII athletes. Each university sets its own educational standards for athletes and their financial aid. For more information about requirements, prospective players should contact athletic directors and coaches at DIII colleges and universities and learn about academic standards from them.

NATIONAL ASSOCIATION OF INTELCOLLIGATE ATHLETICS

The academic standards for this organization are the lowest of all division levels except junior colleges. To be eligible, athletes must graduate from high school and meet two of the following three requirements: finish in the top half of their graduating class, achieve a minimum GPA of 2.0, and/or score at least 860 on the SAT or 16 on the ACT.[8]

NATIONAL JUNIOR COLLEGE ATHLETIC ASSOCIATION

According to this sports organization's 2016–2017 eligibility rules pamphlet, a SA must be a graduate of a high school with a state department of education-approved standard academic diploma, or general education diploma, or a high school equivalency test. Any athletes who had passed

---

[8] "NAIA Eligibility," http://www.playnaia.org cited 3 May 2017.

a state approved equivalency exam — but have not been awarded a certificate or diploma — can establish eligibility by submitting written proof of their successful completion and the member institution keeping proof of it in their audit file.[9]

SAs who enroll in college prior to meeting the minimum requirements are not eligible for participation in a sport or sports. Additionally, any enrollment that takes place prior to meeting the minimum requirements will not be subject to any accumulation or transfer regulations provided the entire academic term takes place prior to meeting the student.

In *Reclaiming the Game: College Sports and Educational Values*, former Princeton University President William Bowen and his co-authors describe how at 33 of America's most academically selective colleges, recruited athletes are nearly four times more likely to be admitted than other applicants of similar academic caliber and these recruits are significantly more likely to be in the bottom third of their class. High schoolers and younger students and their parents are aware of the commonplace success that athletes enjoy in college admissions, and most kids understand that athletic prowess makes them far more likely to be admitted to a top school than academic excellence alone. In fact, it is understood in high school that recruited athletes of even modest scholastic achievement regularly do better getting into select schools than their peers with much higher academic credentials.[10]

Unfortunately, this situation does not encourage students to excel academically. Rather, America's universities created a perverse incentive for kids and teenagers to focus on athletics. After it becomes clear that athletic skill maximizes their chances of being admitted into the college of his or her choice, that athlete will understandably focus on performing better in a sport. Not surprisingly, both SAs and their parents are willing to sacrifice academic achievement and growth to be admitted into a prominent college.[11]

---

[9] "2016–17 NJCAA Eligibility Rules," http://www.njcaa.org cited 3 May 2017.

[10] This overview appeared in Frederick Allen, "When Colleges Recruit Athletes, Everyone Loses," http://www.forbes.com cited 3 May 2017. For the book, see William Bowen, *Reclaiming the Game: College Sports and Educational Values* (Princeton, NJ: Princeton University Press, 2003).

[11] Other readings on important but controversial topics about the education of student athletes are: Jonah Newman, "At Tops Athletics Programs, Students Often Major in

SCHOLARSHIPS

NCAA

The NCAA is the largest athletic association in the U.S. and represents more than 1,000 member schools. Participating colleges and universities are categorized as Division I, II, or III to recognize various member school sizes and acknowledge the level of monetization of each athletic program. Although individual campuses make their own rules, they must be aligned with NCAA values regarding personnel, recruiting, student benefits, athlete eligibility, financial aid, and athletic programs.[12]

Based on its mission, the non-profit organization advocates for SAs and provides valuable resources for member institutions. Students position themselves for NCAA scholarships by embracing eligibility requirements and registering in the Initial Eligibility Clearinghouse. NCAA scholarships benefit undergraduates and graduate students from each of the organization's divisions. While Division I and II scholarships are competitive and used by athletic directors and coaches to lure prime talent into campus athletic programs, the NCAA limits Division III participation in scholarship programs.

NAIA

The NAIA represents a smaller contingent of member schools than the NCAA — or about 350 institutions of higher education located within Canada and the U.S. The organization sponsors athletic Divisions I, II, and III, which are generally comprised of schools outside the scope of NCAA Division I's eligibility requirements, and incorporates a marked emphasis on academics into its student programs. About a dozen

---

Eligibility," *Chronicle of Higher Education* (18 December 2014): 1; P.L. Thomas, "Invisible Young Men: African-American Males, Academics, and Athletics," *English Journal* (September 2014): 75–78; Mitchell Williams and Kevin Pennington, "Community College Presidents' Perceptions of Intercollegiate Athletics," *The Community College Enterprise* (Fall 2006): 91–104.

[12] "Improve Your Chances for an Athletic Scholarship," http://www.collegescholarships. org cited 3 May 2017.

individual sports are supported by its member institutions. Key tenets of the NAIA mission — which fosters principles for SAs — include equal opportunity, fairness and ethical treatment, access to higher education, leadership, sportsmanship, and character building.

The NAIA's rules on financial aid are straightforward. Each school determines how much aid it awards to an individual SA. Under no condition may anyone else provide direct financial assistance to any of them. Scholarships, grants-in-aid, and/or student loans to players are controlled by each institution through the same committee that handles all student loans and scholarships. Financial aid to SAs is limited to the actual cost of tuition and mandatory fees, books, and supplies required for courses in which the player is enrolled, and also room and board based on the official room and board allowance listed in the institution's catalog.

NJCAA

The NJCAA represents two-year schools in higher education. With enough participants, junior colleges compete in separate divisions as NCAA and NAIA athletes do, while sports that draw fewer participants are not split into multiple segments. Scholarships are available for some NJCAA athletes, and academic excellence increases eligibility for school-specific awards.

Each national association sets the maximum number of athletic scholarships their member schools can award to SAs for official team sports. While colleges and universities may or may not award less than the maximum number of them, Table 5.2 for men and Table 5.3 for women contain the annual limits of scholarships as of the 2016–2017 academic year. Typically, incoming athletes at a four-year institution compete for approximately 25 percent of the maximum available scholarships.

According to data in Table 5.2, the maximum scholarship limit for men's sports was 797 in the 2016–2017 academic year. While football had the highest proportion of the total at almost 37 percent, track and field/cross country ranked second at approximately 9 percent, and basketball third at about 7 percent. Conversely, rifle and then bowling, fencing, volleyball, and water polo each had the lowest limits of men's scholarships.

Table 5.2. Men's Maximum Scholarship Limits, by Association and Sport, 2016–2017 Academic Year.

Sport	NCAA		NAIA	NJCAA	Total
	Division I	**Division II**			
Baseball	11	9	12	24	46
Basketball	13	10	17	15	55
Bowling	0	0	0	8	8
Fencing	4	4	0	0	8
Football	148	36	24	85	293
Golf	4	3	5	8	20
Gymnastics	6	5	0	0	11
Ice Hockey	18	13	0	16	47
Lacrosse	12	10	0	20	42
Rifle	3	3	0	0	6
Skiing	6	6	0	0	12
Soccer	9	9	12	18	48
Swimming	9	8	8	15	40
Tennis	4	4	5	9	22
T&F/Cross Country	12	12	17	30	71
Volleyball	4	4	0	0	8
Water Polo	4	4	0	0	8
Wrestling	9	9	8	16	42

Note: The NCAA data excludes partial scholarships but includes the Football Bowl Subdivision and Football Championship Subdivision. Rifle includes women on co-ed teams. Swimming includes diving. T&F is Track and Field.

Source: "College Athletic Scholarship Limits," http://www.scholarshipstats.com cited 4 May 2017.

Of the groups from most to least, the NCAA Division I's limit was 276 or 35 percent of the total, NJCAA's 264 or 33 percent followed by NCAA Division II's 149 or 19 percent, and then the NAIA's 108 or 13 percent. Although football ranked first in scholarship limits among the different associations, the second and third sports were, respectively, ice hockey and basketball in Division I, ice hockey and track and field/cross country in Division II, basketball and tennis each tied for second in the NAIA, and track and field/cross country, and baseball in the NJCAA. Besides associations with zero teams in a sport, golf and tennis existed in each group but had relatively small limits.

The distribution of men's scholarship limits in the table denotes, in part, that SAs in football and then track and field/cross country, basketball, and soccer most likely received more scholarships in 2016–2017 than those qualified to play on teams in other sports. Because they earn revenue for their schools, the former group of sports is important for their schools and also popular among non-athletes on campuses.

Regarding the distribution of scholarships for women athletes, their maximum limits equaled 664 or approximately 83 percent of men's in 2016–2017 based on the data in Table 5.3. While track and field/cross country ranked highest in limits with 11 percent of the total, basketball had 8 percent and soccer and softball each 7 percent. Similar to men's sports, women rifle's limits were less than one percent of the female group's total scholarships followed by only eight each for beach volleyball and triathlon.

Across the different associations, NCAA Division I had 235 or 35 percent of the total women's scholarship limits and then Division II's 186 or 28 percent, NJCAA's 161 or 25 percent, and the NAIA's 82 or 12 percent. Among the group of sports, respectively, female rowing and then ice hockey and track and field/cross country had the highest limits in Division I, rowing and then ice hockey and equestrian in Division II, basketball and track and field/cross country and soccer in the NAIA, and track and field/cross country and softball in the NJCAA. Excluding sports with zero women's scholarships, the lowest limits existed in golf and tennis.

Comparing the maximum number of scholarships by gender in Tables 5.2 and 5.3, NCAA Division I's were both 35 percent, while men had proportionately higher limits in the NAIA and NJCAA — and despite football — were not higher in Division II. Also, there were four more women than men's sports in the latter division. Given their distribution across all team sports in 2016–2017, women had a much smaller variation in scholarship limits than men primarily because of differences between football's large number and those in the other male sports.

Table 5.3. Women's Maximum Scholarship Limits, by Association and Sport, 2016–2017 Academic Year.

Sport	NCAA		NAIA	NJCAA	Total
	Division I	**Division II**			
Basketball	15	10	17	15	57
Beach Volleyball	3	5	0	0	8
Bowling	5	5	0	8	18
Equestrian	15	15	0	0	30
Fencing	5	4	0	0	9
Field Hockey	12	6	0	0	18
Golf	6	5	5	8	24
Gymnastics	12	6	0	0	18
Ice Hockey	18	18	0	0	36
Lacrosse	12	9	0	20	41
Rifle	3	3	0	0	6
Rowing	20	20	0	0	40
Rugby	12	12	0	0	24
Skiing	7	6	0	0	13
Soccer	14	9	12	18	53
Softball	12	7	10	24	53
Swimming	14	8	8	15	45
Tennis	8	6	5	9	28
T&F/Cross Country	18	12	17	30	77
Triathlon	4	4	0	0	8
Volleyball	12	8	8	14	42
Water Polo	8	8	0	0	16

Note: The NCAA data excludes partial scholarships. Rifle includes men on co-ed teams. Swimming includes diving. T&F is Track and Field. Triathlon is a relatively new NCAA sport.

Source: "College Athletic Scholarship Limits," http://www.scholarshipstats.com cited 4 May 2017.

In academic year 2015–2016, colleges and universities awarded $3.3 billion to players in athletic scholarships. Of that amount, the NCAA's portion was 84 percent or approximately $2.8 billion, NAIA's 12 percent or $389 million, and the NJCAA's 4 percent or $131 million. Schools' academic scholarships and other financial aid, meanwhile, totaled $11.1 billion led by the NCAA's 51 percent share at $5.7 billion.

Consequently, this data indicates the value of scholarships allocated by associations to athletes and non-athletes in a recent academic year.[13]

More specifically, the average value of athletic scholarships for men and women that year were, respectively, $5,493 and $6,625 based on a sample of 1,115 NCAA schools and also 228 in the NAIA and 438 in the NJCAA. While women's average exceeded men's amount in the NCAA's Division I by $892 and $1,266 in Division II, females also received $361 more in value as an athlete in the NAIA and an additional $741 if in the NJCAA. Because of Title IX requirements and other legislation, women SAs have surpassed men regarding the value of their scholarships from each of these associations.

With respect to data for men and women SAs, Table 5.4 and then Table 5.5 reveal some interesting but important details about this topic for each group. Table 5.4, in part, contains the values of average scholarships per team of 13 men's sports in NCAA Division I in academic year 2016–2017 and also these sports' number of average, low, and high scholarships per team.

Based on their distribution in Table 5.4, the average scholarship per team across all these sports was $19,102. While those in men's basketball ranked first in value, ice hockey second and football third, lacrosse teams placed 11th, golf 12th, and track and field/cross country 13th. Thus, SAs who played on the three former teams had more valuable scholarships than those in the latter group because their efforts in games resulted in revenue for schools.

According to columns three and four in Table 5.4, men's track and field/cross country, swimming, and golf were lowest in average scholarships per team while the highest included basketball and then ice hockey and football. Meanwhile in column four, the high-average scholarships per team had basketball first, football second, and ice hockey third in value, with lacrosse 13th, golf 12th, and track and field/cross country 11th. As a result, there were large differences in the worth of men SAs' scholarships among these sports because of such things as attendances at

---

[13] "Average Athletic Scholarship Per Varsity Athlete," http://www.scholarshipstats.org cited 5 May 2017 and "2016 Athletic Scholarship Averages for NCAA I Teams by Sport," http://www.scholarshipstats.org cited 5 May 2017.

Table 5.4.   Athletic Scholarship Averages, Division I Men's Teams by Sport, 2016–2017 Academic Year.

Sport	Average Scholarship Per Team			Scholarships Per Team		
	Average	Low	High	Average	Low	High
Baseball	$13,220	$6,298	$25,934	26	14	30
Basketball	$38,246	$26,896	$53,075	13	11	15
Football	$28.388	$19,855	$36,474	85	77	90
Golf	$12,066	$4,050	$24,018	10	6	16
Gymnastics	$18,190	$12,882	$31,573	16	14	19
Ice Hockey	$31,756	$19,934	$35,986	22	16	25
Lacrosse	$12,303	$8,078	$17,483	36	29	43
Skiing	$20,275	$15,478	$24,636	11	10	11
Soccer	$15,008	$5,809	$31,062	21	12	30
Swimming	$16,695	$3,112	$28,651	22	12	36
Tennis	$18,379	$6,104	$42,373	9	6	13
T&F/Cross Country	$11,260	$2,957	$24,059	29	9	59
Wrestling	$12,551	$5,249	$33,596	23	14	31

Note: NCAA is the National Collegiate Athletic Association. The data excludes sports programs that do not award athletic scholarships. Number of scholarships awarded is per team, so for four-year schools typically only 25 percent will be available to incoming SAs. The data for Football is an average of teams in the Football Bowl Subdivision and Football Championship Subdivision. Swimming includes diving. T&F is Track and Field.

Source: "Average Athletic Scholarship Per Varsity Athlete," http://www.scholarshipstats.com cited 8 May 2017.

home games, number of and value of contracts with sponsors, and revenues of each sport from ticket sales and other sources.

With respect to number of scholarships awarded per team in columns five to seven of the table, the overall average was 24, with most of them in football and then men's lacrosse and track and field/cross country. Alternatively, the lowest number had existed for SAs who played on tennis, golf, and skiing country teams. From low in column six to high in column seven, they ranged, respectively, from six each in golf and tennis to 77 in football, and then from 11 in skiing and 13 in tennis to 59 in track

Table 5.5: Athletic Scholarship Averages, Division I Women's Teams by Sport, 2016–2017 Academic Year.

Sport	Average Scholarship Per Team			Scholarships Per Team		
	Average	Low	High	Average	Low	High
Basketball	$36,758	$21,955	$53,185	14	10	16
Equestrian	$10,462	$5,677	$17,196	41	36	47
Field Hockey	$18,331	$10,325	$30,012	20	17	24
Golf	$21,866	$8,870	$39,100	8	6	10
Gymnastics	$40,172	$23,482	$63,337	14	12	16
Ice Hockey	$41,693	$41,208	$42,179	20	20	20
Lacrosse	$12,884	$3,394	$22,842	31	23	38
Rowing	$21,053	$11,507	$31,771	39	19	51
Skiing	$19,084	$15,337	$23,855	12	11	14
Soccer	$17,766	$6,220	$31,363	25	17	33
Softball	$20,715	$7,281	$47,624	19	13	24
Swimming	$18,794	$4,552	$34,850	25	8	35
Tennis	$32,630	$13,457	$58,735	8	7	10
T&F/Cross Country	$14,574	$2,938	$26,308	32	16	11
Volleyball	$31,138	$12,837	$63,281	13	11	16

Note: NCAA is the National Collegiate Athletic Association. The data excludes sports programs that do not award athletic scholarships. Number of scholarships awarded is per team, so for four-year schools typically only 25 percent will be available to incoming SAs. Swimming includes diving. T&F is Track and Field.

Source: "Average Athletic Scholarship Per Varsity Athlete," http://www.scholarshipstats.com cited 8 May 2017.

and 90 in football. These statistics are primarily based on teams' sizes and the number of them in various colleges and universities within NCAA Division I.

Based on the data in Table 5.4, for example, the scholarships of football players on the first team at such popular and prominent schools with large budgets as the University of Alabama, Clemson University, and University of Texas were each worth, as a group, at least $500,000 in academic year 2016–2017. Including scholarships of other athletes on these teams' roster, the total value of their scholarships was approximately $1–$2 million. However, the average amount in scholarships for the 11 football SAs who start for teams in the smallest Division I schools is estimated at $150,000, and the entire group of them at $300,000. Across all men's sports, the table's data denotes the range in investments in athletes by schools with football teams versus those who compete in golf, track and field/cross country, and other sports.

Regarding the data in Table 5.5 across 15 women's sports, the average value of their scholarships per team in 2016 was $23,861 or 24 percent more than men's. While scholarships in ice hockey ranked first followed by gymnastics and basketball, equestrian and then lacrosse and track and field/cross country averaged the least amounts. Except for equestrian and gymnastics, these sports also rated similar among men. With respect to both genders, scholarships in women's ice hockey and gymnastics each exceeded $40,000, with men's basketball third at $38,246. Such things as average number of athletes on teams, costs of their equipment, insurance and uniforms, and other requirements determined these values.

Among the low-valued average scholarships per team was women's track and field/cross country at 15th, lacrosse at 14th, and equestrian at 13th. As did the average values in the low column, the high-valued average scholarships per team occurred in gymnastics and basketball.

While women's gymnastics, volleyball, and tennis had the three highest average scholarships amounts, the least valuable scholarships in column four were in equestrian at $17,196, lacrosse at $22,842, and skiing at $23,855. In short, schools awarded female SAs different scholarship amounts based on the athletic department's budget, type of sport, number of athletes per team, and for other reasons.

Regarding number of scholarships per team in column five of Table 5.5, women's equestrian and then rowing and track and field/cross country had the three highest averages. However, the lowest number of athletes recruited and signed in 2016 performed on golf, tennis, and skiing teams. The average across the 15 sports was 21 scholarships, and they ranged from 41 in equestrian to eight each in golf and tennis. Some sports required more scholarships for SAs than others because senior players had graduated or simply team rosters expanded.

In columns six and seven of Table 5.5 are, respectively, the low and high number of scholarships awarded per team in 2016. The former group of women's sports averaged 15 scholarships and included equestrian with a high of 36 and golf with a low of six. Conversely, the high column averaged 27 and ranged from 51 scholarships for rowing SAs to 10 each for golf and tennis teams. In comparison between low and high number of scholarships per team, only equestrian, golf, and tennis ranked among the group of sports in the two columns, while ice hockey, lacrosse, rowing, skiing, swimming, and track and field/cross country each scored either low or high.

Among the values of men and women scholarships per team across all sports in the tables, women had the highest average by $4,759 and also they averaged $2,090 more in low amounts and $7,587 more in high amounts. In addition, the worth of scholarships varied by group, with men's most valuable being basketball, ice hockey, and football and women's in ice hockey, gymnastics, and basketball. But the lowest averages included men's track and field/cross country, golf, and lacrosse along with women's equestrian, lacrosse, and track and field/cross country. Thus, scholarships averaged different amounts by sport among the two groups of players.

A few team sports had neither high nor low average amounts and were not among the lowest or highest scholarships awarded per team. These included, for example, baseball and men's gymnastics, soccer, swimming, and wrestling, and also women's field hockey, soccer, and softball. Consequently, these sports will likely continue to exist with affordable and popular teams given the value of their SAs' scholarships.

Several websites report statistics and other data and information about athletic scholarships for men and women who play on sports teams in colleges and universities. Here are a few actual but also interesting and significant facts read on various online sources. First, full-ride scholarships enable SAs to attend school at little out-of-pocket cost because they cover such things as tuition, room and board, books, and certain fees related to their classes. Expenses that may not be covered, however, include things like other late fees, parking tickets, fines, or the premium paid for a single dorm room. This type of scholarship is available only to those who play 'head count' sports, known as revenue producers. For men, these include basketball and Division I football, and for women, they are basketball, volleyball, tennis, and gymnastics.[14]

Second, while scholarships for SAs in head count sports provide a full ride, the monetary value of equivalency sport scholarships can be — and usually are — divided by a school among more athletes than there are scholarships. In other words, if a school has 15 scholarships available for a specific equivalency sport, it can divide those scholarships into as many partial scholarships as needed, thereby providing financial support to a larger number of SAs.

Third, athletic scholarships are not only competitive, expensive, and scarce, most athletes do not receive one. For example, about 250,000 high school seniors play basketball annually, but only about 12,000 or 5 percent of them will earn a scholarship to play basketball at the collegiate level. This means an athletic scholarship is not high on the list of possibilities. Thus, SAs should pursue all types of scholarships and financial aid, not just those in team sports.

Fourth, NCAA Division III schools do award athletic scholarships. However, according to *US News & World Report*, some of the best scholarships for athletes come from these schools. Although this sounds confusing, Division III schools are typically smaller private colleges that often give lucrative merit awards for student accomplishments. Even better news is that merit grants often cut tuition by more than 50 percent, which is an excellent benefit for any budding college athlete.

Fifth, despite common references in news media reports, there is no such thing as a four-year scholarship. All NCAA athletic scholarships must be renewed, and thus are not guaranteed year to year, which is something stated in bold letters on the organization's website for SAs. Nearly every scholarship can be canceled for almost any reason in any year, although it is unclear how often that happens.

---

[14] See, for example, David Frank, "5 Facts About Full-Ride Scholarships," http://www.athleticscholarships.net cited 5 May 2017; "14 Surprising Facts About Being a College Athlete," http://www.bestcollegesonline.com cited 5 May 2017; Bill Pennington, "Expectations Lose to Reality of Sports Scholarships," http://www.nytimes.com cited 5 May 2017; "The Facts About 'Guaranteed' Multi-Year NCAA DI Scholarships," http://www.informedathlete.com cited 5 May 2017.

Sixth, although those athletes who receive athletic aid are viewed as ultimate winners, they typically find the demands on their time, minds, and bodies while on college teams even more taxing than the long journey to get there. In some sports, there may be early weight-lifting sessions and exhausting practices, team meetings, study halls, and long trips to and from games. Their varsity commitments often limit the types of courses they can enroll in during a semester. Athletes also might share a frustrating feeling of estrangement from the student body, which views them as being privileged. In this setting, it is not uncommon for first- and second-year SAs to relinquish their scholarships.

Seventh, the NCAA adopted a rule in 2015 to protect athletes from having their scholarship simply cancelled or not renewed for any reason. However, it is still possible for schools to cancel — or choose to not renew — a scholarship for reasons not related to athletic performance, ability, or contribution to team success. Cancellation or non-renewal is possible, for example, if an athlete (a) is ruled to be ineligible for competition; (b) provides fraudulent information on an application, letter of intent, or financial aid agreement; (c) engages in serious misconduct that rises to the level of being disciplined by the university's regular student disciplinary board; (d) voluntarily quits his or her team; and/or (e) violates a university policy or rule, which is not related to athletic conditions or ability such as a university policy on class attendance or an athletic department policy regarding proper conduct on a team trip.

Different aspects of — and problems with — athletic scholarships and their effects on athletes, coaches, sports teams, and schools in higher education have been researched by scholars and reported in the literature. The following is a sample of articles dealing with this subject and its intended and unintended consequences, especially among groups such as the NCAA.[15]

---

[15]The references for these items are: Jacqueline McDowell, "Title IX Exclusion and Marginalization Needs to Change," *Diverse Issues in Higher Education* (14 January 2016): 1; Lynn O'Shaughnessy, "Sports Scholarships Don't Come Easy," *Penton Media, Inc.* (November 2014): 50; Brooke Ross, "Fielding Offers," *Junior Scholastic* (17 March 2014): 1–2; Lynn O'Shaughnessy, "Seven Ways to Capture a Sports Scholarship," *Penton Media, Inc.* (January 2011): 66–67; "How to Become a Scholarship Athlete," *USA Today* (December 2010): 2; "Athletic Scholarships Have a Huge Impact on Black Student

- African–American women are predominantly represented in only two sports, basketball and track and field, and historically did not have the same level of access to scholarships as white women SAs. Moreover, colleges and universities have increasingly added so-called country club sports as golf and tennis or sports such as lacrosse based on a select few or club system, which are usually played by females of European and Asian descent with higher socioeconomic statuses. More attention, therefore, needs to be brought to all women and men, levels of athletics, educational programs, and institutions that are afforded protection under the law. When opportunities are provided, discrimination wanes and people have options to take on identities once denied.

- Some college and university coaches tell male and female teenagers that they have lots of scholarship money to divvy out, but prospects should not assume being recipients. A coach might not know whether he needs a particular athlete until other prospects commit to be on his or her team. What really matters is the scholarship amount contained in the school's official athletic grant-in-aid form. Also, a coach's verbal commitment to an athlete is meaningless. In highly competitive sports programs, more coaches are now offering verbal commitments to talented kids as young as middle schoolers, but there is absolutely no guarantee that anyone who verbally commits to a team will end up on it.

- According to several NCAA coaches, colleges are recruiting younger players than ever before, and many of the SAs are offered full scholarships even before they enter high school. The trend is especially evident in women's sports. It may be a result of Title IX — a 1972 federal law that requires equal funding for men's and women's school sports. To comply with the law, some schools increased the number of women's sports teams and scholarships being offered. This, in turn, led to a growing number of college coaches who need more female athletes, so they end up recruiting younger players. Some parents are

Graduation Rates," *The Journal of Blacks in Higher Education* (Winter 2004): 68; Katherine Baird, "Dominance in College Football and the Role of Scholarship Restrictions," *Journal of Sport Management* (July 2004): 1.

eager to have their middle schoolers secure scholarships by committing to colleges at an early age. But many people worry about the stress this puts on kids to make such big decisions. While some college coaches have concerns about signing young players, they have no choice. If they don't recruit young athletes, other schools will get the best players.

- Former National Football League (NFL) player and National Collegiate Scouting Association speaker Roman Oben shares five things high school prospects need to know to get recruited and offered a college scholarship: (1) the recruitment process can actually start as early as seventh or eighth grade, not when a coach actually contacts an athlete; (2) a talented athlete must initiate communication and convey interest to be noticed. Even if the player is a superstar, he or she must be prepared to start a conversation by calling coaches and asking the right questions; (3) when college coaches first become interested in an SA, they do a majority of their initial scouting by looking at videos before making in-person visits to games, matches, and/or meets. SAs cannot expect these coaches to have the means to travel to watch them compete. Thus, professional film is very important for coaches to evaluate athletes' performances; (4) most opportunities to play college sports are not in Division I programs. While many athletes and their parents feel that the only option for collegiate athletic scholarships are these schools, there are thousands of other colleges and universities that sponsor college athletes and are able to offer financial packages; and (5) SAs and their families ultimately are responsible for connecting with college coaches. Most high school coaches, in fact, do not have the time or resources to make sure their athletes get seen and recruited.

- Despite the public's perception of black college athletes as 'dumb jocks' who are in college only to compete on the athletic field, the evidence denotes that these scholarship athletes actually perform better academically than black students as a whole. Overall, without reference to athletics, approximately 34 percent of African American men who enter college in this country graduate within six years. But 39 percent of black male scholarship athletes earn their diplomas within a six-year period. For black women, the overall graduation rate is 45 percent, but the graduation rate jumps to 60 percent for black women who are scholarship athletes. As of the early 2000s, the graduation rate for black women athletes was actually higher than the national average for all white male college students including athletes and non-athletes.

- Published in 2004, an article examines the relationship between player compensation in college football and competitive balance on the field. It shows that NCAA rule changes restricting football player compensation are not associated with an improvement in football's competitive balance. Although college football is marginally more balanced than professional sports in any given year, an examination of cumulative records spanning numerous seasons proves college football to be as unbalanced as professional sports. The movement to reduce player compensation — coincident with an increasing value to player talent — raises issues over how the financial gain from college football talent should be used. The significant degree of talent (and financial) imbalance among college football teams suggests that more attention should be paid to the determinants of talent distribution in the sport.

COST OF ATTENDANCE

The push to give male and female athletes a stipend to cover the full COA in school has been discussed for decades, but since 2000, the concept found stronger support. In 2003, the NCAA began allowing athletes to receive aid through Pell Grants and need-based scholarships. Eight years later, the NCAA's Division I Board of Directors voted to adopt a $2,000 stipend that would cover an athlete's full COA. Nevertheless, 125 Division I institutions then voted to override the decision, scuttling the increase.[16]

By 2014, the NCAA continued to face a number of lawsuits over the issue, and pressure — including from the U.S. Senate — was building to find a way to close the financial aid gap. Court rulings added additional

---

[16] See such readings in the literature on this topic as "How Colleges Figure 'Cost of Attendance,'" http://www.collegedata.com cited 8 May 2017; "Cost of Attendance Q&A," http://www.ncaa.org cited 9 May 2017; Blair Kerkhoff and Tod Palmer, "They're Not Paychecks, But Major College Athletes Got Extra Scholarship Stipends for First Time This School Year," http://www.kansascity.com cited 9 May 2017.

pressure by bolstering the idea that the NCAA violated federal antitrust law by capping scholarship amounts.

During mid-to-late 2014, the NCAA's Division I Board of Directors voted to restructure how its members govern themselves, granting a greater level of autonomy to the five wealthiest sports conferences. As a result, the Atlantic Coast, Big 10, Big 12, Pacific 12, and Southeastern Conferences were allowed to make their own rules concerning a number of issues with full COA at the top of their list. In January 2015, the conferences voted to approve stipends for athletes. All but one of the 65 institutions voted in favor of the payments.

This change in scholarships authorized schools to provide more dollars for college athletes for elements of attending college and formally defined by federal guidelines with financial aid officers at each school determining the amount. Additionally, based on each school's policies, a student's COA payment could be adjusted based on his or her individual circumstances such as transportation, childcare needs, and unusual medical expenses. The additional funds' intent is to cover the real costs of attending college not covered by the previous definition of a full scholarship — which includes tuition, room and board, required fees, and books. NCAA rules allow SAs who receive a Pell Grant to get the COA or the value of a full scholarship plus the Pell Grant, whichever is greater. Each school must ensure that it also follows applicable federal, state, and school requirements.

In a 2015–2016 survey of the COA expenses at schools in different conferences, the lowest to highest amounts per number of scholarships were budgeted by athletic departments as follows: $600,000 to $1 million in the American Athletic Conference; $500,000 to $2 million in the Atlantic Coast Conference; $750,000 to $2 million in the Big 10; $570,000 to $1.5 million in the Big 12; $250,000 to $655,000 in Conference USA; $315,000 to $850,000 in the Mid-American Conference; $400,000 to $1.5 million in the Pacific 12; and $950,000 to $2.1 million in the Southeastern Conference. For financial, sport-specific, and other reasons, several schools did not report their amounts in the survey.

During early 2017, the NCAA and college sports' major conferences announced a preliminary settlement of $208.7 million with plaintiffs who received athletic scholarships before COA stipends were allowed. If approved, the average class member who played his or her sport for four years would receive approximately \$6,763. Filed in 2014 by former West Virginia football player Shawne Alston and later consolidated with other cases, the lawsuit claimed the NCAA and its conferences violated antitrust law by capping the value of an athletic scholarship at less than the actual cost of attending college. The NCAA and conferences have since changed their rule to allow COA stipends.[17]

In the settlement, proposed class members include Division I men's and women's basketball and also FBS football players from the 2009–2010 through 2016–2017 academic years who did not receive COA as part of their scholarship. The NCAA said class members will be eligible to receive a distribution if they attended schools that have been or will provide COA aid by the 2017–2018 academic year.

This and similar topics have been thoroughly researched by scholars, and articles about them published in the literature. These publications involve such things as the distribution of COAs within small, mid-sized, and large schools, recent increases in stipends to athletes in different sports, and other matters. The following are some typical but important, interesting, and specific news reported in the literature.[18]

First, at the University of Hawaii (UH), implementation of COA meant a payout of \$1,000 to \$2,000 per athlete, depending on the sport. For example, women's and men's basketball players each get \$2,000, while golfers expect to receive \$1,000 (men) to \$1,789 (women). Football is pegged at \$1,500 for each of 85 players. Overall, it can be as much as \$1,000 per player increase at UH from 2015–2016, when the NCAA first allowed its members to begin paying the stipends. And while that is a lot

---

[17] Jon Soloman, "NCAA, Conferences Agree to Pay \$208.7 Million in Cost of Attendance Settlement," http://www.cbssports.com cited 12 May 2017.

[18] Read Fred Lewis, "UH Will Raise the Bar on Its Student-Athlete Stipends," *Honolulu Star* (25 June 2016): 1; Gavin Fowler, "Stipends a New Factor in NCAA Sports," *University Wire* (1 June 2016): 1; Nicole Auerbach, "Athletes' Stipends Mostly go to Food, Rent," *Arizona Republic* (6 January 2016): C.9; "UND Athletes Receive New Stipend," *University Wire* (8 September 2015): 1; Brad Elliott Schlossman, "Breaking News: UND to Pay All Scholarship Athletes Stipends in 2016–17," *TCA Regional News* (2 September 2015): 1; David Briggs, "Universities Deal With New Cost-of-Attendance Stipend for Athletes," *TCA Regional News* (5 July 2015): 1.

of money for UH — which has knocked on doors and looked under sofa cushions for funds — it remains in the shadow of much of its Division I brethren.

The money is designed to be spent for out-of-pocket expenses such as players' home travel, phone costs, clothes, and other things to more adequately address the actual costs of attending college that families might not be able to pay. Overall, UH said it spent $256,100 on COA stipends in 2015, a lot for a school struggling with its budget, yet a fraction of many schools in the Mountain West Conference, where it competes in football. Boise State, which offered as much as $5,100 per athlete, spent more than $1.1 million and Utah State anted up $783,432.

Second, according to a 2015–2016 database compiled by CBS Sports of schools in the 11 Division I FBS conferences, Brigham Young University paid its SAs $4,500 per year, University of Utah spent $3,574 per year on them, and Utah State $3,720 annually. The NCAA, meanwhile, tries to ensure that college players be students first and athletes second. According to published guidelines on the NCAA's website, athletes may not receive a salary, contracts with professional teams, prize money, benefits outside of NCAA sanctioned stipends, or receive representation from agents. Additionally, SAs are not allowed to play with professionals.

While the rule changes seem to benefit collegiate athletes, there are supporters and detractors of the policy. Supporters say athletes should be rewarded financially for their efforts, as they often are unable to work long hours and risk injury while making money for their school. Detractors, however, say paying athletes violates the spirit of 'students as athletes,' and could encourage an even greater focus on athletic, rather than academic, performance.

Third, beginning in the 2015–2016 academic year, NCAA Division I schools were allowed to give their athletes a stipend to cover their full COA at their schools. *USA Today Sports* asked some players competing in the college football playoff what they spent their COA stipend money on thus far. Offensive and defensive linemen, chuckling, said they spent a lot of it on food. Other players were adamant about saving it. This included Alabama receiver Richard Mullaney, who said he's not really into clothes or shoes so he pays his rent and then saves the rest. "We get so little money, I just save it," Clemson linebacker Ben Boulware said. "I spend a little on food if I need to. I get a couple hundred dollars. ... I have a safe in my house, and I lock it all away."

The extra bit of income helped some of the upperclassmen who lived off campus. There were electric, gas, and cable bills, for example, that they do not have to think about when living in on-campus housing. "If I need some shoes, I'm going to go buy me a pair of shoes," Alabama linebacker Reggie Ragland said. "But mostly it's making sure my bills are paid. That's one thing my parents always told me: make sure the bills are paid; you can do whatever you want after that." The stipend also took some strain off players' relatives besides their parents.

Fourth, University of North Dakota (UND) Director of Athletics Brian Faison announced that the department would expand its awarding of full amended grant-in-aid to all athletes who received athletic aid as of the 2016–2017 academic year. UND Athletics provides this same COA to all men's and women's hockey players. The aid includes the cost of tuition, room and board, books, and personal expenses as determined by the Student Financial Aid Office for athletes. The amount that is given to each athlete is determined by their residency status and living situation. These terms, however, have some constraints. For example, tuition will not include tuition for online classes. Similarly, room is based upon the university standard for double occupancy, and board is based upon the school's Unlimited Meal Plus Plan rate. The amount given for books is determined by the NCAA.

Fifth, the vast majority of college football players — 98.3 percent according to the NFL — do not get drafted and advance to careers in professional sports. For most involved in college athletics, it is about playing a sport they enjoy, the experience of being on a college team, and getting an education. Yet, at least a couple of college football coaches had seemed intent on messing it up for the NCAA and college athletes.

At Virginia Tech, for example, coaches put in place a system to take away part of an athlete's stipend for violating rules. According to a display photographed by the *Richmond Times Dispatch* newspaper, players would be fined $20 for missing treatment and $10 for missing study hall or a tutoring session. They were also assessed fines of $100 for flagrant or unsportsmanlike fouls or wearing the wrong equipment and $50 for having a dirty dorm room. The University of Cincinnati football program was supposed to put a similar program in place.

While coaches in athletic departments at schools certainly have the authority to impose these rules, taking away part of the players' newly granted stipend as punishment feels like docking their pay. And, that is probably why Virginia Tech thought about distancing itself from the concept. Cincinnati should also rethink it.

ATHLETICS ENVIRONMENT SUMMARY

This chapter identified, discussed, and referenced — either directly or indirectly — different facts, topics, implications, and viewpoints about the environment of athletics in colleges and universities and their men and women SAs enrolled in sports programs. Although most of them receive full or partial scholarships, public recognition, travel to various places around the country, and complete athletic wardrobes and more benefits, their athletic participation creates problems and requires changes and adjustments to lifestyles. As such, it is fun but also a challenge in college to be committed and successful as a student and athlete. Not only do they practice almost every day and sometimes play in games and/or matches three times in a week, they also attend classes, do homework assignments, prepare for examinations, and try to allocate time for social activities.

Besides spending countless hours outside the classroom doing various activities in their respective sports, they travel to and from various universities in athletic competition. If that is not enough, athletes must also follow the same university rules and regulations as other students, as well as team rules and, ultimately, NCAA rules. All of these rules and regulations can become stressful to men and women players.

In a scholarly study of how SAs at top-tier universities cope with the dual challenges of meeting the expectations of their teams while simultaneously complying with their responsibilities as university students, North Carolina State University (NCSU) researchers found that athletes reported feeling uncertain in three areas: personal uncertainty, such as uncertainty about injury or about balancing school work and sports; social uncertainty, such as uncertainty related to who their 'real' friends are; and future uncertainty, such as uncertainty concerning their post-collegiate careers and whether the time they spend pursuing athletics will hurt their career prospects.[19]

Most of the group reported using a variety of techniques to reduce uncertainty. These uncertainty-reduction strategies included (a) seeking social support from friends, family, or academic counselors; (b) socializing with friends to take a break from sports and school pressures; (c) negotiating with coaches in an attempt to raise their scholarship; and (d) sometimes concealing their athlete status from peers to minimize people befriending them for the wrong reasons, or prevent negative stereotypes. Others came to terms with uncertainty as a natural part of life and turned to prayer to help them cope.

The NCSU researchers suggested that universities should do more to prepare students for life outside of sports. Athletics departments, for example, could work with employers to offer flexible paid or unpaid professional internships around SAs' seasons. In this way, these players would receive work experience in fields outside of sports. Also, university athletics programs could take steps to give players more free time. What is sometimes overlooked amidst a heavy athletics and academic schedule is scholar athletes' need to unwind and decompress. They need more downtime.

In an effort to track the long-term outcomes of past participants in college sports compared with other students on campus, the NCAA collaborated with Gallup Inc. to survey those who graduated from 1970 to 2014. The goal of the study — which included interviews with more than 1,600 former SAs aged 22–71 and titled "Understanding Life Outcomes of Former NCAA Student-Athletes" — was to evaluate their well-being compared with responding graduates who were not college athletes. The responses were gathered as part of the Gallup-Purdue Index, based on online surveys conducted in 2014 with a random sample of 29,560 Americans adults.[20]

---

[19] Matt Shipman, "Study Offers Insights Into Challenges College Athletes Face," http://www.news.ncsu.edu cited 10 May 2017.

[20] Greg Johnson, "Gallup Study Measures Long-Term Life Outcomes of Former Student-Athletes," http://www.ncaa.org cited 10 May 2017.

In the survey, well-being was defined as the interaction and interdependency among many aspects of life. The elements, used to measure well-being, were developed by research and polling company Gallup, and Healthways, a healthcare consultant. The elements included Purpose, or liking what you do each day and being motivated to achieve your goals; Social, or having strong and supportive relationships and love in your life; Financial, or effectively managing your economic life to reduce stress and increase security; Community, or the sense of engagement you have with the area where you live, liking where you live, and feeling safe and having pride in your community; and Physical, or having good health and enough energy to get things done on a daily basis.

Regarding the survey's results, former college athletes were found to be more likely than non-former college athletes to thrive in four of the five well-being elements: purpose, social, community, and physical. In the financial well-being element, former SAs were just as likely to thrive as peers who did not participate in intercollegiate sports. In other areas of postgraduate life, 82 percent of former athletes were employed either full-time or part-time at their desired level, compared with 78 percent of graduates who were not SAs. Additionally, the rates of unemployment were similar for both former athletes and their non-college athlete counterparts.

Most American universities field various men's and women's intercollegiate sports teams. Since all but a handful of these programs lose money from an accounting perspective, why do universities continue to subsidize athletics from mandatory student fees, scarce general institutional funds, public monies from state governments, and contributions solicited from alumni and well-heeled donors that might be directed instead toward reducing the seemingly perpetual escalation of tuition costs?[21]

The issue is not whether college athletes should be paid. Apart from a few walk-ons, most of the players are already compensated via scholarships

---

[21] The source is Allen Sanderson and John Siegfried, "Enough Madness: Just Pay College Athletes," *Chicago Tribune* (3 February 2016): 22. For other economic viewpoints on compensating specific college and university athletes, see Liz Entman, "Elite College Athletes Should be Paid: Economists," http://www.news.vanderbilt.edu cited 10 May 2017; "An Economic Argument for the Paying of College Athletes," http://www.sportsbookreview.com cited 11 May 2017; Dave Zirin, "An Economist Explains Why Athletes Should be Paid," http://www.thenation.com cited 12 May 2017.

or grants that cover most of their expenses. 'Amateur' should not be defined by whether one is paid but, more sensibly, by the nature of the relationship between the player and his or her institution. The issue is that through the NCAA our nation's universities collectively cap their players' compensation, which in other businesses would violate Section 1 of the Sherman Antitrust Act and be a criminal offense.

Finally, as several lawsuits involving various aspects of NCAA control play out, it seems unlikely that the future landscape of big-time intercollegiate athletics will resemble the current incarnation that transfers massive resources from young, poorly represented minorities to the paychecks of coaches and athletic directors who are paid well above what they likely would earn if athletes were compensated reasonably for their services as players.

Chapter 6

ACADEMICS–SPORTS CONTROVERSIES

In contrast to other college and university undergraduate and perhaps graduate students, men and women athletes have less time and also conflicts during their team's sports season or seasons to attend and study for classes, complete and turn in homework assignments as scheduled, prepare for quizzes and examinations, and otherwise achieve high grades relative to their classmates. Indeed, they spend many hours practicing, training, and traveling to and from away games and playing others at home. As a result, many student athletes (SAs) underperform academically and also experience anxiety, pressure, and stress to remain eligible, especially when competing in such demanding revenue sports as football and men's and women's basketball.

While developing the concept, purpose, and scope and then writing the manuscript for *Student Athletes: Merging Academics and Sports*, the author identified and contacted a few professionals in education and requested their comments, opinions, and viewpoints. They were asked a question: From an academic and/or sports perspective, what are some important issues/topics regarding SAs and their current/future role on college and university campuses? In no specific order, each of them replied to the question as follows:

"I think one of the greatest issues for student-athletes is 'athlete and identity.' Too many of these athletes, especially men at all levels (D-III,

D-II, D-I, and NAIA) think they will be playing professionally and are limiting their educational experience as they are over conforming [over generous] with their time they are giving to their sport and under conforming [under allocating] to the time investing in their academics. Put another way, too many athletes are in college to play sports and gain a piece of paper vs. being in college to gain an education and play sports."

— University Sports Management Professor

"This is a good topic. To many casual sports fans it might seem like a simple one but as you know, it is quite complex. There are several perspectives to consider: First, how should a university or college view student athletes? What are the short-run and long-run benefits and costs of having an intercollegiate athletic program? (a) What are the start-up and recurring expenses of an athletic program? (b) How does the athletic program benefit the university in terms of increased enrollment, increased alumni support, and increased revenue from other sources? (c) What support does the university provide student athletes to stay eligible and, hopefully, to earn their baccalaureate degree? Second, what factors are relevant to the student athletes? (a) What support do they receive from the university? (b) Does being a student athlete increase the ability of an individual to attend college and to earn a degree, as opposed to being a non-athlete student? (c) How prepared are they to succeed in the athletic program and to avoid violations that will impact them and the university? (d) What costs and benefits affect a student athlete, and are these costs and benefits visible so an athlete can make rational decisions? Third, what is the role of the NCAA regarding the relationship between it, the university, and the student athlete?"

— University Economics Professor

"The *Journal of Intercollegiate Sport/Journal of Sport and Social Issues/ Journal of Issues in Intercollegiate Athletics/Journal of Sport Management/Journal of Sports Economics*, and *Economic Inquiry* have articles. Finally, economists and others have written for the Knight Commission on Intercollegiate Athletics and the NCAA. The most important topics are: pay for play, the proper role of athletics for student athletes, their mental and physical well-being/the time demands — full time sports occupation + full time student is a clear conflict."

— University Sports Management Professor

"First, time demands — student-athletes can spend 20+ hours a week on their sport, which makes getting ready for their post-collegiate life difficult. They have difficulty pursuing internships or part-time jobs and sometimes have difficulty even pursuing a major that interests them (particularly troublesome majors are education, nursing, lab sciences). The time demands of their sport can impede their ability to get the most out of their college education, which may be why graduation rates are often lower for student-athletes than the rest of the student body. Time demands also can make it difficult for student-athletes to access all of the academic support services they may need, which in turn can result in poor academic performance. Conversely, some student-athletes are so well organized and committed to both sport and academics that they are among some of the most outstanding students I have encountered. Second, identity — student-athletes often identify with their sport first and the college second. If they identify as "athlete" first, their commitment to their education isn't always as high as it could be to help them perform better in the classroom. Conversely, some student-athletes identify as a "Soccer Player" and are committed at a high level to both sport and education. Third, campus involvement — often, student-athletes are unable to be involved in non-sport activities (again time demands). It would be wonderful to be in a situation where they can be involved across the campus outside the classroom. Fourth, behavior — student-athletes have the opportunity to be true campus leaders by exhibiting good sportsmanship and behavior both on and off the playing field. The student body tends to look up to student-athletes. Conversely, bad behavior reflects poorly on them, impacts the greater student body and most definitely the college's reputation."

— University President

"We expect our student athletes to be ambassadors to the rest of the student body. Our expectations are high. They are required to perform community service tasks. They are student's first, athletes second. We expect them to spend quiet study time, and we provide regular study sessions with tutorial assistance on a regular basis. They share their academic progress with their coaches. In short, we have high expectations of our student athletes, and we make sure we work with them on all fronts, physical, mental, and especially in meeting their needs for health and nutrition. Last, we teach them respect for America and all things patriotic. They are expected to observe proper protocol when we play the National Anthem. That is important to display, and our fans appreciate it."

— College President

"This is certainly a deserving topic that is not only complex but somewhat troubling in a variety of ways. I feel that one would need to look at the various levels of athletic programs to get a proper perspective: 1. the Big 5 conferences, 2. other Div.1 conferences, 3. div. 2 conferences and schools. These are simply different worlds for the student athlete and the amounts of wealth made available to the Big 5 conferences. For example, the SEC schools just were just awarded $35,000,000 each for network profits for football and I would guess that the Big ten is in the same ballpark for monetary benefits. Now compare this to the Ivy League schools or to div. 2 schools, it's not the same world for the athlete, the school, the program. The costs are enormous and so are the expectations. The aforementioned contributes to situations such as at UNC, Baylor, Southern Cal., and numerous others over the past 25 years."

— Professor Emeritus

"First, paying student-athletes a salary (Northwestern football team's fight to unionize); Second, letting student athletes control their intellectual property (their jersey or likeness) — Ed O'Bannon case; Third, making them students again (living in regular dorms, etc. — Vanderbilt did this several years ago and took a lot of heat as they technically do not have an athletic director). Fourth, similar to above, not giving them elite status or special protections (Baylor rape cover-up); Fifth, getting rid of the NBA one and done (let them go pro straight out of high school instead of having to fake it in college for a year); Sixth, giving student-athletes some freedom to transfer to another school (particularly when their coach leaves for another school); Seventh, honor their scholarship — coaches are now pulling scholarships every year; Eighth, create more online courses to help student-athletes who travel and miss a lot of class time; Ninth, retool the Academic Progress Rate (APR) to be more stringent (monitor the courses so there's no underwater basket-weaving)."

— University Business Professor

"1. The "time crunch" is much more demanding today that when you and I were in college. Between off-season workouts, in-season workouts, travel (conference expansion) places a large time demand on student-athletes. 2. Most athletes are now in summer school so the academic load is reduced during the season. 3. Academic resources for athletes are improved. The University of Illinois has a center for student-athletes when they can get assistance and are required to attend at a scheduled time. I'm sure you could find information about it online."

— High School Economics Teacher

Based on their replies, the content in prior chapters, and readings in the literature, there are several challenging, controversial, and significant subjects, problems, and other matters relative to the development, growth, and success or failure of SAs on teams in colleges and universities. As a result, this chapter identifies some of these issues and provides various reasons why they exist and, in part, denotes their actual and potential effects economically, educationally, and realistically.

ACADEMIC MOTIVATION AND PERFORMANCE

The data in Chapter 4 reported the academic results of SAs in colleges and universities affiliated with Division I of the National Collegiate Athletic Association (NCAA) and also of member schools associated with the National Association of Intercollegiate Athletics (NAIA) and National Junior College Athletic Association (NJCAA). This section extends the data by revealing and explaining the meaning, motivation, and implication of why and how players perform in the classroom.[1]

---

[1] The readings for this section include such articles as Gary Cutting, "The Myth of the Student-Athlete," https://www.opinionator.blogs.nytimes.com cited 12 May 2017; "Five Reasons Student Athletes Struggle Academically," http://www.gradesfirst.com cited 12 May 2017; Daniel Oppenheimer, "Why Student Athletes Continue to Fail," http://www.time.com cited 12 May 2017; Sarah Ganim, "CNN Analysis: Some College Athletes Play Like Adults, Read Like 5th-Graders," http://www.cnn.com cited 12 May 2017; Brad

The term SA, in part, implies that full-time students who play college sports are also engaged in secondary or extracurricular activities that enhance their education. Their status, the term suggests, is essentially the same as those in schools' choir, debate team, and/or the band. But there are, of course, many athletes who are primarily students first, particularly those in minor or non-revenue producing sports such as men's lacrosse and rowing and women's softball and tennis.

But what is the special status, if any, of athletes in Division I football and men's basketball — that is, on teams in big-time sports programs with revenues in the millions of dollars and a major reason for their schools' national reputation? Are members of these teams typically viewed by the public and fans, and themselves, as students first?

An NCAA survey showed, for example, that by a wide variety of measures, the answer to the question is no. According to results of the survey, football and men's basketball players identify themselves more strongly as athletes than as students and give more weight and emphasis in choosing their college for athletics than with regard to academics, and at least during their sport's season, spend more time on athletics than studies and during the offseason, a large majority of them allocate as much or more time to sports.[2]

The same priority is reflected in many colleges' policies, practices, and programs. Football and men's basketball players are admitted and awarded full scholarships almost entirely because of their skills and athletic abilities. Furthermore, the academic criteria and standards for their admission are less demanding and substantially below those of other students. Given the amount of time and energy such athletes devote to sports, realistically they would have to be academically superior to the average student to do as well as them in their classes.

Wolverton, "NCAA Says It's Investigating Academic Fraud at 20 Colleges," http://www.chronicle.com cited 12 May 2017.

[2] Some recent studies are "NCAA Study of Student-Athlete Social Environments," http://www.ncaa.org cited 13 May 2017; "Student-Athletes," http://www.ncaa.org cited 13 May 2017; "Results from the 2015 Goals Study of the Student-Athlete Experience," http://www.ncaa.org cited 13 May 2017; "NCAA Goals Study of the Student-Athlete Experience: Initial Summary of Findings January 2016," http://www.ncaa.org cited 13 May 2017.

Consequently — based on six years to complete their degree — the graduation rates of football and men's basketball players are considerably below the college average. Even these results actually understate the situation since schools in higher education provide underqualified athletes with advisers, counselors, and mentors who point them toward easier courses and majors and also offer extraordinary amounts of academic coaching and tutoring, primarily designed to keep these athletes eligible to play. In other words, members of these teams are athletes first and students second, both from their own perspective and schools' viewpoint.

Why do a significant proportion of SAs — especially in revenue and other high-profile sports — specifically struggle academically? First is time mismanagement. For them, it may be time to practice, have a lunch date with a girl sitting two rows away in Public Speaking or Principles of Communications, scheduling a video game session with a roommate, or any number of other activities and events college students pack into their day. Managing the pressures of athletics and also being a normal college student is extremely difficult for players, in part, because of other things that distract their academic focus.

Second, SAs typically step onto the field or court in an athletic role in which they are very good at and usually love to do. This confident preparedness — while beneficial to that role — fails to provide the mindset needed for them to surrender pride and admit that they are not good or qualified at something else. When that is academic-related, a major problem occurs. Being scared or too intimidated to ask for and use an advisor, counselor, or tutor is a big reason SAs struggle academically.

Third, their motivation can be an academic killer. Sadly, some players look at academics as the necessary evil of being an SA. While some manage to navigate through classes with enough focus to remain eligible for a sports season, others forget or entirely fail to realize or appreciate the true purpose of their scholarship. The problem is not always a lack of caring, but rather a lack of background needed to understand the importance of their progress toward a degree. Once identified, however, an athlete often treats classes like a competition and realizes a rapid improvement. Not a lost cause, he or she simply lacks the necessary experience to attack and excel in the classroom as they do in their sport.

Fourth, a combination of small actions will contribute to their success academically. Many SAs have not been exposed to the pressures they face in college nor experienced the relief provided by being organized. These activities include such things as preparing and keeping notes in separate notebooks or simply knowing how many study hall hours to complete in a week. These small things can pile up and overwhelm SAs who are not used to balancing the demands that come with the title.

Fifth, communication is probably the most obvious and definitely one of the common reasons for having problems while being in school. Lacking it is a struggle every SA must deal with and overcome at some point. For example, when is that meeting? What time is practice? Did I forget to email my advisor? These simple tasks can become hard to organize, manage, and control when any or all of the previous issues exist in some way.

Academic struggles are often related to things other than intellect or the simple desire or ability to be successful educationally. The beauty of these and similar perceived problems is that each of them is coachable and can be solved. Time management, direct communication with advisors and tutors, and organization tools are all built-in perks that athletes should utilize, among many other options. Problems like these are no longer reasons or justification for men and women players to struggle in their classes while excelling in a sport.

Another possible but intriguing reason is that some SAs do not think their teammates take schoolwork as seriously as them. When asked to assess how much their teammates cared about sports, athletes were close by guessing 8-plus on a 10-point scale in a questionnaire. However, when asked to evaluate how much their teammates cared about academics, they guessed only 7-plus or far below the 9-plus average.

Why is this important? Because when an athlete thinks that the rest of the team does not care about academics, that person tries to fit in by pretending not to care either. This, in turn, creates a distressing and self-perpetuating cycle. Tight-knit SAs will seek ways to fit into a culture that they perceive as neglecting academics by defaulting into majors of dubious merit and spending less time doing homework, knowing that their habits are observed by teammates. When teammates observe those habits, it reaffirms the false conviction that caring about academics is an unfortunate aberration best suppressed.

A professor described this process particularly well: "There are student athletes who want to excel in the classroom, but think their teammates would judge them for it, so they study a little less, or take an easier major. And it turns out, that's how virtually everyone on the team feels, but there's never an opportunity to realize, oh wait, all of us really care about what's happening on the academic side."

This is a phenomenon that psychologist's call 'pluralistic ignorance' — when private preferences differ from perceptions of group norms. It leads people to engage in public behaviors that align more with the perceived norms than with their true preferences. The tragedy is that the norms are false in reality, and everybody would be happier if they just behaved in line with their true preferences.[3]

A Cable News Network (CNN) investigation, interestingly, found in public universities across the country that many students within schools' basketball and football programs read only up to an eighth-grade level. The data obtained through open records requests also showed a staggering achievement gap between college athletes and their peers at the same institution. This was not an exhaustive survey of all schools with major sports programs because CNN chose a sampling of public universities where open records laws applied. The network sought data from a total of 37 institutions, of which 21 or 56 percent of them responded. Some schools denied requests for entrance exam or aptitude test scores by claiming the information did not exist while others cited privacy rules. A few simply did not provide it in time.[4]

Officials at the universities from which CNN collected data said they recognized the low scores and gave several reasons for them. Some athletes, for example, do not aim or try for high scores when taking entrance exams, looking only to score high enough to become NCAA eligible. Also, many times low scores are indicators of learning disabilities. However, entrance exams are just one factor taken into consideration when deciding whether to accept or reject a SA's application. The officials

---

[3] Joshua Levine, *et al.*, "Pluralistic Ignorance Among Student-Athlete Populations: a Factor in Academic Underperformance," https://www.link.springer.com cited 13 May 2017.

[4] *Idem*, Sarah Ganim, "CNN Analysis: Some College Athletes Play Like Adults, Read Like 5th-Graders."

also believed excellent tutoring and extra attention from academic support allows these players to perform well both off and on the field, and many cited their relatively high graduation rates.

In 2015, the NCAA investigated allegations of academic misconduct on 20 campuses. The cases at various stages — from preliminary inquiry to awaiting a hearing with the Division I Committee on Infractions — involved a variety of missteps including allegations that players received impermissible assistance from professors, academic advisors, or people outside of an athletic department.

Eighteen or 90 percent of the cases were in Division I and one each in Divisions' II and III. The officials declined to name any of the colleges. The NCAA's vice president for enforcement, Jonathan Duncan, said the association was investigating potential academic violations at several prominent but accredited colleges.

Many of the cases involved people who had relationships with an athletic department or a particular sport but not necessarily employed by the department. These included such individuals as professors, academic advisers who worked outside of athletics, and people in the registrar's office. Head coaches were also involved and, in some cases, they urged members of their staff — secretaries, athletic trainers, people in the weight room — to get this male or that female athlete eligible. The association also interviewed other people involved in players' lives including agents, amateur coaches, and/or financial planners, and anybody who took inappropriate steps to help players gain eligibility. Results of the cases were not reported or publicized by the NCAA.

Since the arrests of 10 men — including four assistant college coaches and an Adidas executive — in September–October 2017, NCAA President Mark Emmert reported widespread distrust in both the NCAA and its schools in a commissioned poll in which 79 percent of Americans agreed with the statement that major schools put money ahead of the interests of their athletes. Said Emmert, "We cannot go into the next basketball season without seeing fundamental change with the way college basketball is operating. We need to act. We need to demonstrate that we [NCAA and schools] are, in fact, capable of resolving these issues."[5]

---

[5] See Will Hobson, "NCAA President: Major Changes Needed to Restore Public Trust," *Charlotte Observer* (31 October 2017): 4B. In response to an FBI investigation, former

PAY-FOR-PLAY

College athletics is a relatively big, entertaining, lucrative, and popular business. Millions of taxpayer dollars are spent updating stadiums, training facilities, and other areas of athletic departments, all for male and female amateur athletes to compete. Money floods into schools' athletic departments and athletes benefit in many ways. But, do they deserve to be paid for their performances on courts, fields, and other places?

This argument exists and been perpetuated for decades. Obviously, the idea of SA has been flipped to athlete-student, and an NCAA regulation that 50 percent of them must graduate is very loose. However, in order to keep the façade of a so-called student-first mentality, college players are not paid. Despite stipends for food and other essentials, athletes are not fully compensated for their services.

Some people are aware enough to realize that men and women SAs on athletic scholarships are essentially already paid because they receive free tuition, a dorm room, meal plans, and some money for books and miscellaneous expenses. At bigger, wealthy, and more successful universities, athletes also receive academic counseling, tutoring, life-skill training, and perhaps nutritional advice. Certainly, not all of them or even a large majority is on a full scholarship. Even so, those in the revenue-producing sports receive compensation in the form of educational benefits and living expenses. To an economist, this is a payment or pay.

Beyond that and commonly overlooked, however, is that athletes also receive free professional coaching, strength and fitness training, and support from athletic trainers, nutritionists, and physical therapists. Before becoming professionals, football and basketball players pay $2,000 to $3,000 per week for advice, guidance, and training in the weeks leading up to their pre-draft workouts.

Using these valuations and adding in the value of a scholarship, some men and women players on teams at schools in a major conference and on full scholarship likely receive a package of education, room, board, and coaching/training worth between $50,000 and $125,000 per year

---

Secretary of the State Condoleezza Rice leads a committee to determine the type of changes to restore public confidence in college athletics, particularly football and men's basketball programs.

depending on their sport and whether they attend a public or private university. In addition to that, the best college athletes gain valuable publicity from playing on sports teams. As such, here are other reasons whether or not to compensate college and university players.

Oppose Pay-for-Play

Most male and female athletes will never be in professional sports but rather seek gainful employment elsewhere beyond their brief career in college. If collegiate sports shift from amateurism to professionalism, this would discourage academic involvement, which is fundamentally the purpose of schools in higher education. Paying them a salary could existentially threaten other athletic programs such as golf, soccer, tennis, and swimming. Furthermore, any sort of compensation or extra payment in addition to outright replacement of scholarships might entirely or partially detach athletics from academics.

This is both wrong in principle and impossible in practice. How would schools disperse salaries? Would star players get paid more than others? Would all players be paid the same amount? Would basketball players get paid more than those in football because there are fewer athletes on a basketball team? What about other types of sports or women's teams? Do schools pay all athletes irrespective of their gender, role, and level of participation? Consequently, there are confusing, numerous, and complex unanswerable questions about implementing pay-for-play.

According to some academic and sports officials, paying male and female college athletes would not be necessary, fair, and/or feasible. They should not be paid in order to keep a clear divide between amateur and professional sports. Paying college athletes would create a completely new playing field, and the consequences would be costly. Because football and men's basketball are typically the most or even the only revenue building sports, program-based pay would be drastically unfair. This means that top athletes in such sports as lacrosse, soccer, and volleyball would be guaranteed to make substantially less money than the second string on the football team, if they were even paid at all. That is, not mentioning women's sports.

On individual pay, how would coaches and school officials evaluate top players across different sports? Is it more important to win championships, break conference and/or school records, or simply be the top player on a team? There is also a problem with the availability of funds, but that seems to be irrelevant or ignored. Assuming it would be a good idea and fair to compensate players on just sports teams that generate revenue like football and basketball, profits earned by these teams are typically how athletic departments subsidize and support smaller sports. Taking away funding from minor sports would have a major impact on college athletics. Funds for baseball, softball, swimming and tennis, for example, would shrink and many programs would be eliminated altogether.

To compare models in pay-for-play schemes, a coach could offer a recruit a salary instead of a scholarship. Does $100,000 give a SA a better deal than a $65,000 scholarship? Undoubtedly, a $100,000 salary is impressive. A future Heisman Trophy winner in football might command more money, but $100,000 is reasonable for an 18-year-old high school recruit. But since it is a salary and not a scholarship, it is subject to federal and state income taxes. Tuition and college expenses would not be deductible because the income level surpasses the Internal Revenue Service (IRS) eligibility limit.

Based on that situation, a player paid a salary would owe approximately $23,800 in federal income tax and $6,700 in state taxes for a total of $30,500. In cities that levy an employee payroll tax, the salaried student's taxes go up to about $2,400 per year. As a result, total income taxes increase to $32,900. Furthermore, as an employee, the player would have to pay at least $2,000 in other taxes such as social security, for a total of $34,900. This leaves the college player with $65,100. Since college costs amount to about to $65,000, the player is left with $100.

Paying SAs to play sports is infeasible without ignoring fiscal responsibility and legally mandated equality. Title IX, for example, requires equal opportunities for women at schools who receive federal funding. This mandate includes a literal one-to-one gender ratio. Any benefit afforded to a male athlete must likewise be granted to a female one. Compensating athletes could existentially threaten other sports programs. With few exceptions, only some Division I football and men's basketball teams are able to financially sustain their programs. All others in Division I and those in other NCAA divisions are non-revenue programs and rely on subsidies from the university and its donors. Undoubtedly, schools would eliminate many of them.

Expressed in a different way, there are several current, controversial, and valid criticisms of pay-for-play. In no particular format or sequence, four of them appeared in the literature. Listed, they are as follows:[6]

- Amateur male and female players who receive compensation' seem like a complete disaster. They do not know how to manage their money, and there would not be anyone to guide their financial decisions. Sports media personality Colin Cowherd states: "I don't think paying all college athletes is great; not every college is loaded, and most 19-year-olds (are) gonna spend it — and let's be honest, they're gonna spend it on weed and kicks!"

- Unfair and perhaps conflicting compensation schemes might exist between players on teams. For example, would players be compensated in cash, by check, or with deposits into their bank account? Will each player receive the same amount or adjusted by some formula? What about payments to top-level talent? Should they receive more because they were All-Americans, first or second team All-Conference, or All-League? In theory, this would bring problems between players due to one or more teammates potentially receiving more, less, or the same amount of money for their performances?

- Athletes might not attend and/or study for class. If schools give these teenagers and young adults money, they would have little to no incentive to be at their daytime or evening classes. Unfortunately, many of them do not want to be there anyway. Combined with the fact that some may be receiving grades without doing any work, money will only add to the problem.

- Various sports officials believe pay-for-play removes athletes' competitive nature and passion for the game. In their view, players would

---

[6]Malcolm Lemmons, "College Athletes Getting Paid? Here Are Some Pros and Cons," http://www.huffingtonpost.com cited 13 May 2017 and Ekow Yankah, "Why N.C.A.A. Athletes Shouldn't be Paid," http://www.newyorker.com cited 13 May 2017.

take on a 'pro mindset' where the primary motive is always money. Thus, they lose the hunger and passion seen in college sports. This, in turn, will be traded for lackadaisical plays and half-hearted efforts sometimes displayed by professionals in their games.

Support Pay-for-Play

To make a pay-for-play system succeed and even thrive throughout college sports programs in America, every Division I football and men's basketball team would have a salary cap, just as the professional franchises do — except the amounts would be vastly lower. In basketball, for example, the cap would be about $650,000, and in football approximately $3 million.

It is ludicrous, therefore, to argue that the college Power 5 programs cannot afford these amounts. Indeed, the combined $3.65 million is less than one-half the $9 million that University of Michigan football head coach Jim Harbaugh earns in a season. Moreover, schools might also drop the number of scholarships in college football to 60 from the high 70s/low 80s, which is closer to the size of a National Football League (NFL) roster.

Another option to consider is impose a minimum salary, for example, at $25,000 per player in each sport. Obviously, this would not make many amateur athletes rich. But it would also give them enough to live like typical college students. With respect to free-market economics, minimum salaries consume only half the cap space. The rest of the money may be used as a recruiting tool, so that a star player could be offered additional payment as an inducement to sign with a particular school. In other words, one university might decide to offer a star halfback in football $40,000 while another might offer him $60,000. The player would make a choice based not on a recruiter's sweet-talking promises — or not solely on that offer — but mostly on cold, hard cash.

According to Entertainment Sports Programming Network (ESPN) college basketball analyst, former player for Duke University, attorney, and renowned supporter of compensation reform Jay Bilas, regardless how many billions of dollars are passed around between the NCAA, its broadcast partners and various sponsoring corporations, the players themselves still receive zero dollars in cash for their performances. They are in a money-wind machine but locked in a strait-jacket.

In simple terms, Bilas explained why college athletes deserve to be paid. One, it is a multibillion dollar business where the only people who are restricted in their earnings, in any way, are the athletes. Two, 'it will ruin the game' doomsday scenarios are ridiculous. Three, other sports will not be canceled because some players are being paid. Four, implementing a new system is much easier than those in charge want you to believe. Five, it won't dramatically change the quality of the top teams. Six, good players would stay in school longer. Seven, nobody would put up with this in any other walk of life.[7]

Several proposals outline ways to encourage, publicize, and promote pay-for-play plans in NCAA Division I football and men's basketball programs. The arguments have been specifically tailored for the two sports at schools who receive bonus money from the NCAA, in part, because these colleges and universities and their coaches enjoy considerable revenue from television contracts and sponsorships generated by football bowl games and 'March Madness' appearances in basketball.

The first argument is that athletic scholarships do not provide a free education. In the 1950s, the NCAA approved the addition of living stipends to athletic scholarships that previously included only tuition and fees. Now, a 'full ride' scholarship includes only tuition, fees, room, board, and books. Depending on the school attended by athletes, the scholarship can be worth anywhere from $80,000 to $300,000, although $40,000 to $150,000 over a four-year period might be more accurate. In any case, that range in amounts does not cover the full cost of attending college.

The second argument is that the majority of SAs do not know the economic value or opportunity cost of their scholarship. Although all realize they are getting a scholarship — which allows them to attend school

---

[7]Maurice Peebles, "7 Common Sense Reasons Why College Athletes Should be Paid (According to Jay Bilas)," http://www.complex.com cited 12 May 2017. Besides supporting a pay-for-play system for male and female players, Bilas also has publicly complained about the NCAA's rules regarding student-athletes transferring from a school to another one. One case is basketball guard Cameron Johnson being restricted by the University of Pittsburgh to play at the University of North Carolina in Chapel Hill. In designing rules, he believes the NCAA thinks mostly of schools first rather than the best interests of athletes. For this dispute, read Hank Tucker's article, "ESPN Analyst, Former Duke Player Bilas is Body's Loudest Critic," *Charlotte Observer* (12 July 2017): 4B.

and play a sport — most do not know the actual or true worth of their agreement with a school. In fact, they generally have very little understanding about entering a 'plantation-like' system in which their scholarship is not guaranteed, renewed yearly, and therefore can be terminated at any time by the school. SAs are also led to believe by coaches and others they will play and receive a college degree while possibly picking up a few fringe benefits along the way. This is not, of course, entirely accurate.

The third argument is that schools offer more than education, which is possible but not probable. More specifically, many administrators, athletic directors, and coaches and their staffs claim that colleges and universities offer more than an education — for example social clubs, concerts, fraternities, lectures, intramurals, and sororities — in settings that enrich the college experience. Due to the plantation effect, for the most part, athletes are not able or available to take advantage of those events and organizations. For instance, few if any scholarship athletes would be allowed to play in intramural games for their coach's fear of them being injured. SAs are also overscheduled already with study halls, practices, weight training sessions, film study, individual workouts, more practice, travel, and competition. In fact, these activities are an attempt to help athletes maintain focus on their sport.

The fourth argument is that, at least from an economic perspective, the NCAA operates as a cartel. The late Cornell University economist Alfred Kahn examined the operation of the NCAA's college football and basketball systems and offered lessons about the determinants and effects of market supply and demand. Specifically, he utilized economic principles to calculate the average value of college football players at a typical university. He noted that total ticket revenues for football and men's basketball were $757 million in 1999, which exceeded the total ticket sales for all professional baseball, football, and ice hockey games that year. Based on these results, the NCAA has been a very successful business entity engaged in capitalism.

According to cartel theory, the NCAA enforces collusive restrictions on payments for factors of production including player compensation, recruiting expenses, and assistant coaches' salaries, and also the organization restricts output and defeats potential rival groups. Kahn noted, along with other research scholars, that the NCAA can also impose sanctions that range from scholarship reductions, elimination from postseason play to program death penalties — football, for example, at Southern Methodist University — and possibly even threaten a school's academic accreditation. However, restriction of payments to players is the primary way in which the NCAA acts to restrict competition.

Pay Proposals

To improve conditions in college sports, especially for athletes, some people suggest the NCAA should get out of the commercial business of football and basketball. Rather, the group should follow the Ivy League example of providing a truly amateur environment where players are actually students first. That move would be significant and certainly put athlete second in the SA term.[8]

It does not seem pragmatic or realistic, however, that either the NCAA or any of the major Division I universities are in a hurry to agree and actually turn away millions of dollars per year in profits. Therefore, it is time to consider some pay-for-pay proposals. Although California and Nebraska passed state legislation enabling colleges and universities to compensate their athletes, they are blocked by the NCAA from doing it. Therefore, one or more proposals to adopt, implement, and enforce pay-for-play are as follows.

First is the Big 10 conference's plan and/or work study proposal. At the very least, the NCAA would follow former NCAA President Miles Brand's suggestion and allocate to athletes significantly more money

---

[8] See Oliver Tonkin, "Oliver Tonkin, Paying Student-Athletes Will Harm Academic Institutions," *University Wire* (23 October 2014): 1; Allen Sack, "College Athletes are Students First and Should Not be Paid," *Deseret News* (16 March 2008): G.3; Jarad Welch and Brad Marshall, "Should Student Athletes be Paid to Play?" http://www.usatoday.com cited 12 May 2017; Joe Nocera, "A Way to Start Paying College Athletes," http://www.nytimes.com cited 12 May 2017; John Thelin, "Here's Why We Shouldn't Pay College Athletes," http://www.time.com cited 12 May 2017; Jon Soloman, "10 Ways College Athletes Can Get Paid and Remain Eligible for Their Sport," http://www.cbssports.com cited 12 May 2017; Brittany Anas, "CU-Boulder to Enter Student-Athlete 'Pay for Play' Debate," *The Daily Camera* (20 June 2011): 1; Dennis Johnson and John Acquaviva, "Point/Counterpoint: Paying College Athletes," http://www.thesportjournal.org cited 14 May 2017.

and/or resources in cost of living to their full scholarships. Since players are supposedly only allowed to spend 20 hours per week with sport-related activities, this distribution might actually be paid as 20 hours of work study or as a monthly living stipend. This would provide athletes with the needed income for such things as clothes, laundry, sundries, travel, and other small-item expenses.

During previous meetings, officials from the Big 10 reviewed a similar proposal that would help schools' athletes pay expenses not covered in their athletic scholarship. Commissioner Jim Delany reported some athletic directors and university officials seriously discussed using some of their growing television revenue to give athletes a portion of it. This proposal also had the support of current NCAA president Mark Emmert.

Second is a Southeastern Conference (SEC) game-pay proposal. At a conference meeting, former University of South Carolina football coach Steve Spurrier put forth a proposal to pay his players at least $300 per game. With the support of several other SEC coaches, this type of a proposal could provide athletes anywhere from $300 to $1,000 based on their time played per game and/or season. Since most players are not involved more than 30 minutes a game, a player could be paid on a per-minute of competition basis. At a rate of $20 per minute, a player might net at least $600 for a game and approximately $6,000 to $7,000 per season.

Regarding the pay-for-play dilemma, third is a professional league proposal recommended by Middlebury College professor Peter Plagensa. He agrees with scholars like Stanley Eitzen — Professor Emeritus of Sociology at Colorado State University. That is, the current policies, regulations, and rules of colleges and the NCAA amount to little more than a plantation system.

Eitzen suggested that big-time college football and basketball schools continue to maintain the multimillion-dollar industry by making SAs professional at a certain age. This proposal allows universities to hire players as college staff — much like administration officials, cafeteria personnel, or groundskeepers — at moderate salaries plus room and board. Universities could also grant athletes free academic classes until they earn a degree and even after their playing career expired.

Fourth is a revenue sharing proposal. Former Heisman Trophy winner and current minor league baseball player Tim Tebow revealed on the

Daily Show about joking with his college coach prior to a national championship football game about getting a cut of his bonus money to ensure a victory. This brought up another pay-for-play possibility to the surface: head coaches sharing bonuses and other performance incentives with their players.

Most coaches in big-time programs are paid huge bonuses based on their team's record and ranking, all a result of player performances. For instance, according to 2009 Internal Revenue Service (IRS) income tax reports, Duke University head basketball coach Mike Krzyewski received approximately $2.2 million in bonuses and incentives. Under this proposal, coaches would be required to share 25–50 percent of their bonuses with players. It seems fair, practical, and reasonable to expect athletes to get a portion of that money. After all, they put the coaches in a position to earn it.

PLAYER SCANDALS

During mid-2016, the NCAA's Division I Council clarified the academic integrity rules for member schools' SAs in an important way. This was the first legislative change to the division's approach to academic integrity issues since 1983. The new rules established clear and consistent guidelines with respect to academic integrity issues and also how to govern such matters when considered an NCAA violation.[9]

Designed by the Committee on Academic Performance and Academic Cabinet, the legislation struck a balance between a school administration's role in deciding academic integrity issues on campus and the NCAA's collective role in reinforcing and upholding its core academic principles.

Each school determines the purpose, scope, and content of its policies, and must follow them when an academic integrity issue involving an athlete occurs, regardless of circumstance. Under the rules, only conduct that violates a school's academic misconduct policies may become an NCAA academic misconduct violation. Specifically, the misconduct must have resulted in a falsification of the student-athlete's academic record,

---

[9]The reference is Michelle Brutlag Hosick, "D1 Council Adopts Academic Integrity Proposal," http://www.ncaa.org cited 22 May 2017.

involved a school's staff member and/or boosters, or allowed the student to compete while ineligible.

Since schools cannot know or predict every type of academic integrity issue, some misconduct committed by their staff members or boosters that does not violate a school's academic misconduct policies may still violate NCAA rules regulating impermissible academic assistance. In fact, the new rules defined impermissible academic assistance as (a) conduct involving a staff member or booster that falls outside of a school's academic misconduct policies; (b) provides a substantial impact on the student-athlete's eligibility; and (c) is not the type of academic assistance generally available to all students. Based on NCAA rules and those of various U.S. colleges and universities, the following is an overview of some major scandals, infractions, and/or violations involving athletes and their schools.[10]

*University of North Carolina–Chapel Hill: In a fraudulent 'paper class' scheme in the African and Afro-American Studies Department, several athletes took advantage of it and reaped short-term benefits, which allowed them to remain eligible for NCAA competition. They did not, however, encourage or lobby former department manager Deborah Crowder to create or perpetuate the sham classes or steer themselves into the classes. And unlike the administration, they were not in the position to audit and regulate the academic department. Nevertheless, why did they participate knowing the classes were unethical besides being illegal?

Although inappropriate to entirely blame athletes, they share responsibility for sustaining the fraud. But, why did individuals like Crowder and

---

[10] Read Cameron Miller, "Miller: What Role Did UNC Athletes Play in the AFAM Academic Fraud Scandal?" *University Wire* (4 November 2014): 1; Marc Tracey and Dan Barry, "Baylor's Pride Turns to Shame in Rape Scandal," *New York Times* (10 March 2017): A.1; Mike Henderson, "AD Mark Coyle Discusses Fallout From Football Sex Assault Scandal," *University Wire* (21 February 2017): 1; Tim Sullivan, "Confessions of a UC coach and 'Slimeball'," *Cincinnati Enquirer* (27 December 2015): C.1; "Louisville Sex Scandal," *University Wire* (22 October 2015): 1; Nicholas Fouriezos, "UGA Football Scandal," *Atlanta Journal* (17 October 2014): B.1; Arian Campo-Flores, "School President Hits Back at NCAA Over Shapiro Scandal," *Daily Bankruptcy Review* (22 March 2013): 1; Blair Kerkhoff, "Wall of Shame: A Rundown of the 10 Scandals That Have Rocked — and Sullied — College Athletics," *Pittsburgh Post* (4 September 2011): D.1.

former department chairman Julius Nyang'oro engage in the behavior that, when uncovered, shamed a well-respected university? To some people, the real cause was the university's unwise and perhaps unfair admittance of elite athletes underprepared for the challenges of college-level academics. Thus, admitting students solely on the basis of their ability to contribute to the school's athletic teams, and without any regard for their ability to succeed in the classroom, not only disrespects the academic mission of the institution, it also demonstrated callous neglect of these athletes' long-term future.[11]

In mid-October 2017, the NCAA Committee on Infractions could not conclude academic violations in the case. Therefore, the committee did not sanction the institution with any penalties. Approaching the release of the infractions committee's report, the university and its supporters feared the worst: postseason bans, vacation of victories and potentially championships. There was none of them. The infractions committee ruled, essentially, that it could not determine that violations occurred in association with a long-running scheme of bogus African Studies courses that University of North Carolina–Chapel Hill's accrediting agency found lacked integrity.[12]

*University of Georgia: Considered a Heisman Trophy candidate, junior running back Todd Gurley received at least $400 to sign 80 pieces of memorabilia according to multiple sources. As a result, the school

---

[11] To avoid serious sanctions against its athletic programs, the University of North Carolina released documents in late May 2017 to counter NCAA allegations. The school challenged the organization's jurisdiction and disputed the number of athletes who enrolled in a system of bogus classes. The university also cited assertations by someone in the scandal that office administrator Deborah Crowder wasn't specifically trying to help athletes. Her interviews with NCAA investigators were included in the school's response. For more details about it, see Dan Kane, "North Carolina's Response Challenges NCAA's Jurisdiction in Academic Scandal." *Charlotte Observer* (26 May 2017): 1B, 2B and Luke Decock, "Battle Lines Between UNC, NCAA Never More Sharp." *Charlotte Observer* (26 May 2017): 2B.

[12] See Andrew Carter, "Why NCAA Had no Penalties for UNC in Long-Awaited Report on Academic Scandals," www.newsobserver.com cited 25 October 2017. The only violations that the NCAA infractions committee concluded in this case were that two former staff members in the African Studies Department — Julius Nyang'oro and Debby Crowder — failed to cooperate during the investigation. The university, meanwhile, was essentially found innocent of the other three charges it faced: those of impermissible benefits, lack of institutional control, and failure to monitor.

suspended him indefinitely while investigating claims he violated NCAA rules by receiving improper benefits.

After considering ways to punish people who jeopardize college athletes' eligibility, state legislators sponsored an existing law that authorized colleges to sue anyone who coerced athletes into breaking NCAA rules in specific situations. It allowed colleges to sue for lost revenue caused by self-imposed disciplinary actions, which included suspensions that occurred when players received improper benefits. The current law allowed for misdemeanor charges, but legislators sought to expand its criminal component. In other words, such athletes as Gurley should be protected from those who could capitalize on their image with no risk or consequences.

*University of Miami: Former Health and Human Services secretary in the Clinton administration, Chancellor Donna Shalala, boosted the school's standing in academic rankings, secured visits from a host of dignitaries, and raised more than $2 billion to fund new buildings and cutting-edge research. Nevertheless, the NCAA investigated the school's football and men's basketball programs because former booster Nevin Shapiro violated NCAA rules by providing gifts to some athletes. After pleading guilty in 2010 for operating a $930 million Ponzi scheme, Shapiro was penalized and sent to prison.

Although the investigation did not diminish fundraising or undermine support for Shalala, the incident negatively affected the morale of students, faculty, players, and alumni. It is unclear what Shalala knew about Shapiro's actions. But a photo published in 2011 by Yahoo! Sports had her with Shapiro at a Miami Beach bowling alley three years earlier. She was smiling at a check just given to her for the Hurricanes' basketball program. Later, the university returned the donation.

While the NCAA tossed information obtained in depositions, it pressed ahead with the inquiry and presented the school with allegations, details of which were not public. The university had to respond and appeared before the NCAA's committee on infractions. As a result, sanctions were imposed in 2013 involving some of the school's coaches and sports programs.

*Baylor University: While at an off-campus party, football player Tevin Elliott poured liquor for freshman Jasmin Hernandez and other underage students. But for some reason, he then insisted her friends had gone somewhere. When Hernandez expressed doubts about it, he pulled her by the wrist to go outside. But the farther they strayed into darkness, she argued her friends were back at the party and they should return. Without a word, Elliott picked her up and made his violent intentions clear.

Despite telling Elliott she was gay, he raped her behind a secluded shed. Later, Hernandez appeared on ESPN and assumed her rape was a horrible but isolated incident at Baylor. Even after Elliott was convicted in 2014 and sentenced to 20 years in prison, Baylor officials said they considered him to be a solitary bad actor preying on a campus of goodness.

Since the rape, allegations of sexual assault by Baylor football players multiplied, causing incalculable damage to the university's reputation and leading to resignations and firings, including those of the school's president, football coach, and athletic director. Lawsuits cluttered the courts, with more than a dozen women claiming they had been assaulted amid a campus culture that put them at risk.

*University of Louisville basketball's coaching staff, for several years, allegedly paid for escorts to dance and engage in sexual acts with potential recruits at parties in the area. An ESPN report claimed there were nearly two dozen stripping and sex parties from 2010 to 2014 inside Billy Minardi Hall, the on-campus dorm for athletes and other students and named for the university men's basketball head coach Rick Pitino's late brother-in-law.

If Pitino knew about this, that is somehow an even bigger problem. If he was unaware of this type of outrageous behavior, should he be dismissed for negligence? In response to calls for his dismissal or resignation, the school's president declined to comment and its athletic director backed Pitino's claim of innocence. There is no way this scandal can be totally blamed on a graduate assistant coach, who could not afford to consistently turn a residence hall into a strip club. Because of these allegations, this could mean what college sports fans call the 'Death Penalty' from the NCAA.

Besides those incidents, others were costly, newsworthy and unethical, and also severely affected athletes and their respective schools' sports programs for years or even decades. For example, already on probation in 1985 for football recruiting violations, Southern Methodist University paid 13 players approximately $61,000 from a booster slush fund. Because the athletic director and members of his department knew about the fund, the school's football program was shut down for two years and eventually, it had only one winning season between 1989 and 2008.

Implicated in gambling scandals during the early 1950s, some University of Kentucky basketball players were involved in a point-shaving scheme during the 1948–1949 season. The SEC ruled the school could not play a conference schedule in 1952–1953 and three months later, the NCAA declared there would be no games for the Wildcats that season. Essentially, this was college sports' first death penalty.

In 2004, Baylor University basketball coach Dave Bliss encouraged his players to lie to investigators about a murdered athlete and say that he paid for his tuition by dealing drugs. The Bears were put on probation for five years, prohibited from playing non-conference games and in the Big 12 tournament for one year, and lost scholarships and sacrificed recruiting visits for two years. Then, in a bidding war for a wide receiver — who got regular monthly payments from an assistant coach and also a sports car — the Oklahoma State University football program received a four-year probation starting in 1989, had no bowl games for three years or any on television for two, and was penalized with reduced scholarships.

During the early 2000s, four University of Michigan basketball players received more than $600,000 from a booster. The Wolverines and NCAA joined to give the school's program a two-year postseason ban, forced it to vacate victories for five seasons, and removed banners from the arena and athletes' names from the record books. Also, University of Southern California football player Reggie Bush and his family accepted $300,000 in illegal gifts from sports agents. Besides getting their victories removed, the Trojans were banned from postseason play for two years and docked 30 scholarships over three years.

After the Oklahoma Sooners had been placed on a three-year probation for major recruiting violations in the 1980s, a crime spree by players involved rape charges, a shooting, and a quarterback caught selling cocaine to an undercover government agent. The three-year probation for the recruiting violations included a two-year ban on television games and bowl appearances along with scholarship reductions. Several years later, an academic advisor falsified 57 Pell Grants for University of Miami football players and received $220,000 in kickbacks, plus someone at the school made $400,000 in illegal payments to players. The Hurricanes lost 31 scholarships over a three-year period, was given a one-year bowl ban by the NCAA, and the adviser served three years in federal prison.

During the late 1990s, University of Minnesota basketball team tutor Jan Gangelhoff wrote numerous term papers for at least 20 players and head coach Clem Haskins participated in the fraud. The school spent four years on probation, lost five scholarships, had all its team records erased from six years of postseason tournaments, and had to return money earned from the tournaments. Finally, Memphis University basketball player Derrick Rose allegedly had somebody else take his high school exams. Also, the NCAA found a booster had provided Rose's brother, Reggie, with $1,700 in travel expenses. As a result, the school surrendered its national runner-up trophy, forfeited an NCAA-record 38 victories, and was placed on probation for three years.

To determine how often crimes involving college athletes get prosecuted and what factors influence them, ESPN's Outside the Lines obtained police reports involving all football and men's basketball players on rosters from 2009 to 2014 from campus and city police departments covering programs of 10 major schools — Auburn, Florida, Florida State, Michigan State, Missouri, Notre Dame, Oklahoma State, Oregon State, Texas A&M, and Wisconsin. Some police departments, however, withheld records citing state disclosure laws and not all information was uniform among jurisdictions.[13]

Available reports showed that Florida had the most athletes named as suspects — 80 in more than 100 crimes. Even so, the athletes either never faced charges, had charges against them dropped, or not prosecuted 56 percent of the time. When Outside the Lines examined a comparison set of cases involving college-age males in Gainesville, Florida, 28 percent of the crimes ended without a record of charges being filed or the charges eventually being dropped. Florida State had the second-highest number of athletes named in criminal allegations or 66 men's basketball and football

---

[13] Paula Lavigne, "Lawyers, Status, Public Backlash Aid College Athletes Accused of Crimes," http://www.espn.com cited May 23, 2017 and "How OTL Completed Its Investigation," http://www.espn.com cited 23 May 2017.

athletes. In 70 percent of those incidents, the athletes never faced charges, had charges against them dropped, or not prosecuted. In comparison, cases ended up without being prosecuted 50 percent of the time among a sample of crimes involving college-age males in Tallahassee, Florida.

Investigators found that interaction between high-profile college athletes and law enforcement officials is not as simple as the commonly held perception that police and prosecutors simply show preferential treatment, although that occasionally occurs. Rather, the examination of more than 2,000 documents indicted that athletes from the 10 schools primarily benefited from a confluence of factors, which is a reality at major sports programs. These include the immediate access to high-profile attorneys, intimidation felt by witnesses who accuse athletes, and the higher bar some criminal justice officials feel needs to be met in high-profile cases.

Other factors found from the examination of the 10 schools were first, athletic department officials inserted themselves into investigations many times. In fact, some tried to control when and where police talked with athletes while others insisted on being present during player interviews, alerted defense attorneys, conducted their own investigations before contacting police, or in one case, mishandled potential crime-scene evidence. Also, some police officials were torn about proper procedure — unsure when to seek a coach's or athletic director's assistance when investigating crimes.

Second, some athletic programs had, in effect, a team lawyer who showed up at a crime scene, jail, or police department — even before an athlete requested legal counsel. Sometimes the lawyers, contacted by athletic department officials, were often successful in giving athletes an edge in evading prosecution from minor offenses to major crimes. Third, the high profiles of the athletic programs and their athletes had a chilling effect on whether cases were even brought to police and how they were investigated. Numerous cases never resulted in charges because accusers and witnesses were afraid to discuss wrongdoing, feared harassment from fans and the media, or were pressured to drop charges in the interest of the schools' sports programs.

A Gainesville police officer said everyone is at fault for athletes having such leverage. "It's the fault of the athletes, it's the fault of the victims, it's the fault of society, it's the fault of the media, because everyone paints this picture and holds athletes up on a pedestal sometimes and we all are making them invincible," he said. "The fans are making them invincible, and the victims themselves, they look up to them at the same time. So to think that they can be victimized by this person is sometimes a reach for them."[14]

OTHER TOPICS

Thus far, this chapter highlighted and discussed data, facts, situations, and other types of information about men and women SAs in colleges and universities and their academic motivation and performances, pay-for-play proposals and reasons to oppose or support them, and player scandals in schools of higher education. Besides those things, there are other current and interesting but also newsworthy and controversial topics and subjects that in different ways challenge, concern, and/or influence athletes in various ways including their academic progress and sports. In no specific order, these appeared online in articles of the literature and are summarized for readers in this final but important and concluding section of the chapter.[15]

Topic 1: *Sexual Risk-Taking Behaviors, Gambling, and Heavy Drinking Among U.S. College Athletes.* In an exploratory study, researchers empirically examined the prevalence patterns of sexual risk-taking behaviors — such as unprotected sex and having multiple sex partners — in relation to levels of gambling problems and heavy episodic drinking (HED) among U.S. college athletes.

---

[14] *Idem,* "Lawyers, Status, Public Backlash Aid College Athletes Accused of Crimes."

[15] For these topics, see Michael Sanserino and Sam Werner, "Cost of College Athletics May Rise Amid Challenges," *TCA Regional News* (10 June 2014): 1; Huang Jiun-hau, *et al.* "Sexual Risk-Taking Behaviors, Gambling, and Heavy Drinking Among U.S. College Athletes," *Archives of Sexual Behavior* (June 2010): 706–13; "Are College Athletes Being Mistreated?" *Florida Times Union* (5 April 2014): B.8; Doug Robinson, "UCLA's $280M Deal Adds to NCAA Hypocrisy," *Deseret News* (28 May 2016): 1; Nick Selb, "Foreign Athletes Face Unique Challenges," *University Wire* (5 November 2013): 1; Kaitlin Mulhere, "Student Athletes More Likely to Thrive After College Than Non-Athletes, Survey Says," http://www.time.com cited 12 May 2017; "After the Game," http://www.ncaa.org cited 12 May 2017; Craig Greenlee, "Student-Athletes Making Their Voices Heard on Controversial Issues," http://www.diversseducation.com cited 23 May 2017.

Data from a representative national sample of 20,739 players were derived from the first NCAA national survey of problem gambling and health-risk behaviors. Among those who were sexually active during the past year, males reported significantly higher prevalence of unprotected sex at 10.2 percent and multiple sex partners at 14.6 percent than females at 7.9 percent and 9.3 percent, respectively. Using the DSM-IV Gambling Screen classification, as the level of gambling severity increased, the prevalence of sexual risk-taking behaviors also increased among female athletes but decreased among males.

Regarding the effect of heavy drinking, while both male and female HED athletes reported elevated sexual risk-taking, the effect of HED was twice as large in females as males. It is important to know that the definition of sexual risk behaviors in the study took into account committed sexual relationships. Hence, the results need to be interpreted with the refined sexual risk measures in mind.

Further investigations are warranted to help better understand and explicate the interrelationships of sexual risk-taking behaviors, gambling, and heavy drinking among this and other groups of men and women athletes. The findings, however, suggested new directions for future research and practice and also highlighted the importance of a more inclusive multicomponent approach to address these co-occurring youth risk behaviors.

Topic 2: *Are College Athletes Being Mistreated?* When Northwestern University athletes received a first positive response to their attempt to form a union in 2014, it upset the collegiate world. Although this was only a first step and did not affect public universities, the attempt raised a number of questions about how college athletes are actually treated by school officials, coaches, and other groups. The fact that Northwestern students raised the issue was ironic since those athletes have some of the highest graduation rates in the college universe. Still, they sometimes spent more than 40 hours per week on sports. Does that make them students or employees of the university? Do they receive special treatment, or are they being taken advantage of? Or is it a little bit of both?

According to results of a survey, some people responded that a small stipend for expenses was reasonable for athletes assuming payments represented actual amounts. While oversight is needed, spending 40 hours a week seemed irrelevant. Postgraduate prepaid insurance for them may be supportable, presuming the athlete does not become a professional. Should athletes be allowed to share in profits from selling memorabilia that includes their name or image? Respondents said that is reasonable since colleges benefit from athletes' personal fame as performers.

What about non-revenue sports? While athletes are in school, a stipend for them is acceptable but not health insurance after college. They can get coverage other ways. Also, revenue from the sale of memorabilia should be included in stipends. However, if athletes in revenue-producing sports get stipends and additional benefits, there will be a movement to extend them to non-revenue producing sports, which may result in the elimination of these programs at many schools.

Topic 3: *Does UCLA's $280 million megadeal add to NCAA hypocrisy?* When UCLA signed a $280 million contract with sports apparel giant Under Armour in 2016, it added fuel to the ongoing discussion about NCAA hypocrisy and its unfair treatment of athletes. Referring to this deal, UCLA quarterback Josh Rosen said, "We're still amateurs, though, got to love non-profits." This launched another series of media rants against the supposedly tyrannical, hypocritical, filthy-rich NCAA and how it takes money with one hand and holds athletes down with the other while preaching the virtues and religion of amateurism.

Students are still subsidizing most athletic programs through their fees, most of which are hidden in a generic line item simply titled 'fees.' Those might have been easier to justify years ago before college athletic departments turned into big businesses and games became an every-night-of-the-week, made-for-television event, and before conferences and schools signed lucrative television contracts and shoe-company deals and sold luxury boxes and stadium-naming rights. But it makes less sense now. At least athletes are getting something tangible — free education, prestige, tutors, use of plush locker and weight rooms — that are better than neighborhood gyms and also an opportunity to play a game, with some seen by millions of fans on television.

At least athletes have a choice. If they feel exploited and no longer want to play sports, they should move on to something else. But other students have little to no choice. At some schools, they are forced to pay for athletics and be season-ticket holders whether the team wins or loses. The *Washington Post* reported that students at 32 or 61 percent of universities in the Power 5 conferences — the richest, most elite football schools in the country — paid $125.5 million in athletic fees during the 2014–2015 academic year.

Meanwhile, college athletic programs are bringing in record revenues. In 2014–2015, for example, these amounts included $180 million at the University of Texas, $171 million at Ohio State, $151 at the University of Alabama, and $139 million at Louisiana State University. That year, 24 other schools each surpassed $100 million in revenue.

Why pick pockets of regular or traditional students? Why not pay back investors — students — since the college sports business is flush with cash? Why not reduce athletic fees and lower tickets prices or eliminate taxpayer subsidies for athletic departments? More and more money pours into football and men's basketball programs, but schools never get ahead — they simply spend more. It's like a drug; they need more and more money to feed their habit.

There is an arms race underway in college football and basketball in which every big school tries to top the others. As a result, they spend hundreds of millions of dollars on new stadiums or renovations of them, plush locker rooms and new study halls, indoor and outdoor practice facilities, and football and basketball centers.

When the University of Utah joined the Pacific 12 in 2011, this meant the Utes would share in the conference's newly -signed television deal — $250 million annually or $20.8 million per school. As a new conference member, Utah began receiving a full share in 2014. But instead of cutting student athletic fees and other subsidies, the school simply spent more and built a $32 million football center and $36 million basketball center that contained player lounges, hydrotherapy tubs, a yoga room, a rooftop terrace, and big-screen televisions. Not only were student fees and subsidies not reduced or eliminated, they continued to rise dramatically along with ticket prices to games — which included a chintzy $2 per ticket fee to pay for a video board and restrooms.

The school's marketing deal with Under Armour expired at the end of the 2016 football season and undoubtedly will lead to considerably more money. But, don't expect it to be passed along to students or fans. Most students simply want an education. What does getting a degree in accounting, chemistry, or engineering have to do with paying for the school's so-called Triple-A professional football team? Why should students be forced to pay for hydrotherapy tubs and big-screen televisions for football players?

A few years ago, student debt in the U.S. reached a reported $1.3 trillion, and about 70 percent of graduates with bachelor's degrees left school in debt. The graduating class of 2015, for example, averaged approximately $35,000 of debt. If considering fair treatment in the NCAA model, students should come first. After all, universities are about education first — or are they?

Topic 4: *Foreign Athletes Face Unique Challenges.* With college sports being a booming business in America, it is sometimes easy to forget that athletes often viewed as celebrities or 'big men or women on campus' are, for the most part, no different from other college students. Though most SAs are recognized primarily for their athletic endeavors, all of them have school-work, social lives, and perhaps families to focus on, along with the complex maturation process that every college student endures. This transitional phase may be tough, as nearly all students will attest. But the challenge becomes more difficult when the commute from hometown to campus is not merely a quick drive up an interstate or the cheapest flight an airline offers. For international students coming to the U.S. from overseas countries, the adjustment to life as a college student and also athlete can be daunting.

At some universities, there are one or more international players on varsity rosters according to athletic departments' websites. Many of them arrived on campus under similar circumstances — with excitement for a new challenge — but unsure of how to adapt to their environment. A redshirt junior from a foreign country, who played on the men's water polo team, said that "the first [semester] was really rough. I wasn't very good at English. I would say the language barrier was the hardest thing at the beginning, but everybody helped me, so [the transition] was pretty smooth."

Like many international SAs, he was drawn to the school's athletic tradition and location in sunny and eclectic Southern California, but did not know how to best acclimate to his new surroundings. Fortunately, in this case, the structured routine athletes are subject to helped him grow accustomed to life as a college student.

"My freshman year was just amazing," the athlete said. "I would do tutoring five hours a week and they were all helping me. It was really, really helpful. It was kind of hard because I was out all the time, either in class, tutoring or practice, but it helped me a lot." Even more important than the academic resources were his teammates, who gave him an already established initial group of friends. "It wasn't too hard, to be honest," he said. "All the guys were really nice to me and ready to help all the time, so it was a really easy adjustment." Creating a strong team bond early in the school year is crucial for making international SAs feel at home, reported the director of the school's academic services. Thus, unity is the easiest way for international players to quickly feel relaxed in their new environment.

Topic 5: *Student Athletes More Likely to Thrive After College Than Non-Athletes, Survey Says.* Former men and women athletes are more likely to be engaged at work, involved in their community, and driven to meet goals, according to results of a recent survey. Even though players have considerable time demands due to training periods and competitions, they also were more likely than non-athletes to report participating in a club on campus or joining a fraternal organization.

The survey polled 1,670 former NCAA athletes ranging in age from 22 to 71 and compared their responses with more than 22,000 non-athletes. About 60 percent of SA participants were male and nearly half of them competed in Division I athletics, the most competitive division. The NCAA partnered with Gallup to track the long-term effects of participating in intercollegiate athletics and, for the first time, it compared those outcomes to other students.

Based on the survey's results, a slightly greater share of SAs were thriving in four out of five areas of well-being: purpose or liking what you do and being motivated to achieve goals; social or having strong relationships; community or liking where you live and feeling safe; and physical or being healthy and energetic.

Former athletes and non-athletes were equally likely to be thriving in financial well-being. Overall, less than four in 10 participants were considered thriving on that measure, based on questions such as whether they worried about money in the past week. In addition, 42 percent of former

SAs and 39 percent of non-athletes said they were engaged at work, based on measures such as having the opportunity to work on projects that interest them and having a coworker or boss who encouraged them. But the gap was more significant for female workers, with 48 percent engaged at work compared with 41 percent of non-athletes.

Topic 6: *Student-Athletes Making Their Voices Heard on Controversial Issues*. When the University of Missouri's black football players threatened a boycott in support of a protest about racial injustices on their campus in 2016, it was a light-bulb moment for athletes' activism. Indeed, more than 30 of them would not participate in meetings, practices, or games until university president Tim Wolfe was removed from his position. Wolfe had been under intense public scrutiny as a result of his alleged negligence in addressing minority students' complaints about the hostile racial climate at the university. Besides Jonathan Butler — a graduate student who staged a hunger strike to call attention to the plight of black students — the football coaching staff and athletic department plus Southeastern Conference officials also supported the players.

If the boycott occurred, the school would have to pay a $1 million penalty to opponent Brigham Young University for not playing the game. The economic ramifications of this move produced the desired results. Two days after the players' boycott was announced, Wolfe resigned.[16]

The situation at Missouri, however, did not set a precedent. In recent years, college athletes have joined together in order to speak about issues of deep concern to them. For example, the football players at Grambling State University went on strike in 2013 to protest poor facilities and travel arrangements in which they had to endure 15-hour bus rides one way from Grambling, Louisiana to Kansas City and Indianapolis due to severe reductions in Louisiana's state budget for higher education.

Led by Northwestern University quarterback Kain Colter, there was a movement by players in 2014 to unionize as a means to be recognized as employees of the school. And at the University of Oklahoma in 2015, head

---

[16] Former State University of New York Provost and Executive Vice Chancellor Dr. Alexander Cartwright has led the University of Missouri's flagship campus in Columbia since August 1, 2017. For more details about his role and expectations, see Melissa Korn, "Troubled Campus Gets a New Leader," *Wall Street Journal* (25 May 2017): A3.

football coach Bob Stoops and basketball coach Lon Kruger, and approximately 100 athletes attended a campus demonstration in response to an online video that went viral. In the video, several members of a fraternity had made racist chants.

Given the impact of what transpired at Missouri, coupled with situations involving athletes at Grambling, Northwestern, and Oklahoma, more protests may likely take place in the future. "I get the sense that college athletes are a little more emboldened by what's happened and by the support they've gotten from fans, people in the media and college faculty members," says Kevin Blackistone, a sports columnist for the *Washington Post* and panelist on ESPN's Around the Horn television program. "There's so much money involved, and there's been so much attention on this issue of health and welfare and equitable treatment of college athletes in revenue-generating sports. That's why I think we'll see more of this."[17]

Some people wonder if the scope of activism will go beyond college campuses. The question now is whether or not SAs will be motivated enough to stand up for controversial national issues in collegiate sports. These include such topics as due process, adequate but equitable scholarships, and guarantee of a sufficient education leading to employment after their playing days are over.

Public opinion about men and women college athletes and the issues they face seems to be more newsworthy and favorable for them than in the past. Even so, there are those who argue that scholarship jocks have no basis for their concerns and about how to be treated while in school. For sure, there are many college coaches who hold fast to the notion that athletes should be satisfied with not having to pay for tuition, books, plus room and board out of their or parents' pockets.

Fear of reprisal has been one of the chief reasons why black athletes, in general, have been reluctant to be more vocal in public about their problems. That trend, however, has started to shift in a different direction. These male and female athletes seem more unified in their numbers when they choose to take a stand. It also helps that many schools are opting to

---

[17] Kevin Blackistone, "Can College Athletics be Reformed? Blame '39 TV Game for Crisis," *Dallas Morning News* (8 December 2003): 1.

eliminate one-year renewable scholarships, and instead offer athletes four-year guaranteed scholarships.

When it comes to SAs having the willingness to speak out or become more aware about equitable treatment, some people see it as ironic that the team concept — which coaches instill in their players — enables them to maintain a united front in a protest. Knowing there is strength in numbers, athletes are beginning to have some understanding of the power of leverage they possess. It is no secret that players should be empowered to protest like their non-jock counterparts.

The sentiments about punishing athletes who participate in protests go way beyond the negative comments, for example, about Missouri's black football players that appeared on various media outlets online. About a month after the school's president stepped down from his post, a state legislator proposed a bill that bars SAs from taking part in boycotts. Under the bill's provisions, athletes who strike lose their scholarships. Furthermore, coaches who support them would be fined and any school employees showing support would be fired. After undergoing a public firestorm of harsh criticism, the politician withdrew his proposed legislation.

As an effective mean of communication, the growth of social media plays an increasingly significant role in helping to galvanize people for a common cause. For instance, when a Missouri student announced his hunger strike on Twitter, he received more than 30 hits. When the school's black football players joined the protest, the post received 55,000 hits. What has happened since then, students who want some sort of change on their campus are inspired to engage in mass-movement protests.

Although there have been highly publicized and well-intentioned but controversial protests involving athletes in recent years, it remains to be seen if the desired changes will come to full fruition. In fact, a sociology professor at George Mason University does not believe any trends are emerging nor think that any lasting changes are coming right away. He said, "I don't see these recent protests as a sign of a continuing trend. Some people are trying to attach what went on in Missouri to everything under the sun — including the resignation or the firing of the president there. That was going to happen anyway. So, as for the extent of the change, I'm not so sure it's going to measure up to the media coverage of the events."[18]

---

[18] *Idem*, "Student-Athletes Making Their Voices Heard on Controversial Issues."

Chapter 7

REFORMS:
ACADEMICS–SPORTS

Besides officials in the National Collegiate Athletic Association (NCAA), National Association of Intercollegiate Athletics (NAIA), and National Junior Collegiate Athletic Association (NJCAA), those in other national sports organizations and also college and university administrators, faculty and athletic directors, and various sports authorities, experts, and scholars are aware and more knowledgeable of the academic, personal, and social circumstances, relationships, and/or problems associated with being a male or female student athlete (SA) while enrolled in American schools of higher education.

As a result, these organizations and professionals have collectively researched and authored articles, books, reports, and studies to expose, examine, and perhaps improve the lives and careers of men and women players on athletic teams. This chapter discusses the types and sources of past, current, and future reforms, including similar topics highlighted before in the book.

NAFCAR/DRAKE GROUP

To generate and exchange ideas and then circulate them among colleagues and other people, the National Association of Faculty for Collegiate Athletic Reform (NAFCAR) was founded in 1999 when Jon Ericson — a former professor and provost at Drake University — invited a distinguished group of college faculty, authors, and activists to a 24-h think tank on how to end academic corruption in college sports. Included in the conference were members of faculty senates, journalists, athletic directors, and members of such organizations as the NCAA and Knight Foundation Commission on collegiate sport. From the meeting emerged a non-profit organization that, one year later, changed its name to the Drake Group (DG), which then elected officers and adopted bylaws.

The mission of the DG is to defend and instill academic integrity in higher education, rather than the corrosive and perhaps illegal aspects of commercializing college sports. Its vision is to create an atmosphere on schools' campuses that encourages personal and intellectual growth for all undergraduate and graduate students, and demands excellence and professional integrity from the faculty charged with teaching athletes and their classmates.

More specifically, DG's goals are to (a) ensure that universities provide accountability of their trustees, administrators, and faculty by publicly disclosing information about the quality of education male and female athletes receive; (b) operate as a major lobby for proposals that ensure quality education, particularly for students who participate in intercollegiate athletics; (c) support college faculty and staff whose job security and professional standing are threatened when they defend academic standards in intercollegiate sports; (d) influence public discourse on current issues and controversies in sports and higher education; and (e) coordinate local and national reform efforts with other groups that share the organization's mission, goals, and/or proposals.[1]

A founding member, University of New Haven management professor Allen Sack, stresses that DG is concerned primarily with faculty behavior rather than with the management, policies, and rules of organizations like the NCAA. He says the organization supports any action the NCAA takes to defend academic standards and will work with it if feasible and whenever possible. The group's members are not experts on the business and operations of college sports and cannot tell the NCAA and those who

---

[1] For more information about its role as an organization, see "History: The Drake Group, Inc." https://www.thedrakegroup.org cited 27 May 2017; "Vision, Mission and Goals." https://www.thedrakegroup.org cited 27 May 2017; and "Group Seeks to Reform Market-Driven College Athletics." http://www.asanet.org cited 27 May 2017.

manage intercollegiate programs how to complete their affairs. They are, however, experts about matters in higher education and know what is necessary to defend the integrity of the classroom.

Professor Sack describes the current situation with college sports as a family feud because DG is most upset with those faculty who seem to have little concern for or interest in the integrity of their profession. When men and women student athletes (SAs) do such things as cut classes, miss exams, and fail to study and yet the faculty ignore such behavior and then support them when they play games, especially on school nights, the message being sent is that learning in classrooms is not as important or necessary as activities in the athletic department. In some cases, college and university coaches and their assistants will not tolerate or accept any interference from faculty and other school officials with their game plans.

REFORM MOVEMENT

Since 1999–2000, controversies and different problems in schools' sports programs and the need to reform intercollegiate athletics in order to provide better opportunities for men and women SAs to succeed has been highlighted and discussed in the literature. Next are some historical but important and relevant comments, opinions, and viewpoints about academic reforms for athletes and how things evolved chronologically as potential and actual solutions.

During the late 1990s/early 2000s, for example, some critics strongly contended that the enormous interest in college sports led to the blending together of intercollegiate athletics with entertainment, which in turn, caused commercialization of it to grow. In fact, a survey conducted by the American Council on Education showed that the majority of Americans believed sports were too dominant and overemphasized by officials on college and university campuses. As such, this increasingly jeopardized the purpose and essential mission of these schools. In fact, the situation reached crisis proportions and threatened to undermine the integrity of a system of higher education widely acknowledged to be best in the world.[2]

---

[2]At the American Council on Education's discussion, the participants settled firmly on a shared perspective that intercollegiate athletics programs at all levels must respect the

This problem could, of course, create serious damage to schools and their SAs if left unchecked. It is true that well-functioning Division I football and men's basketball programs generate sufficient revenue to support a wide range of popular non-revenue sports, including many played by women such as soccer, swimming, tennis, and volleyball. As a result, all athletes, and particularly low-income and minority students, have a real and once-in-a-lifetime opportunity to receive an education and graduate with an undergraduate and/or graduate degree.

According to the beliefs of former Indiana University and NCAA President Myles Brand, for various reasons, the situation was at a crucial juncture during the early 2000s. The value system of the entertainment industry and resulting commercialization, in Brand's view, had distorted the purpose, role, and scope of intercollegiate athletics and negatively affected some schools in higher education. Extreme solutions were considered, such as eliminating intercollegiate athletics altogether or simply acceding to the trend toward professionalization and therefore lose the benefits and long-term effects of a well-functioning intercollegiate athletic program.[3]

Brand believed that benefits could be preserved to provide a revitalization of the reform movement. To do so, however, would require the leadership of university chancellors, provosts, and presidents who needed help and support from their governing boards, athletic directors, and faculty committees, and also from each other especially at the conference level.

These leaders, however, faced pressure from schools' athletic departments and boosters to try to gain an advantage through such things as new facilities and higher salaries, and sometimes, they had to deal with

---

primacy of the academic enterprise and remain firmly grounded in it; intercollegiate athletics provides a significant educational opportunity when aligned with the mission of the institution; institutions must enable their SAs to have access to the same range and quality of academic pursuits as other students; and academic integrity cannot be compromised by our colleges and universities, or by members of their campus communities. For more details about the meeting, see "The Student-Athlete, Academic Integrity, and Intercollegiate Athletics." http://www.acenet.edu cited 5 July 2017.

[3] Myles Brand, "Academics First: Reforming Intercollegiate Athletics." *Vital Speeches of the Day*, Vol. 67, Issue 12 (1 April 2001): 367–71.

entrenched athletic directors and coaches whose actions were not always in the best interests of the university. But Brand had great confidence in school officials and firmly believed they were best positioned to effectively lead a reform movement to take back intercollegiate athletics from commercialization and emphasize academics first.[4]

For further evidence that reforms were needed almost two decades ago, the different ways in which SAs and their coaches on some campuses avoided academic requirements had risen to an art form. As a result, the NCAA's initiatives in 2002–2003 followed a series of outrageous and highly publicized incidents of admitted or alleged academic fraud. At the University of Georgia, for instance, an assistant basketball coach gave a passing grade in a course he taught to an athlete who failed to attend class. At Fresno State, a team statistician was paid by, of all people, an academic adviser, to write players' term papers and complete their assignments. And at St. Bonaventure, a basketball player who supposedly had a degree from a junior college had, in fact, earned only a welding certificate.[5]

One NCAA initiative — which was phased in over three years actually relaxed eligibility standards — although the ultimate outcome may have been positive. It allowed entering athletes, who were admitted with low Scholastic Aptitude Test (SAT) or Admission College Test (ACT) scores, to play as freshmen if their secondary school Grade Point Average (GPA) was high enough in a mix of 14 core courses. The change essentially permitted colleges to take risks on recruiting and accepting marginal students, many of them minority teenagers, who received inadequate preparation for standardized tests at lousy and underperforming urban and rural high schools.

The counterbalancing effect, however, is that once in college, these students must meet newly toughened "continuing eligibility" requirements. The danger, of course, is that toughening the standards for schools and their athletes could create incentives and opportunities for more, not less, academic fraud and also steer more students into questionable academic majors where good grades are easy to achieve. Undoubtedly, some coaches would

---

[4] *Idem.*

[5] See, for example, "Reform and College Sports." *Knight Ridder Tribune News Service* (31 December 2003): 1.

do whatever it took to meet and overcome any requirements the NCAA imposed — honestly or fraudulently.

Regarding the reform of college athletics from a historical perspective, optimistic and pessimistic views were expressed of the movement by critics and perhaps published in the literature. It was supposed to be just another college football season opener in 1939 when Fordham University and Waynesburg College met in a horseshoe-shaped cement stadium on an islet beneath the Triborough Bridge. Not much mention of the game was made in local newspapers because Fordham was a powerhouse and Waynesburg a cream puff. Indeed, Fordham romped to a 34–7 victory before 9,000 fans. That, in part, explained why the phrase "college athletic reform" rolled off more lips during the early 2000s than ever before.[6]

An emissary from NCAA President Myles Brand's office, Wally Renfro, admitted in writing to the nation's sports editors that, "The past six months have been especially turbulent for university administrations that are striving to better integrate their athletics programs into the academic missions of their institutions. Why are coaches being paid so much? How will the arms race be brought under control? Why are student athletes not getting a greater share of the revenue pie in college sports? Can higher education reforms resolve the problems in intercollegiate athletics, or are governmental intervention the answer?"

According to ex-college athlete and athletics administrator John Gerdy: "I believe we're [reformers] beginning to build a critical mass that is raising the right questions. None of these groups — school trustees, faculty, or student athletes — is going to do it on their own. It (college athletics) needs to be hit on all levels. If it doesn't happen within the next five or ten years, economics will drive us out of business, or the courts will. So we really need to do something."[7]

In September 2003, Vanderbilt University Chancellor Gordan Gee announced that he was disbanding the school's athletic department. Although no men or women sports teams were actually cut or athletic scholarships lost, Gee tried to pull athletes back into the academic

---

[6]The primary reference is Kevin Blackistone, "Can College Athletics be Reformed? Blame '39 TV Game for Crisis." *Dallas Morning News* (8 December 2003): 1.

[7]*Idem.*

community. Thus, he became the public face of a movement to reform college sports. Gee's success or failure may have foretold the future of an extracurricular activity, a \$3 billion annual industry. Behind the crowds and television hype, pressure was building either to turn class-skipping athletes into students or recognize that — at least at the big-time sports schools — it was simply too late to turn back the clock. That pitted reformers against an army of alumni boosters, politicians who control state schools, television networks, and commercial interests — all of whom would feel the impact of downsizing college sports.[8]

More than 10 years ago, a study of 93,000 NCAA Division I male and female athletes showed 77 percent of them graduated within six years, up from 76 percent in 2005. That kind of progress among mostly scholarship athletes — who entered college from 1996 to 1999 — revealed, in part, the merit of academic reforms actually adopted by the NCAA. It was also a solid model for local school districts to improve the graduation rates of their high school players. The sooner these students understood they were students first, the better their chances of succeeding in college.[9]

As reformers realize, there are always new and perhaps less costly but more conscientious ways to improve the graduation rate of men and women SAs. Leading the effort, for example, have been such people as James Bowers, a former school board member, and Jim Greco, a longtime parent activist in city schools. They wanted to change existing policies, which barred failing SAs from participating in their sport for six weeks. Instead, they campaigned to require players with a GPA below C to be placed on academic probation for the next six-week marking period. During that time, the athletes must attend tutoring sessions and provide their coaches a daily written progress report.

These requirements are far more beneficial to failing athletes, who typically fall further behind in their studies during suspension and often end up dropping out of school. The reforms that Bowers and Greco

---

[8]A reading for this topic is "A Whole New Ball Game? The Push to Reform — and Scale Back — Collegiate Athletics is Gaining Yardage." https://www.bloomberg.com cited 27 May 2017.

[9]"NCAA Approves Academic Reforms." http://www.chronicle.augusta.com cited 28 May 2017.

proposed deserved serious study. Similar to the NCAA's enhanced initial-eligibility and progress reports toward degree requirements implemented in 2003, they set the bar higher for SAs. While the NCAA inched toward a goal of an 80 percent graduation rate for Division I schools, a policy change at city school districts based on the Greco–Bowers proposal could have put athletes in urban schools on a similar course for success.

Unless Congress got involved, America's system of higher education — as of 2008 — would continue to be hostage to the professionalized collegiate sports entertainment industry. Sadly, that system included many catholic schools, which, rather than being leaders in college sports reform, were willful participants in this money-focused, win-at-any-cost industry.

A growing sense of frustration existed in 2008 among reform-minded faculty and other educators over the lack of bipartisan follow-up in Congress on the strong effort of retired House Ways and Means Committee chairman Bill Thomas to have the NCAA provide justification for its tax-exempt status. In the long term, congressional scrutiny of the tax-exempt status of the NCAA and its franchisees could explode the status of SAs, and thus have a negative impact on the professional level of play in their big-time athletic programs by forcing the National Basketball Association (NBA) and National Football League (NFL) to operate their own minor leagues.[10]

Then during the spring of 2009, the NCAA announced the latest nuance in its academic reform program. Titled the Coaches Academic Progress Rate (CAPR), it included coaches' career Academic Progress Report (APR) scores, which in turn, measured and reported the retention and eligibility rates of their teams' players. This followed the initiation of the non-coach APR four years earlier, which was designed to improve athletes' eligibility, retention, and graduation rates while punishing under-achieving teams and institutions.[11]

---

[10] See, for example, "Time for Accountability in Sports: Corrupt Collegiate Athletics Overshadow Faltering Academic Mission." https: //www.thefreelibrary.com cited 29 May 2017.

[11] Read Michelle Brutlag Hosick, "NCAA Releases Academic Progress Report for Coaches." http://www.ncaa.org cited 29 May 2017. The Head Coach APR Portfolio

Before the NCAA published and distributed its CAPR in 2010, it also should have concentrated on the serious drawbacks of and problems with the current reform movement. Academic reforms must establish minimum admission standards that mandate mastery of the most basic academic competencies.

After nearly 30 years of work with athletes' educational aspirations, some experts on the topic recommended the following steps to upgrade existing academic reform. Initially, preparedness standards must be raised. The NCAA's decision to change initial-eligibility standards by removing minimum standardized-test scores in favor of a sliding scale resulted in the intended and greater access to higher education. Although more players compete on the court, field, and in other facilities, they are less likely to be competitive in the classroom. Theoretically, prospective players could establish athletics eligibility without a single correct answer on a standardized exam.[12]

KNIGHT COMMISSION

Following an 18-month study of schools' sports finances, the Knight Commission on Intercollegiate Athletics released a report in 2010 that called for financial reforms in college sports. It included principles for reining in spending by colleges on athletic programs. Titled "Restoring the Balance: Dollars, Values, and the Future of College Sports," the report indicated that expenditures in big-time college sports increased by 38 percent — nearly twice as much as spending on academics — from 2005 to 2008. In fact, the 10 public institutions that spent the most on college

---

includes the single-year team APR for head coaches at each institution he or she has been a head coach, along with the average single-year APR in the specific sport for comparison purposes. Interim head coaches are not included in the database. Hiring and separation dates for each institution at which a person held a head coaching position are also included on each coach's page, and years in which a coaching change occurred are indicated in each individual report.

[12] See Gerald Gurney, "Now We Must Reform Athletics Reform." http://www.chronicle. com cited 29 May 2017.

sports were on pace to exceed $250 million annually in athletics expenses, on average, in 2020.[13]

The Commission's report was particularly timely given the shifts in athletic conference affiliation that dominated the news, which have been based at least in part on the desire to increase revenues to cover skyrocketing spending. This gave new urgency to the finding of a survey sponsored by the group in 2009, in which a majority of university presidents agreed.[14]

More specifically, the Commission's blueprint for financial reform offered three important but necessary principles. These were as follows: (a) requiring that financial reports be public and transparent; (b) rewarding institutions that make academic values a priority; and (c) treating athletes as students first and foremost, and not as professionals. Furthermore, the Commission recommended that financial reports filed by each institution with the NCAA should be made public and include an additional measure comparing spending in athletics and academics. "Academic reform in intercollegiate athletics began in earnest when graduation rates were first shared publicly," said the Commission's co-chairman. "We believe the same will be true for financial reform when there is far greater transparency on athletic expenditures. These bigtime sports budgets are beginning to have a significant impact on college students, and financial data ought to be transparent and readily available to students, parents, trustees, and taxpayers who have a stake in the spending."[15]

The Commission's second recommendation involved rewarding practices that prioritize academic values. Its members believed college teams should not be able to compete for a conference or national championship if they failed to reach core academic benchmarks. The group of reformers

---

[13] The reference is "Restoring the Balance: Dollars, Values, and the Future of College Sports." http://www.knightcommission.org cited 30 May 2017.

[14] For more specific information including data, please read "Knight Commission on Intercollegiate Athletics; Knight Commission Calls for College Sports Reform, Recommends Public Transparency of Finances and New Financial Incentives: Restoring the Balance: Dollars, Values, and the Future of College Sports Reveals Huge Disparities Between Spending on Athletics and Academics." http://www.knightcommission.org cited 30 May 2017.

[15] "Knight Commission Calls for College Sports Reform." http://www.knightfoundation.org cited 1 June 2017.

recommended that teams only be allowed to compete in postseason championships if they achieve an APR that predicts at least a 50 percent graduation rate of SAs under the NCAA's graduation measure.

The Commission also recommended that revenue distribution be more closely tied to schools' academic values. Its report called for the NCAA to create a new revenue distribution account called the Academic–Athletics Balance Fund. Division I institutions would be eligible if their teams have APR scores that predicted at least a 50 percent graduation rate and also if they appropriately balanced their investments in athletics and education. The Commission preferred that the new fund be created by reallocating revenue awarded for success in the men's basketball tournament of the division.

Kirwin's descriptions of transparent injustices — such as any athletes who lose their ability to play over trivial NCAA rules violations and lack of insurance coverage, scholarships voided for those who are hurt or lose their touch, legal waivers that allow the NCAA to control the likenesses of college stars long after they graduated — touched a nerve among educators and sports officials. As such, these were some basic reforms that addressed problems discussed by former NCAA President Brand and acknowledged by college and university athletic directors and administrators. It is unfair, for example, to recruit and then sign poor male and female students to scholarships to play on a sports team and to waive their tuition but then expect them to survive on campus without money.[16]

NCAA REFORMS

Based in Indianapolis, Indiana since 1999, the NCAA is a non-profit association that regulates athletes of more than 1,000 institutions, conferences, and organizations, as well as individuals. As of 2015, the vast majority of those who participated in NCAA sports — more than 460,000 young men and women each year at 1,084 institutions across three divisions and in 23 different sports — the experience is exactly what it intends to be: a meaningful extension of the educational process that provides the

---

[16] *Idem.*

opportunity for students to compete fairly against other students, in an educational environment.[17]

While the NCAA's member schools spend roughly $13.8 billion per year on their sports programs — including $2.7 billion on direct scholarship support — athletic spending represents a very small proportion or only about 4 percent of total institutional spending. Furthermore, these colleges and universities generate far less revenue from athletics than they spend on them. In fact, the deficit of operating expense over generated revenue is greater than $6 billion per year collectively. Next are facts and also varying opinions on whether the NCAA and academic institutions had done enough to protect the interests of their SAs by initiating, implementing, and enforcing reforms.

During April 2004, the NCAA approved an academic reform package aimed at improving the educational success of schools' men and women players. As part of a broader effort that included several other measures, the association modified the way it reported graduation rates, instituted a new method to gauge the academic progress of athletes, and created a system of penalties against institutions with poor records of graduating athletes.

---

[17]The readings for this section include "The Pro and Cons of Making Major Reforms in the American Collegiate Athletic System," *Congressional Digest*, vol. 94, issue 6 (June 2015): 8; Ted Hutton, "NCAA Adopts Landmark Academic Reform Package," *Knight Ridder Tribune News Service* (10 January 2005); Teddy Greenstein, "NCAA OKs Tough Reform Measures Based on Academic Standards." *Knight Ridder Tribune News Service* (29 April 2004); Sandra Meyer, "NCAA Academic Reforms: Maintaining the Balance Between Academics and Athletics." *Phi Kappa Phi Forum* (Fall 2005): 15–18; Teddy Greenstein, "NCAA Puts Number on Academic Reform; Goal of New APR Formula: Hold Schools, Athletes Accountable." *Chicago Tribune* (1 March 2005): 1; Rodney McKissic, "Classroom Wake-Up Call: NCAA's Academic Reforms Hold Colleges Accountable for Student-Athletes' Academic Performances." *Buffalo News* (16 June 2005): 1; Ted Hutton, "NCAA Board Adopts Strict Academic Reform." *Knight Ridder Tribune News Service* (10 January 2005); "Latest Academic Progress Rates Data Shows That Academic Reform is Taking Hold.," *US Federal News Service*, Washington, D.C. (1 March 2006); Gerald Gurney and Jerome Weber, "Rethinking the NCAA's Academic Reform." *American Association of Collegiate Registrars and Admission Officers*, Washington, D.C. (2007); Robert Kuwada, "Boeh Discusses Recent NCAA Reforms." *"McClatchy-Tribune Business News"* (30 October 2011); Jeff Schultz, "NCAA Can't Reform With so Many Private Agendas." *TCA Regional News* (24 May 2014); Zachary Zagger, "College Player Compensation Issue Rages On Despite Reforms." http://www.law360.com cited 26 May 2017; "Managing Student-Athletes' Health Issues." http://www.ncaa.org cited 28 May 2017.

Starting in 2005, the NCAA began examining a sports program's academic performance annually rather than through the six-year window of graduation rates. Programs can earn points for having high rates of SAs who maintain eligibility by keeping their grades up, and also of their retention and graduation. The NCAA measures the progress rate of each Division I team at the start of each academic year. The new standards also raised the requirements for progress toward a degree. After two years, an athlete must have completed 40 percent of the school's requirements for graduation, as opposed to 25 percent under the old system. At the end of three years, athletes must have completed 60 percent toward graduation, and after four years 80 percent. Most players on teams are on a five-year academic calendar.

Schools' sports programs may face penalties — including scholarship loss, stricter limits on the recruitment of potential athletes, and bans from championship tournaments — if their progress rates consistently fall below a "cut line" when compared with three measures. These are all Division I teams in all sports, all Division I teams in that particular sport, and the academic performance of an institution's general student body.

An academic reform package aimed at dramatically strengthening the educational success of SAs and holding colleges and universities and their teams accountable was unanimously approved by the NCAA Division I board of directors. The board also approved a number of "student-athlete-friendly" measures related to the cost of attendance, summer financial aid, and medical expenses. The comprehensive, three-year effort to improve the academic progress, retention, and graduation rates of SAs was the most far-reaching effort of its kind in the history of the association.

According to former NCAA President Myles Brand, "These are strong and well-thought-out reforms that are critically necessary to ensuring that SAs are academically successful. For the first time ever, the NCAA will have the ability to hold institutions and teams accountable for the academic progress of their student athletes."[18]

---

[18] *Idem*, Myles Brand, "Academics First: Reforming Intercollegiate Athletics" and "Show Colleges the Money, University Sports in Need of Some Commercialism." *Chicago Tribune* (6 April 2005): 1–2.

Contemporaneous penalties, such as the loss of a scholarship for one year if an SA on scholarship leaves the school in poor academic standing, began in the 2005–2006 academic year. Two years later, the NCAA's board of directors reviewed whether the contemporaneous penalties needed to be more stringent. Historical penalties associated with academic failure over time may include scholarship reductions, recruiting limitations, ineligibility for NCAA championships, and in the most extreme cases, restricted membership status for the institution in the NCAA. These penalties started in three years rather than four as originally proposed.

ACADEMIC PROGRESS REPORT

An Academic Progress Rate (APR) is calculated by the NCAA and includes all scholarship SAs entering an institution. The package also established a graduation success rate based on a six-year timeframe for graduation and included all scholarship players entering the institution. The incentives/disincentives program requires that institutions submit to the NCAA annual documentation showing compliance with the APR.

For the most part, NCAA officials believe the historic legislation they approved during the early 2000s would compel SAs to study and learn as vigorously as they hit the weights. The plan penalizes schools whose teams fail to meet academic standards. Schools that fall short of guidelines are warned before the next year, and continued shortcomings may result in a loss of scholarships and then the loss of postseason eligibility. No postseason means zero postseason revenue.

The NCAA's so-called "incentives and disincentives" legislation was the final piece of a three-part package of academic reform. The first part required high school students to complete more core courses to be eligible as college freshmen. The number of courses rose from 13 to 14 in 2005–2006 before increasing to 16 two years later. The second part addressed continuing eligibility, requiring SAs to complete 40 percent of their college degree coursework by their second year, 60 by the third, and 80 by the fourth.

But those measures were small compared to the massive package approved in 2004. Up until then, there was no penalty for a school that failed to graduate its athletes. According to NCAA statistics, only 21 or approximately 33 percent of teams that qualified for the NCAA men's basketball tournament had graduated more than 50 percent of their players. After calculating graduation targets, schools were notified whether they had been at risk for penalties if standards had already been in place.

An official spoke about some academic reforms instituted by the NCAA and about the role of academic/athletic advisors in carrying out the reforms, even when they did not necessarily agree with rules they must monitor and follow. Among these is the mandatory academic support for SAs, initial eligibility legislation and graduation rates, and roles of coaches and academic/athletic advisors. The proper niche of intercollegiate athletics in higher education had been a topic of debate for decades. Issues stemming from lack of institutional control over athletics programs, unethical conduct by institutional staff members, academic scandals, and so on had cast a negative light on college sports.

Criticism abounds about how institutions in higher education can change the culture of intercollegiate athletics and make it compatible with each institution's mission. Some of them contend that sports and higher education will never be compatible. Others believe that more restrictions — more rules to catch the perennial "cheaters" — help to establish and control ethics. Then integrity can be restored, if indeed missing.

Inextricably involved in controversies about reforms are schools' academic/athletic advisors who have, perhaps, one of the most challenging jobs in higher education. Their primary concern is the integrity of their institutions and the welfare of athletes. They act as liaisons between the academic and athletics communities and are primarily responsible for ensuring that players have as much academic success as their ability can afford. Many people, however, view academic/athletic advisors as eligibility brokers, i.e., those who keep athletes eligible to play. In reality, the only people who keep players eligible are themselves.

Ever since it was discovered that basketball player Kevin Ross spent four years at Creighton University in the early 1980s without learning to read, there has been mounting pressure on colleges to better educate their athletes. In 1986, for example, the NCAA passed Proposition 48, which consisted of rules geared toward helping high school athletes considered academic risks to make the transition to the college classroom. Concerns about the new academic reform package came mainly from coaches who believed that some of their colleagues might have players take an easier route to graduation rather than jeopardize their eligibility.

For more details about the reforms' accountability, a team offering the full complement of 13 scholarships can accumulate a maximum of 52 points — 13 times two points times two semesters — each year. Each member can earn two points per semester, one for academic eligibility and another one for remaining in school. If two players are academically ineligible for one semester, that is minus one point for each of them. If another player leaves for the NBA in the second semester and becomes academically ineligible, that is minus two points. The team has 48 points, which is divided by the total possible of 52 points. The resulting figure is an APR score of 923, or two points shy of the NCAA cut line.

Beginning in 2006, the program was subject to an increasing series of sanctions. Teams with annual poor academic rates could be shut out of the NCAA basketball tournament or a major bowl game, although unclear about the bowl bans because those football games are not controlled by the NCAA. The first of these more severe sanctions would be handed down in the 2008–2009 academic year. The most frequent offenders could be slapped with restricted membership and have their teams barred from postseason play as early as 2009–2010.

In 2005, the NCAA did more than release a new set of numbers that measured the academic success of Division I SAs; it also introduced a new language. Forget about old-school terms such as graduation rate and grade-point average. The new lingo included such terms as confidence boundary, contemporaneous penalties, and quarter school variance. They were all part of the NCAA's APR, an annual survey that measured how teams from every school perform in the classroom.

This is a complicated formula that makes Bowl Championship Subdivision computations look like elementary school arithmetic. But more importantly, the numbers can be used to determine penalties that include a loss of scholarships and banishment from postseason play. NCAA President Myles Brand once said the APR scores — which measure the eligibility and retention of SAs — put schools on notice.

According to NCAA data, for example, 7.2 percent of the 5,720 men's and women's Division I sports teams fell below 925. About 50 percent of all schools had at least one team that fell below that mark and could lose at least one scholarship. Furthermore, the data showed that football, base-ball, and men's basketball were the only sports whose average APR fell below 925. The 284 Division I baseball teams posted an average APR of 922, while the 234 football and 326 men's basketball squads compiled an average APR of 923.[19]

The APR cutoff score of 925 translates to a graduation rate of 50 per-cent using current measurements. The University of Florida (UF) and Florida State's football graduation rates were less than 50 percent in the 2005 NCAA report, as were those of the UF and University of Miami's baseball teams.

As a result, the NCAA levied penalties based on academics for the first time, and this came after years of embarrassing graduation rates among many of the nation's top football and basketball teams. The 325 schools and the more than 5,000 teams who played Division I-A sports in 2005 were given APR scores. The final piece of the academic reform package was the establishment of a Graduation Success Rate, which is based on four years of the APR and carries more severe penalties. These include those schools banned from bowl games and postseason tourna-ments, being put on restricted status, and eventually being kicked out of the NCAA if the failures continue.

After 2005, the NCAA's academic reform efforts firmly took hold on campuses nationwide. Second-year APR data, for example, showed that 99 Division I sports teams at 65 colleges and universities — or less than 2 percent of 6,112 Division I sports teams nationwide — would lose scholarships for poor scholastic performances by their SAs in 2006. In the prior year, APR data indicated that as many as 350 Division I sports teams could have faced scholarship losses or about 6 percent of squads nation-wide. "We are encouraged by the response on many campuses to

---

[19]This book's Chapter 4 — "Student Athletes Academic Performance" — contains the APR scores of school's affiliated with NCAA Divisions I, II, and III. Other data is avail-able from the organization's headquarters in Indianapolis, Indiana, and also within online reports.

academic reform," said NCAA President Myles Brand. "The goal of academic reform is to improve academic behaviors and increase graduation, not unnecessarily penalize teams."[20]

Based on the 2004–2005 academic data, the next year began the penalty phase of academic reform, as last year's data were used to identify poor-performing teams and warn of possible scholarship losses. More serious consequences — which include limits on postseason competition and restricted membership status — await teams that continue to academically underperform, as part of the historical penalty structure.

The phased-in approach to the APR and the accompanying penalty structure changed the way Division I athletics communities thought about players' academic performance. The data showed that the average APR for all Division I SAs was 955, and the average for males at 943 and females at 969. In sports with most penalties, the average APR for baseball equaled 931, football 929, and men's basketball 927.

The degree to which the NCAA shifted its focus from the protection of athletes to the generation of income for itself and its member institutions was apparent in 2007 when the House Ways and Means Committee — the Congressional seat of legislation related to federal tax policy — required the NCAA to respond to a number of questions, the burden of which was to ask if the NCAA abandoned its educational mission to the extent that it could no longer justify its status as a tax-exempt organization. The cornerstone of President Brand's plan for academic reform was the installation of a complex program designed to provide an exemplary educational and athletic experience in an environment that supports the primacy of the academic mission of its member institutions, while enhancing the ability of SAs to earn a four-year degree.

During August 2011, university presidents and NCAA administrators formed five working groups to chart a course toward positive change for athletes. After meeting with schools' athletic directors, coaches, faculty athletics representatives, and compliance staff, and also with conference officials and various SAs to gather facts, seek input, and craft legislation,

---

[20] *Idem*, Myles Brand, "Show Colleges the Money, University Sports in Need of Some Commercialism." *Chicago Tribune* (6 April 2005): 1–2.

the groups adopted changes to improve intercollegiate athletics. Table 7.1 contains two of them for each group.

With respect to other topics besides those in the table, the NCAA published the *2013–14 Sports Medicine Handbook*. Its primary purpose is to provide information used to effectively and quickly identify players who are at risk or experiencing emotional symptoms. Like most medical problems, early identification of mental health problems usually means less disruption to an athlete's life, fewer severe health complications, and a less complicated but quicker recovery from injuries.

There are chapters about mood, anxiety, eating, and substance-related disorders, and another one on management and treatment issues. In the handbook, the NCAA discussed why and how coaches should be involved in managing mental health issues that arise in their athletes. The NCAA stressed that the coach's role is not to be a therapist to affected players, but rather to identify and refer actual and potential healthcare problems. That is not to say, however, they should be uninvolved in players' treatment. Coaches have considerable power and influence with members of

Table 7.1. NCAA Status Reports, Sample Topics by Working Group, Updated April 2014.

Working Group	Topic	Adopted	Impact
Academics	Postseason eligibility	2011	Multiyear 930 team APR
	Two-year transfers	2011	Minimum 2.5 transferable GPA
Enforcement	Four-level violation structure	2012	Focuses on conduct breaches
	New penalty structure	2012	Creates consistent penalties
Resource allocation	Eliminate foreign tours	2012	Reallocates resources
	Reduce scholarships	2012	Reallocates resources
Rules	Live scouting	2013	Simplifies scouting rules
	Expenses	2013	Creates consistent definitions
SA well-being	Multiyear grants-in-aid	2011	SA receives multiyear aid
	Eliminate restrictions	2011	Schools pay former SAs degree

Note: Abbreviations are National Collegiate Athletic Association (NCAA), student athlete (SA), Academic Progress Report (APR), and Grade Point Average (GPA).

Source: "Reform Efforts," http://www.ncaa.org cited 27 May 2017.

their team or teams. That power and influence can be used by them to encourage and support treatment, which may have a positive effect on treatment outcome.

Despite issues and other problems mentioned thus far involving SAs, NCAA President Mark Emmert reportedly believes nothing is wrong with his organization — nor with the wobbly, creaking edifice that is big-time college sports — that a few minor, well-intentioned tweaks can't fix. Several years ago, for example, he endorsed an expanded athlete grant-in-aid allowance, some slightly stricter minimum academic requirements, less costly overseas travel, more thoughtfulness and collegiality in the Cash-4-BCS-Bids conference realignment scramble, and definitely fewer rules about what recruiters can and cannot spread atop complimentary stuff because everyone agrees that more regulation is completely absurd.[21]

That, to some extent, is why the NCAA is doomed: because Emmert and his fellow campus power brokers are fixated on behavior issues and recruiting scandals, and because they are disgusted with the shameless, grasping likes of violations by coaches. While appearing before the Knight Commission in mid-2011, Emmert had reason to be a semantic stickler. Amateurism still rules the day. Players cannot be paid for their athletic labor, or be viewed as such. Otherwise, they might qualify for workman's compensation, or be allowed to collectively bargain. The Internal Revenue Service might take another look at the tax-exempt status of university athletic departments. College sports as currently constituted likely would implode.

CONFERENCE REFORMS

In 2011, the NCAA Division I board of directors approved some sweeping reforms. These included giving athletic conferences the option of adding money to scholarships for players, allowing schools the option to make scholarships multiple-year agreements rather than renewing them every year, and imposing tougher academic requirements on incoming recruits.

---

[21] Patrick Hruby, "Why the NCAA's New Reforms Won't Fix College Sports." http://www.theatlantic.com cited 5 July 2017.

In addition, some conferences voted to add up to \$2,000 in spending money for scholarships and thereby cover what the NCAA called full cost-of-attendance. While some college administrators wanted a higher amount than \$2,000 per scholarship athlete, some schools and conferences expected to have a difficult time to provide additional funds. Because of a private agenda, the Southeastern Conference's (SEC) Mike Slive effectively gave the Pac-12 a pat on the head but then added: "While I don't necessarily concur with all of their proposals, it is encouraging that we are all working toward an environment that puts the student-athlete front and center."

Because it was about players, a number of the Pac-12's proposals make sense. For example, to increase the value of scholarships as stipends and also insurance coverage, guarantee scholarships as long as the student is in good academic standing, and liberalize transfer rules. The NCAA finally realized that simply being a multibillion-dollar non-profit entity is not enough anymore.

The issue, however, is that the five major conferences and also smaller schools have an agenda. Nevertheless, the NCAA wants to do the right thing. While the value of scholarships must increase, resolution can be a problem because everybody has their own goals, plans, and strategies. In other words, the SEC does not care too much about what happens in the Atlantic Coast Conference (ACC), Big Ten, Big 12, or Pacific-12. That is because its primary concern is member schools. Thus, each conference wants only what benefits their dozen or so members.

In recent years, the NCAA began to institute reforms, in part, to reduce the time SAs are allowed to practice but also increase the time available for studying. The organization took bold action to loosen transfer rules and allow male and female athletes to transfer to other schools. For instance, the graduate transfer rule passed in 2006 permitted athletes to use their final year of college eligibility to play immediately at another school without having to sit out a year as the case for undergraduate transfers. Even before the O'Bannon ruling, the so-called Power 5 conferences — ACC, Big 12, Big Ten, Pacific-12, and SEC — had voted to allow aid packages for athletes up to the full cost of attendance.

These conferences, in fact, were granted greater autonomy from the NCAA in 2016. "All of those [reforms] are focused on the student aspect. I think they are being done in an altruistic manner, that is, for the educational purposes of the student," said one observer. "But quite frankly, they will have benefits also for the legal case, because all of the resources put behind that help support the case that the purpose of the person being admitted to the school was to get an education."

Presidents and chancellors of Pac-12 schools voted in 2014 to adopt a reform package that included guaranteed four-year athletic scholarships, liberalized transfer rules within the conference, and postgraduate medical coverage for all athletes. As of that year, these changes were the most progressive package put forward by an athletic conference, which could have previously been adopted by schools or conferences. The reforms came when the Power 5 conferences had the autonomy to vote on and create their own benefits as college sports faced ongoing litigation threats about the treatment of and compensation for athletes.[22]

The conference's first reform was *guaranteed four-year athletic scholarships while in good standing.* A scholarship will not be reduced or canceled if the athlete remains in good standing and meets his or her terms of the agreement. Starting in 2015–2016, all the conference's scholarship agreements offered to recruits would be multiyear agreements for no less than four academic years.

Second is *return to school for athletes who don't graduate.* Pac-12 athletes are allowed to return to school to complete their degree. Starting in 2016–2017, if a Pac-12 athlete leaves a university in good standing and completed half of his or her degree, the athlete can return and receive necessary educational expenses for remaining terms of the scholarship agreement.

Third is *enhanced medical support for current and former players.* Starting in 2015–2016, Pac-12 schools will be required to provide direct medical expenses for documented athletically related injuries to former players for a period of four years after they leave their team or university.

---

[22] Joe Soloman, "Pac-12 Adopts Reforms Hoping to Help College Athletes." http://www. cbssports.com cited 28 May 2017; "Pac-12 Universities Adopt Sweeping Reforms for Student-Athletes, Guaranteeing Scholarships, Improving Health Care, and More." http:// www.pac-12.com cited 29 May 2017; "Pac-12 Passes Reforms for Athletes." http://www. espn.com cited 29 May 2017.

Fourth are *liberalized transfer rules within the Pac-12*. The conference removed the financial-aid penalty that applied to its transfer rule. Effective immediately, an athlete who transferred within the Pac-12 can receive an athletic scholarship from the second school immediately provided the athlete is eligible to receive the aid.

Fifth is *increased athlete representation at Pac-12 meetings*. The conference has schools' athletes attending meetings, workshops, and other types of groups to discuss policies and other things. Although they have meaningful impact with their voice, athletes cannot vote at conference council meetings, where each school is represented by an athletic director, senior administrator, and faculty representative for one vote per school.

The Pac-12's presidents and chancellors also reaffirmed their support for incorporating the full cost of attendance for the conference's scholarship SAs. The 65 institutions that compose the five major conferences and 15 representative athletes voted on this important issue at the inaugural meeting in January 2014. Also, they discussed the next steps to strengthen protections for players against excessive time demands of intercollegiate athletics. The conferences continued to examine this subject with its council and fellow major conferences.

The conference's presidents and chancellors reaffirmed their support for stipends to cover the full cost of attendance. Pac-12 commissioner Larry Scott said that figure likely will range between $2,000 and $5,000 per athlete depending on the university. The institutions in the five major football conferences — granted autonomy by the NCAA in 2014 and 15 representative athletes — vote on the issue at the group's inaugural meeting in January.

SCHOOL REFORMS

A professor's findings in his research suggested that colleges and universities should do more to prepare students for life outside of athletics. For example, schools' athletics departments may be able to work with employers to offer flexible paid or unpaid professional internships around SAs' seasons. In this way, they would receive work experience in fields outside of sports.[23]

---

[23] For the School Reforms Section, see Professor Lynsey Romo, "Study Offers Insight Into Challenges College Athletes Face." https://www.news.ncsu.edu cited 28 May 2017; Erik

In addition, some college athletics programs could take steps to give their players more free time. What is sometimes overlooked amidst a heavy athletics and academic schedule is the scholar athletes' need to decompress, relax, and unwind. Study participants reported having to make a concerted effort to see family and friends, often at the cost of time that could have been devoted to schoolwork. As such, they needed more downtime.

To recap initiatives regarding reforms of SAs by schools and their officials, the NAFCAR adopted an ambitious platform designed to restore academic integrity, fulfill obligations as faculty, and protect the welfare of all students at a meeting in 2000. The group's call for institutions to eliminate athletic scholarships, publicly disclose significant information about the classroom performance of sports teams, and put the faculty in charge of academic counseling for athletes was discussed.

The alliance's founder, Don Ericson, acknowledged that past efforts to rouse faculty opposition to the perceived abuses of big-time sports and commercialism went nowhere. What is different this time, he said, was the group's focus on academic abuses. "No one in the past . . . has been willing to confront the academic corruption head-on and expose it in such a way that it cannot be explained," said Ericson, a professor of rhetoric and communication studies at Drake University.

The platform of the alliance called on universities to (a) remove academic counseling of athletes from the control of athletics departments and abandon the practice of providing special academic support to these

---

Lords, "Professors' Group Seeks to Reform College Sports." *The Chronicle of Higher Education* (7 April 2000): 1; Tom Witosky, "Deck: Colleges; Critics Propose NCAA Reforms." *Des Moines Register* (27 March 2000): C.5; Ron Higgins, "Coaches, AD's Question Academic Reforms." *The Commercial Appeal* (18 June 2003); "SEC Faculty Leaders Urge Reform of Intercollegiate Athletics." *U.S. Newswire* (2 May 2003); Carol Simpson Stern, "The Faculty Report in the Reform of Intercollegiate Athletics." *Academe* (January/February 2003): 64–70; Scott Ferrell, "Area Colleges Adjust to NCAA Academic Reforms." *The Times* (18 January 2005): C.1; Eddie Comeaux, "Rethinking Academic Reform and Encouraging Organizational Innovation: Implications for Stakeholder Management in College Sports." http://www.researchgate.net cited 2 May 2017; Mara Rose Williams, "College Athletics: Professors Place Low Priority on Reforms Emphasizing Academics." *McClatchy-Tribune Business News* (15 October 2007); "Rationalize Sports Recruiting: UC Regents Approve Reforms to Student-Athlete Policies." http://www.daily-cal.org cited 3 May 2017.

players; (b) eliminate athletics scholarships, expand the availability of need-based aid for all students, and publicly disclose information about the majors, advisers, and courses taken by all athletes without revealing individual grades; (c) reduce the number of intercollegiate athletics games; and (d) stop using the term "student-athlete" and instead refer to those who participate in athletics as either students or athletes.

Instead of watching the NCAA men's basketball regional finals in 2000, a small but committed group of college academics fired its first official shot at trying to reform intercollegiate athletics. "We believe strongly that the time has come for faculty members across the country to wake up to what has happened on so many college campuses with their sports programs" said Jon Ericson, a Drake University professor of rhetoric and communications. "Whether we will be successful is another question. It is going to be a big challenge."

Ericson made his comments after the DG for Reform of College Athletics adopted a five-step platform they contend would help restore academic integrity to intercollegiate athletics. "College athletics have been transformed into a multibillion dollar entertainment industry that has compromised the academic mission of the university," the group said in a public statement.

To resolve those problems, the group adopted a package of proposals they want faculty members at all Division I schools to consider. Those included such things as abandonment of the term "student-athlete" by faculty and administrators, and removal of all academic counselling and support programs from the control of athletic departments. In addition, the group urged universities to stop providing academic support services on the basis of athletic status and disclose all academic majors and courses taken by all students without revealing the names of individual students or their grades.

The group also encouraged colleges and universities to make public the academic courses and average grades and instructors on a per team basis, reduce the number of intercollegiate athletic contests, and eliminate athletic scholarships as well as impose rules mandating that no athlete loses financial aid.

During 2003, athletic director Todd Turner said the NCAA would have an appeals process for SAs wishing to change majors, saying that "we don't want to deny doing something for athletes that is in their best interests. If a player leaves school in good academic standing, it should not count against the school's graduation rate. But if an athlete is not in good academic standing when leaving school, then it should count against the school. If a school performs beyond the academic norm, the NCAA may reward the school with additional revenue, more scholarships, recruiting benefits, additional graduate assistants, academic enhancements, and a public recognition program."

The meeting was the first of its kind of SEC faculty leaders, who came together in 2003 to consider the role of academics in intercollegiate athletics. Virginia Shepherd, President of the Vanderbilt University Faculty Senate and co-organizer of the meeting, said the meeting far exceeded organizers' expectations and that the group's vote on the issues in the final report was nearly unanimous. "I think the voices that are being heard now from the presidents down to the faculty to the governing boards are that we need reform, but we want to retain athletics and we want the best academic situation and options for those student athletes," she said.

The group, assembled on May 1 as a collection of faculty leaders from 12 SEC schools, had adjourned as the newly formed SEC Association of Faculty Leaders. Shepherd said they now are "an organized faculty voice that the presidents and chancellors will listen to" as they consider reform efforts. "I don't want to go so far as to say we are going to set policy," Shepherd said of the new leadership group, but "the support we're going to give to our chancellors and presidents is going to be very important."[24]

Among the recommendations issued from the meeting, the group urged that competition scheduling should be based on academic considerations instead of on revenue considerations and the NCAA and the SEC should examine the length of athletic seasons, number of competitions, and athletes' non-traditional season activities and their impact on student welfare and academic performance. The faculty discussed issues related to the proposed NCAA reforms in intercollegiate athletics and concluded that athletes who are admitted to member institutions should have a strong likelihood of academic success, that the six-year graduation rate of them

---

[24] "SEC Faculty Leaders Urge Reform for Athletics." http://www.scout.com cited 5 July 2017.

should equal or exceed that of the other students at the institution, and that processes should be in place to guarantee institutional control of the quality of all academic programs.

Among its general conclusions, the faculty group endorsed the efforts of the presidents and chancellors of the Bowl Championship Conference schools to formulate and enact proposals for significant reform of intercollegiate athletics and urged the presidents and chancellors to continue their cooperative efforts and engage their faculties in this process. In addition, the group recommended that faculty at their colleges and universities play an increased and significant role in oversight of athletic department activities, policies, and personnel decisions. In order to identify best practices, the group agreed to share information about the academic oversight bodies at their respective institutions.

Colleges and universities have an obligation to create opportunities for students to pursue their educational goals. Intercollegiate athletics requires a major allocation of financial resources. "Universities must be judged by their achievements as academic institutions, not as sports franchises" observed Myles Brand, Indiana University and NCAA President. We need, he added, "to make certain that athletics programs enhance and support the larger academic mission of the university."

Given that fourteen principles and the recommended practices have been set forth as above to implement change, what can be done to ensure that they are enacted and enforced? As the Knight Commission report states, "Change will come, sanity will be restored, only when the higher education community comes together to meet collectively the challenges its members face." As for the faculty's role in this process, on some campuses a fundamental reordering of the structures and practices of institutional governance may be needed before the faculty can begin to assume its appropriate responsibility for the oversight of the institution's athletics program.

In those institutions with a strong tradition and practice of shared governance, however, campus-wide recognition of and dedication to these principles as part of institutional governance should make it much easier for the faculty — if it is willing to become engaged and assume an appropriate role in athletics reform. Hasten to add that, as was observed in "The Role of the Faculty in the Governance of College Athletics," it is doubtful that faculty efforts alone will be sufficient to refocus the priorities of major athletics programs. On the other hand, faculties are in a unique position to advocate adherence to meaningful academic standards."[25]

Enactment and enforcement of requisite reforms to establish a proper balance between sports and education will require members of the faculty to work as much as possible with support or at least sympathetic administrators, trustees, and athletics program staff, including coaches, to invest time and energy in this project. The American Association of University Professors (AAUP) urges the adoption by faculty senates of resolutions embodying the principles set forth here and calls upon administrations to work with the faculty to implement policies consistent with the practices recommended in this report. They also encourage individual faculty members to continue to speak out with independence and candor about the issues addressed. At the same time, the association wants to emphasize the need for institutions to ensure that faculty members — who do bring public attention to these matters and actively work for reform — are afforded protections against retaliation for exercising their academic freedom.

As with efforts being undertaken by the DG and by faculty senates at Pac-12 and Big-Ten universities, faculty members at one institution may find it useful to form coalitions with members of other senates at other institutions and with other external groups who share the same principles and goals in order to promote these recommended practices and assist in advancing the reform of intercollegiate athletics programs. But ultimately faculty must take responsibility at their own institutions for the proper functioning of athletics programs and the appropriate treatment of college athletes as students.

SCHOLARSHIP REFORMS

College sports teams must stay on track to graduate at least 50 percent of their SAs in order to avoid the risk of losing scholarships for a year. The

---

[25] A report prepared by the Special Committee on Athletics and established by the Executive Committee of the Council of the American Association of University Professors, it was titled "The Role of the Faculty in the Governance of College Athletics." http://www. aaup.org cited 5 July 2017.

long and the short of it is, it may be easier for some kids to be admitted to participate in NCAA sports, yet harder to remain eligible. The NCAA has been pushing tougher academic standards for years. Now the organization has put penalties for underperformance. In 2005, for example, NCAA athletes were required to pass at least six hours in the fall to be eligible in the spring. Those players are also on a 40–60–80 scale where they must complete 40 percent of their degree work before the start of their third year, 40 percent by the end of their sophomore year, and so forth. That 40–60–80 academic progress is now backed by penalties.

For a male or female athlete to have to accomplish that much is hard because it requires more of them and puts more stress on us. That viewpoint is also shared by coaches who now have the potential loss of scholarships hanging over them if their program is not making progress toward graduation. Coaches have always considered academics in recruiting. But now it becomes an even greater factor in the recruiting process.

There are increasing concerns about the educational experiences of Division I athletes in big-time college sports. Calls for reform have come from within colleges and universities and beyond. The literature of innovative management offers ideas that can help mitigate the academic and athletic divide and offer new ideas for athletic departments. Specifically, this body of literature is placed within the context of academic support centers for SAs to underscore the importance of new ways of thinking and to shed light on the centrality of the champion in the successful implementation of innovation. The article also introduces the Career Transition Scorecard, a practitioner-as-researcher model that fosters evidence-based practices among practitioners in athletic departments as they improve the well-being of all Division I athletes.

When a coach offers a recruit a scholarship, he acts as an agent for the university. A celebrity coach's offer of a scholarship to a recruit is a powerful implied offer of both admissions and financial aid. It places enormous pressure on the director of admissions and the president of the university to admit the committed recruit irrespective of his academic qualification or institutional fit. To deny admission would certainly create media headlines and angry fans and donors. Instead, require the institutions' examination of academic records and a tentative approval of admissions *before* offers of athletic-related aid are extended to recruits.

Scholarships should not be offered unless there is some assurance that the recruit will be admitted to the college of his choice and has a reasonable chance of graduating. Without a serious review of the recruit's academic qualifications, his verbal commitment will often rule out the recruit's options to attend other colleges.

- *Abandon the National Letter of Intent (NLI) and Releases for Transferring.* The NLI document clearly disadvantages the athlete. By signing the contract, the recruit ends the formal recruiting process. The document presumes that the athlete has committed to the institution, and it attaches eligibility penalties for attending a different school or transferring prior to the completion of an academic year. Should the coach who recruited him or her leave for a more lucrative job, the student remains bound to the institution under penalty of loss of athletic eligibility.

- *Redesign official visits to follow those offered to the general student body.* Abandon the orchestrated entertainment offered by hosts and volunteer recruiters. Official visits for prospective athletes should be designed to be learning opportunities about the institution and the athletic program rather than the circus and party atmosphere they have become. Recruits should stay in campus residential facilities rather than five-star hotel suites. Their visits should be similar to the process offered to other prospective students by the campus and simulate common campus life.

- *Limit official visits to three institutions.* Prospective athletes may take as many as five official visits paid by the institutions. De-emphasizing and reducing the number of official campus visits to three would represent a cost savings to institutions and possibly reduce the party atmosphere.

- *Require police background checks of recruits and all athletic personnel.* Information that could legally be gathered on the past criminal activities of recruits should be sought and reported to the president of the university *before* offers of admissions or financial aid are executed. Police background checks should periodically be conducted for coaching staffs and all full-time athletic staff.

Taylor James wakes up for 6 a.m. rowing practice with the knowledge that she will have a busier day than most University of California-Berkeley students could ever imagine. Then she returns from practice at 9 a.m. for her classes, which end around 3 p.m. The senior legal studies student has another workout in the afternoon and also must squeeze in a three-hour rehab session for her spinal surgery. But after she graduated, James still calls her time in athletics the best part of her UC Berkeley experience.

Because of a new proposal adopted by the UC Board of Regents, students throughout the University of California system will have the same amount of support as James during her athletic career. At a Wednesday meeting, a 14-point proposal to reform athlete policies throughout the University of California system — introduced by Lt. Gov. Gavin Newsom — was approved by the regent's educational policy committee. In response to an alleged lack of system-wide athlete policies, Newsom's plan consisted of changes to policy in seven groups — administrative accountability, admissions, financial support, academic support, injury support, student life, and annual reporting. The plan's points provide a wide range of support among coaches and other officials.

GOVERNMENT PROPOSALS

There are other proposals and viewpoints regarding admissions to implement support mechanisms for struggling players. Former U.S. President Obama's point made on education, for example, delivered a tough message of reform during the keynote luncheon of the NCAA's 106th annual convention in Indianapolis. "You can implement far reaching reforms to reassert the educational mission of the universities and colleges," said U.S. Secretary of Education Arne Duncan. "I don't believe you can meet these challenges by doing business as usual."[26]

Duncan was talking about two of the most controversial measures ordered by NCAA President Mark Emmert: career-long scholarships for

---

[26] References for Government Proposals are: Joel Gehrke, "House Democrats Probe NCAA Neglecting College Athletes' Educations." *The Examiner*, Washington, D.C. (20 May 2014); "Moran Introduces NCAA Reform Bill." *Congressional Documents and Publications*, Washington, D.C. (1 December 2014); "California Congressman Cardenas Introduces Law to Help Protect Collegiate Student-Athlete Academic Progress." *Congressional Documents and Publications*, Washington, D.C. (20 November 2013).

SAs and $2,000 a year stipends to cover living expenses. "I don't know what the NCAA membership will ultimately decide about these initiatives but it seems clear that they are steps in the right direction to protect SAs and put their interests first." Emmert has experienced push back from some Division 1 programs to his proposals, but other university and college presidents agree change is needed.

Duncan pulled no punches in the address at the Indiana Convention Center as he spoke of the Penn State football child molestation allegations and the Ohio State football scandal, which cost head coach Jim Tressel his job. Duncan also referred to the recent multibillion-dollar television contracts negotiated for college sports. "The narrative for 2012 is that college sports are all about the deal, all about the brand," said Duncan. "It's all about the bigtime college football program saying, 'Show me the money.' I think it is a problem that the BCS conferences use zero percent of their bowl game revenue for educational components or to support student academic success."

Congressman Tony Cardenas — a member of the House Committee on Oversight and Government Reform — introduced legislation in 2013 to protect collegiate athletes as they achieve academic goals, while also protecting their health. The Collegiate Student-Athlete Protection Act (CSAP) requires that universities and colleges who profit most from the exploits of amateur athletes trading athletic performance for the opportunity to achieve a high level of postsecondary education, to guarantee that opportunity.

Institutions that receive more than $10 million per year in media revenue — whether through their own contracts or those of their athletic conferences — will be required to guarantee a fair opportunity to earn a college degree, within an appropriate timeframe, to male and female athletes who maintain proper academic standing. The goal of the CSAP Act is to ensure that an inability to compete does not leave the scholarship contract null and void, allowing universities latitude on continued funding for an agreed-upon scholarship. It would also protect current and former players who can be left to pay for costly medical expenses incurred from injuries suffered while participating in intercollegiate athletics.

To achieve these goals, the CSAP Act requires alternate academic scholarships for any athlete involuntarily removed from completing a degree at a college or university, but who maintains their academic standing. It also requires life skills and finance workshops including explanation of the full rights provided in scholarships and what SAs can expect to pay in health care costs. To protect them, they will also be afforded the same due process procedures as other students of the institution, including the reduction of athletically related student aid.

In 2014, U.S. House democrats investigated whether colleges and universities provided athletes good education in exchange for performance on the field, in a letter to the NCAA that raises questions about the "student-athlete" designation that historically prevented college athletes from being paid or receiving workman's compensation for injuries. Public reports suggested that the NCAA oversees a system in which its member institutions may be requiring SAs, particularly in high-revenue sports, to sacrifice their educational goals for the financial interests of college athletics. House Oversight and Government Reform Committee ranking Democrat Elijah Cummings of Maryland and Rep. Tony Cardenas, D-Calif, wrote to NCAA President Mark Emmert, citing, among other things, "that between 7 percent and 18 percent of student-athletes in the basketball and football programs of more than 20 NCAA member schools could read no higher than at the eighth-grade level."[27]

If the NCAA doesn't answer this line of questioning to their satisfaction, it's at least theoretically possible that the lawmakers could take steps to end the "student-athlete" designation at the heart of the NCAA system. "Our concerns are further heightened because the NCAA has relied on the designation of NCAA players as "student-athletes" — a term coined by the NCAA more than 50 years ago — to avoid potential financial liability," congressmen Cummings and Cardenas wrote.[28]

North Virginia congressman Jim Moran, a ranking Member on the Interior Appropriations Subcommittee and senior member of the Defense Appropriations Subcommittee, introduced legislation in 2014 that would establish a Presidential Commission on Intercollegiate Athletics Reform. "Recent scandals involving intercollegiate athletics programs at a number

---

[27] *Idem*, "House Democrats Probe NCAA Neglecting College Athletes' Educations."

[28] *Idem*, "California Congressman Cardenas Introduces Law to Help Protect Collegiate Student-Athlete Academic Progress."

of the nation's most prestigious institutions reveal the absence of policy and practice that would ensure a level of academic integrity, athlete welfare, and financial soundness appropriate for non-profit institutions of higher education," said Rep. Moran. "We need to give our colleges and universities the tools they need to sustain healthy intercollegiate athletic programs that benefit the schools and protect our SAs. The challenges of reform are so complex and important to higher education that a blue ribbon commission of experts and Members of Congress should be convened to objectively study these concerns and offer recommendations for reform."[29]

---

[29] *Idem,* "Moran Introduces NCAA Reform Bill."

Chapter 8

SUMMARY

After the book's Abbreviations and Introduction, the contents in Chapters 2–7 include several interesting but also historical, interrelated, and special topics about male and female student athletes (SAs) and, in part, their role as players on teams in fall, winter, and/or spring sports programs of American colleges and universities (sponsoring schools or institutions). For information about these athletes from the literature and other sources, there were several tables of data in both the chapters and appendix.

To identify, highlight, and summarize — for such readers as academic officials and professionals, athletic directors, coaches, and sports fans — the most important and relevant matters regarding SAs is the essential purpose of Chapter 8. Following in the book are the Appendix and then the Bibliography, Index, and About the Author.

Within seasons of two sports periods and various academic years, Chapter 2 has the number and distribution of men and women sports programs in public and private schools representing Divisions I, II, and III of the National Collegiate Athletic Association (NCAA). In addition, there is similar data for years but different colleges and universities of the National Association of Intercollegiate Athletics (NAIA) and National Junior College Athletic Association (NJCAA).[1]

---

[1] "NCAA Sports Sponsorship and Participation Rates Report 1981–1982 to 2014–2015," http://www.ncaa.org, cited 13 March 2017; "Sports Sponsorship, Participation and Demographics Search," http://www.ncaa.org, cited 8 March 2017; "NJCAA Participation

The chapter denotes why some team sports are more prevalent than others, like cross country and soccer in the fall, basketball and indoor track in winters, and baseball for men and softball for women in the spring. Readers, for example, also learn and understand when, whether, and to what extent each sport expanded or declined among schools and reasons for their growth, popularity, and success or lack thereof among SAs and the general student body.

In Chapter 2, there are comparisons of data between schools' sports programs relative to being members of the NCAA, NAIA, and NJCAA, and a discussion for why they varied over time and in size across seasons. It is especially appropriate, newsworthy, and unique to compare and reveal the progress of men's and women's sports at schools that sponsored them. To verify and report results of the analysis, the actual data was obtained from the three associations and also articles, books, Internet sources, and studies in the literature.

Based, in part, on information and results in the previous chapter, the population of schools' male and female SAs and changes in them is the focus and primary topic of Chapter 3. Covering two multiyear periods and a few academic years during each fall, winter, and spring sports season, there is data regarding the number and distribution of men and women athletes in sports programs of colleges and universities associated with Divisions I, II, and III of the NCAA, and also with respect to institutions affiliated with the NAIA and NJCAA.[2]

Among men's sports, the majority of SAs in the NCAA's divisions had participated in football, baseball, and outdoor track, while relatively few teams existed in bowling, equestrian, and triathlon. In contrast to that group, women mostly played on teams in outdoor track and then soccer and indoor track. Furthermore, tables in the Appendix list the number and proportion of male athletes by sport and race — white, Hispanic, black, or

---

Figures-Men's Division," http://www.njcaa.org cited 18 March 2017; "NJCAA Participation Figures-Women's Division," http://www.njcaa.org cited 18 March 2017.

[2] "Men Student Athlete Participation," http://www.naia.org cited 26 April 2017; "Women Student Athlete Participation," http://www.naia.org cited 26 April 2017; "Sport Sponsorship, Participation, and Demographics Search," http://web1.ncaa.org, cited 8 March 2017.

other races. Similar data is also available in tables for the number of female SAs on teams of schools in the NCAA, NAIA and NJCAA.

Given the contents in Chapter 3, SAs' population growth between different academic years and within sports and their seasons are examined in pages of the text. Besides history and tradition, such things as Title IV, budgets of athletic departments, experiences and preferences of academic administrators and students, and teams' success in winning conference titles and national championships affected decisions about which sport or sports schools' offered and supported each season. At the end of the chapter, the Notes section contains readings to use in further researching these topics by faculty, scholars, and anyone else interested in players and their participation in sports within schools of higher education.

The fourth chapter of the book primarily analyzes but also critiques the academic performances of men and women SAs on teams in seasons of sports programs of schools in each division of the NCAA — although similar data was not available for athletes in institutions associated with the NAIA and NJCAA. The data, which was provided by the NCAA in tables for Division I players, consisted of Academic Progress Reports, Graduation Success Rates, Eligibility Rates, and Retention Rates.[3]

These documents, as a group, represented the educational achievements of Division I male and female SAs by sport for fall, winter, and spring seasons during several academic years. For NCAA Divisions II and III, however, there is data about the academics of men and women athletes from two different tables, each titled Academic Success Rates and Federal Graduation Rates.

While their academic scores improved, the gap between male and female SAs on teams in Division I sports programs gradually decreased from the 2009 to 2014 academic years. More significantly, women's results were closer than men's to 100 percent in eligibility and also for

---

[3] "Average APRs by Sport for Men's Teams," http://www.ncaa.org cited 16 March 2017; "Graduation Success Rate Trends for Division I Women's Sports," http://www.ncaa.org cited 13 April 2017; "ASR Trends for Division II Men's Sports," http://www.ncaa.org cited 16 March 2017; "Federal Graduation Rate Trends for Division II Women's Sports," http://www.ncaa.org cited 16 March 2017; "Average Federal Graduation Rates and ASRs for Division III Women's Sports (Voluntary Schools," http://www.ncaa.org cited 21 April 2017. Other data may be available at schools and the NCAA.

them to return to school as seniors to complete requirements for their undergraduate degree.

In Division II, meanwhile, academic rates tended to be highest each year for male athletes on teams in fencing and skiing but lowest for those in basketball and football. For female SAs, scores were the most in field hockey and gymnastics but least in basketball and bowling. Regarding results for Division III athletes — who played without athletic scholarships — women outperformed men on average each reporting year by at least nine percentage points. Besides Title IX, these differences between genders' success and graduation rates occurred because of such things as SAs' commitment and dedication to their education, college and university admission standards and recruiting policies, and athletes' skills and performances while in high school.

The topics in Chapter 5 — Athletics Environment — includes such elements as the commercial aspects of sports programs in schools of higher education; differences in academic standards of SAs on sports teams in each division of the NCAA and also within the NAIA and NJCAA; men's and women's athletic scholarship limits by Association and sport for the 2016 academic year; and historical data about the cost of attendance of athletes. In some way, each of these topics had likely influenced or impacted players and their programs and schools.

To measure the results of athletes' environment while in school, tables of data for some of these topics appear within the chapter or Appendix. One table, for example, lists in columns the net revenue for a group of men and women sports in Divisions I and II for Fiscal Year 2014. It shows that football and men's basketball and tennis in Division I, and women's gymnastics and water polo in Division II were the only team sports whose amounts exceeded zero dollars. For both genders, sports with the largest or worst negative net revenues included ice hockey, soccer, and track and field.[4]

---

[4] "Total Generated Revenues and Expenses by Sport, Division I-Football Bowl Subdivision, Fiscal Year 2014," http://www.ncaa.org cited 30 April 2017; "Total Generated Revenues and Expenses by Sport, Division II With Football, Fiscal Year 2014," http://www.ncaa.org cited 30 April 2017; "College Athletic Scholarship Limits," http://www.scholarshipstats. com cited 4 May 2017; "Average Athletic Scholarship Per Varsity Athlete," http://www. scholarshipstats.com cited 8 May 2017.

In addition to that type of data, other tables contain the median expenses — with and without football — for each male and female sport in Division III and also the average value of scholarships per team of sports in Division I for seasons in 2016–2017. Besides discussing the advantages and disadvantages of athletes getting cost of attendance stipends, Chapter 5's Notes section has references to further research the implications, problems, current status, and future of this issue.

Based on contents in Chapters 1–5, readings in the literature, and also comments, opinions, and viewpoints of college and high school educators, the next chapter is titled Academics–Sports Controversies. Among concerns and many important subjects or topics, some of the most prominent of them are motivational methods, models, and techniques to increase and then sustain the academic performances of men and women SAs, opposition to and support of pay-for-play proposals for college and university athletes, and reasons for athletes' scandals and ways to minimize and also penalize violations.[5]

In identifying and analyzing each controversy, the chapter refers to results of cases, reports, and studies authored by the NCAA and scholars and thus reported in such diverse sources as academic journals and also popular magazines, newspapers, and periodicals. Besides those mentioned before, other topics in the research are players' sexual risk-taking behaviors, gambling, and heavy drinking; abuse and mistreatment of college athletes; hypocrisy, if any, of megadeals between businesses and schools; challenges of foreign athletes to prepare for and compete on teams in American colleges and universities; SAs' post-college careers; and athletes' participation and leadership in boycotts and protests, and reacting to racial injustices.

---

[5] "Five Reasons Student Athletes Struggle Academically," http://www.gradesfirst.com cited 12 May 2017; "NCAA Study of Paid? Here Are Some Pros and Cons," http://www. huffingtonpost.com cited 13 May 2017; Cameron Miller, "Miller: What Role Did UNC Athletes Play in the AFAM Academic Fraud Scandal?" *University Wire* (4 November 2014): 1; Huang Jiun-hau, *et al.* "Sexual Risk-Taking Behaviors, Gambling, and Heavy Drinking Among U.S. College Athletes," *Archives of Sexual Behavior* (June 2010): 706–13; "Student Athletes More Likely to Thrive After College Than Non-Athletes, Survey Says," http://www.time.com cited 12 May 2017.

Given the tables of data and contents in various parts of the book, Chapter 7 reviews the beginning, historical progress, and success of reforms to merge academics and sports in order to improve the performances of male and female SAs while in school and their careers after graduation. In fact, the chapter has sections that involve such important matters as actions of the Drake Group, policies of the Knight Commission and NCAA, reforms established and enforced by sports conferences and their schools, coaches' recruitment of athletes and whether, when, and how to award them scholarships, and also proposals from politicians.[6]

During late 2011, the executive director of Boston College's Chief Executives Club at the Carroll School of Management said this about changes in college sports: "In pursuit of their strategic mission, the needs of higher education institutions have diverged from the interests of their student-athletes. Reform in college athletics is needed to ensure that higher education re-balances the role of intercollegiate sports and offers better alignment of the well-being of student-athletes with the institution's mission. Failure to do so will lead to a future where athletics no longer serves to develop and educate student-athletes — the primary purpose of higher education." Furthermore, "Leaders in higher educational institutions must find sustainable solutions that realign this imbalance, and in the process improve the quality of the student experience for the benefit of all. It is higher education, led by the university presidents, and aided in part by the NCAA, that must recalibrate the balance between athletics and a school's mission."[7]

---

[6] "Reform Efforts," http://www.ncaa.org cited 27 May 2017; "The Student-Athlete, Academic Integrity, and Intercollegiate Athletics," http://www.acenet.edu cited 5 July 2017; Myles Brand, "Academics First: Reforming Intercollegiate Athletics." *Vital Speeches of the Day*, Vol. 67, Issue 12 (1 April 2001): 367–71; "NCAA Adopts Landmark Academic Reform Package," *Knight Ridder Tribune News Service* (10 January 2005); "The Role of the Faculty in the Governance of College Athletics," http://www.aaup.org cited 5 July 2017; "SEC Faculty Leaders Urge Reform of Intercollegiate Athletics," *U.S. Newswire* (2 May 2003); Carol Simpson Stern, "The Faculty Report in the Reform of Intercollegiate Athletics," *Academe* (January/February 2003): 64–70; "Moran Introduces NCAA Reform Bill," *Congressional Documents and Publications*, Washington, D.C. (1 December 2014).

[7] See Warren K. Zola, "Time for Transformative Change in Intercollegiate Athletics," http://www.huffingtonpost.com cited 10 July 2017. In his article, Zola made specific recommendations regarding academic standards and integrity, interests, and experiences of student athletes, and their accountability.

APPENDIX: TABLES

Table A2.1. School Sponsorships, by NCAA Division and Sport, 1981–1982 and 1990–1991 Academic Years.

| | Divisions | | | | | | | |
| | I | | II | | III | | Total | |
Sport	**1981**	**1990**	**1981**	**1990**	**1981**	**1990**	**1981**	**1990**
Fall								
Football	187	193	121	120	189	221	497	727
Men's Cross Country	256	285	161	162	233	248	650	695
Men's Soccer	182	192	10	108	233	267	521	567
Men's Water Polo	28	32	8	10	13	15	49	57
Women's Cross Country	183	280	92	154	142	232	417	666
Women's Field Hockey	95	76	42	13	131	128	268	217
Women's Soccer	22	82	10	51	48	185	80	318
Women's Volleyball	226	270	156	193	221	278	603	741
Winter								
Men's Basketball	273	295	190	204	278	296	741	795
Men's Bowling	6	0	4	0	3	0	13	0
Men's Fencing	43	28	9	1	27	20	79	49

(*Continued*)

Table A2.1.   (*Continued*)

Sport	Divisions						Total	
	I		II		III			
	1981	1990	1981	1990	1981	1990	1981	1990
Men's Gymnastics	59	38	10	1	10	4	79	43
Men's Ice Hockey	48	48	24	15	58	60	130	123
Men's Indoor T&F	209	225	96	86	117	145	422	456
Men's Rifle	49	28	17	9	17	13	83	50
Men's Skiing	20	13	13	12	22	20	55	45
Men's Squash	8	3	0	0	13	20	21	23
Men's Swimming	181	159	57	49	139	157	377	365
Women's Badminton	7	0	1	0	3	0	11	0
Women's Basketball	273	284	176	206	256	296	705	786
Women's Bowling	6	0	2	0	3	0	11	0
Women's Fencing	39	25	10	3	27	20	76	48
Women's Gymnastics	99	67	42	19	38	17	179	103
Women's Ice Hockey	9	0	0	0	8	0	17	0
Women's Indoor T&F	127	221	51	86	61	140	239	447
Women's Rifle	10	0	2	0	4	0	16	0
Women's Skiing	15	11	4	11	14	19	33	41
Women's Squash	7	0	0	0	9	0	16	0
Women's Swimming	161	163	57	54	130	179	348	396
Wrestling	146	111	68	49	149	120	363	280
Spring								
Baseball	254	271	148	156	240	265	642	692
Men's Crew	31	24	6	6	11	13	48	43
Men's Golf	263	266	134	126	193	211	590	603
Men's Lacrosse	50	51	18	20	70	86	138	157
Men's Outdoor T&F	230	241	140	121	207	204	577	566
Men's Sailing	6	0	1	0	8	0	15	0
Men's Tennis	267	273	172	153	251	266	690	692

(*Continued*)

Table A2.1.   (*Continued*)

Sport	Divisions						Total	
	I		**II**		**III**			
	1981	**1990**	**1981**	**1990**	**1981**	**1990**	**1981**	**1990**
Men's Volleyball	33	24	15	10	15	24	63	58
Women's Crew	28	7	5	2	10	3	43	12
Women's Golf	83	104	22	18	20	23	125	145
Women's Lacrosse	39	33	13	12	53	73	105	118
Women's Outdoor T&F	180	239	101	117	146	197	427	553
Women's Sailing	4	0	1	0	6	0	11	0
Women's Softball	152	174	116	161	164	245	432	580
Women's Tennis	246	279	145	154	219	278	610	711

Note: The National Collegiate Athletic Association is NCAA. Before 1981, the NCAA did not publish sports sponsorship reports for men and women by division. The word 'and' is represented by the symbol &. Swimming includes diving.

Source: "NCAA Sports Sponsorship and Participation Rates Report 1981–1982 to 2009–2010," http://www.ncaa.org cited 19 March 2017 and Frank P. Jozsa Jr., *College Sports Inc.: How Commercialism Influences Intercollegiate Athletics* (New York, NY: Springer, 2013).

Table A2.2. School Sponsorships, by NCAA Division and SPORT, 2000–2001 Academic Year.

Sport	Divisions			
	I	**II**	**III**	**Total**
Fall				
Football	236	157	231	624
Men's Archery	1	0	0	1
Men's Cross Country	305	230	325	860
Men's Rowing	28	6	26	60
Men's Soccer	198	171	361	730
Men's Water Polo	23	6	17	46
Women's Archery	3	0	0	3
Women's Cross County	318	255	350	923
Women's Field Hockey	76	25	147	248
Women's Soccer	274	199	378	851
Women's Volleyball	308	271	396	975
Winter				
Men's Basketball	321	288	382	991
Men's Fencing	22	7	23	52
Men's Gymnastics	21	1	4	26
Men's Ice Hockey	58	7	67	132
Men's Indoor T&F	252	107	194	553
Men's Rifle	27	2	16	45
Men's Skiing	12	9	23	44
Men's Squash	8	0	18	26
Men's Swimming	149	52	184	385
Men's Wrestling	90	41	104	235
Women's Badminton	0	0	3	3
Women's Basketball	318	288	414	1020
Women's Bowling	22	3	0	25
Women's Fencing	26	3	17	46

(Continued)

Table A2.2.   (*Continued*)

Sport	Divisions			Total
	I	**II**	**III**	**Total**
Women's Gymnastics	67	7	16	90
Women's Ice Hockey	27	2	34	63
Women's Rifle	31	2	12	45
Women's Skiing	14	10	24	48
Women's Squash	8	0	22	30
Women's Swimming	185	67	227	479
Spring				
Baseball	285	232	343	860
Men's Golf	293	188	269	750
Men's Lacrosse	55	30	123	208
Men's Outdoor T&F	270	150	239	659
Men's Sailing	8	1	16	25
Men's Tennis	278	180	316	774
Men's Volleyball	22	19	42	83
Women's Equestrian	9	7	31	47
Women's Golf	206	85	146	437
Women's Lacrosse	71	26	141	238
Women's Outdoor T&F	286	160	250	696
Women's Rowing	82	14	42	138
Women's Softball	249	250	378	877
Women's Tennis	312	217	362	891
Women's Water Polo	27	8	15	50

Note: The 2000 Season is actually 2000–2001. The word 'and' is represented by the symbol &. Swimming includes diving and synchronized swimming.

Source: "Composition and Sport Sponsorship of the NCAA in 2000–2001," http://www.ncaa.org cited 19 March 2017 and Frank P. Jozsa Jr., *College Sports Inc.: How Commercialism Influences Intercollegiate Athletics* (New York, NY: Springer, 2013).

Table A2.3.   Men teams, NAIA Season and Sport, 2008–2014 Academic Years.

Sport	2008	2009	2010	2011	2012	2013	2014
Fall							
Archery	0	0	0	0	1	1	1
Cross Country	84	100	101	100	93	100	100
Rowing	2	2	2	2	2	2	2
Soccer	205	210	207	204	197	191	193
Volleyball	16	16	15	17	18	21	22
Winter							
Basketball	256	252	249	246	236	229	228
Bowling	11	16	22	23	28	34	36
Football	89	86	85	86	80	82	87
Gymnastics	0	0	0	0	0	1	1
Ice Hockey	2	2	2	2	5	5	7
Rifle	1	1	0	0	0	0	0
Rodeo	6	7	8	8	7	7	7
Table Tennis	1	1	0	0	0	0	0
Skiing	4	4	2	3	3	3	3
Swimming	9	11	6	10	6	5	5
Track and Field/Indoor	19	27	28	26	22	29	36
Weightlifting	0	1	0	0	0	0	0
Wrestling	32	39	37	39	41	43	48
Spring							
Baseball	203	201	202	197	186	183	183
Equestrian	3	3	2	2	3	3	2
Golf	166	171	174	175	171	171	169
Lacrosse	6	8	13	12	13	19	22
Sailing	1	1	2	2	1	2	1
Tennis	97	97	99	101	98	100	102
Track and Field/Outdoor	36	47	48	48	45	53	64
Water Polo	5	4	3	3	2	2	2

Note: NAIA is National Association of Intercollegiate Athletics. Academic Years are actually 2008–2009 to 2014–2015. Swimming includes diving. The table excludes NAIA's "Other Sports."

Source: "Intercollegiate Teams by Division," http://www.naia.org cited 27 April 2017.

Table A2.4. Women Teams, by NAIA Season and Sport, 2008–2014 Academic Years.

Sport	2008	2009	2010	2011	2012	2013	2014
Fall							
Archery	0	0	0	0	1	2	2
Cross Country	86	100	101	103	96	103	103
Field Hockey	3	2	2	2	2	2	2
Soccer	206	209	204	200	195	194	196
Volleyball	236	232	231	235	226	220	216
Winter							
Basketball	253	251	241	243	232	226	227
Bowling	10	18	23	24	26	34	36
Gymnastics	0	0	0	1	0	1	1
Ice Hockey	1	1	1	1	1	1	2
Rifle	1	1	0	0	0	0	0
Rodeo	6	7	8	8	7	7	7
Table Tennis	1	1	0	0	0	0	0
Skiing	4	4	2	3	3	3	3
Swimming	12	14	8	12	6	5	6
Track and Field/Outdoor	20	26	29	26	24	31	38
Wrestling	6	6	8	9	9	9	14
Spring							
Equestrian	5	5	3	3	4	4	4
Golf	121	128	129	135	138	142	143
Lacrosse	6	7	10	13	15	17	25
Rowing	2	2	4	3	2	2	2
Sailing	1	1	2	2	1	2	1
Softball	197	201	198	201	194	193	190
Tennis	112	113	113	113	109	110	112
Track and Field/Outdoor	39	48	50	48	46	55	65
Water Polo	6	5	4	4	2	1	3

Note: NAIA is National Association of Intercollegiate Athletics. Academic Years are actually 2008–2009 to 2014–2015. Swimming includes diving and synchronized swimming. The table excludes NAIA's "Other Sports."

Source: "Intercollegiate Teams by Division," http://www.naia.org cited 27 April 2017.

Table A3.1. Men and Women Student Athletes, by Race and Sport, NCAA Divisions I–III, 2015–2016.

| | Race | | | | | | | |
| | White | | Black | | Hispanic | | Other | |
Sport	M	W	M	W	M	W	M	W
Baseball	28,433	0	1,415	0	2,230	0	2,477	0
Basketball	7,576	8,598	8,422	5,444	504	569	2,182	1,979
Beach Volleyball	0	634	0	50	0	54	0	171
Bowling	4	362	0	159	0	29	4	49
Cross Country	10,596	12,022	1,229	1,186	1,131	1,040	1,456	1,350
Equestrian	12	1,206	0	16	3	30	0	105
Fencing	370	373	25	37	36	59	216	252
Field Hockey	0	5,131	0	108	0	105	0	688
Football	36,530	0	27,826	0	2,646	0	6,658	0
Golf	6,824	3,678	191	97	230	206	1,431	1,312
Gymnastics	225	1,072	19	118	19	66	57	246
Ice Hockey	3,064	1,751	43	7	49	24	946	507
Lacrosse	11,570	9,762	462	347	300	323	1,134	943
Rifle	134	147	3	4	8	8	18	35
Rowing	1,755	5,536	29	177	91	409	468	1,347
Rugby	93	215	18	38	15	40	37	79
Sailing	397	0	3	0	22	0	36	0
Skiing	311	360	1	0	5	3	100	73
Soccer	15,125	20,943	1,924	1,230	3,055	2,021	4,699	3,164
Softball	0	15,449	0	957	0	1,479	0	1,794
Squash	285	243	12	12	14	19	177	132
Swimming	7,124	9,833	213	177	444	457	1,674	1,933
Tennis	4,586	5,290	334	550	505	444	2,667	2,649
Track/Indoor	15,678	17,204	5,516	5,478	1,201	1,107	2,825	3,091
Track/Outdoor	17,106	18,303	6,264	5,956	1,729	1,438	3,242	3,365
Triathlon	3	17	0	0	1	3	0	1

(Continued)

Table A3.1.   (*Continued*)

	Race							
	White		Black		Hispanic		Other	
Sport	**M**	**W**	**M**	**W**	**M**	**W**	**M**	**W**
Volleyball	1,291	12,621	116	1,742	206	789	286	1,966
Water Polo	684	754	10	10	84	121	236	251
Wrestling	5,275	0	575	0	504	0	721	0

Note: Abbreviations are National Collegiate Athletic Association (NCAA), Men (M), and Women (W). Other student athletes include American Indian/Alaskan Native, Asian, Native Hawaiian/Pacific Islander, Two or More Races, and Nonresident Alien. The NCAA Divisions are I, II, and III. Swimming includes synchronized swimming.

Source: "Sport Sponsorship, Participation, and Demographics Search," https://www.web1.ncaa.org cited 8 March 2017.

Table A3.2.   Men and Women Student Athletes, by Race and Sport, NCAA Division I, 2015–2016.

| | Race | | | | | | | |
| | White | | Black | | Hispanic | | Other | |
Sport	**M**	**W**	**M**	**W**	**M**	**W**	**M**	**W**
Baseball	8,222	0	566	0	751	0	891	0
Basketball	1,358	1,600	3,153	2,456	90	129	871	805
Beach Volleyball	0	517	0	43	0	45	0	153
Bowling	0	158	0	80	0	14	0	31
Cross Country	3,378	4,317	446	553	388	343	587	734
Equestrian	1	620	0	6	1	23	0	52
Fencing	223	212	17	22	20	22	129	147
Field Hockey	0	1,378	0	24	0	36	0	357
Football	11,240	0	13,453	0	771	0	2,916	0
Golf	2,078	1,246	85	58	91	84	687	788
Gymnastics	211	722	18	90	19	51	56	195
Ice Hockey	1,086	499	16	4	17	7	514	345
Lacrosse	2,650	2,890	91	92	71	66	327	296
Rifle	109	127	1	4	6	7	10	26
Rowing	1,009	4,244	16	140	46	283	307	986
Rugby	39	118	16	32	8	23	7	40
Sailing	229	0	0	0	16	0	23	0
Skiing	83	126	0	0	3	2	66	40
Soccer	3,168	6,499	567	622	696	644	1,446	1,379
Softball	0	4,320	0	425	0	573	0	724
Squash	108	83	2	1	5	2	84	65
Swimming	2,794	4,277	68	84	145	187	714	975
Tennis	1,160	1,238	99	171	152	133	1,233	1,368
Track/Indoor	5,554	7,137	2,722	3,498	484	531	1,334	1,651
Track/Outdoor	5,987	7,311	2,963	3,541	615	547	1,501	1,737

(Continued)

Table A3.2.   (*Continued*)

	Race							
	White		**Black**		**Hispanic**		**Other**	
Sport	**M**	**W**	**M**	**W**	**M**	**W**	**M**	**W**
Volleyball	285	3,428	9	773	16	215	84	823
Water Polo	390	433	3	7	33	62	148	163
Wrestling	1,867	0	185	0	183	0	266	0

Note: Abbreviations are National Collegiate Athletic Association (NCAA), Men (M), and Women (W). Other student athletes include American Indian/Alaskan Native, Asian, Native Hawaiian/Pacific Islander, Two or More Races, and Nonresident Alien. Swimming includes diving and synchronized swimming.

Source: "Sport Sponsorship, Participation, and Demographics Search," http://www.web1.ncaa.org cited 8 March 2017.

Table A3.3. Men and Women Student Athletes, by Race and Sport, NCAA Division II, 2015–2016.

	Race							
	White		Black		Hispanic		Other	
Sport	M	W	M	W	M	W	M	W
Baseball	8,503	0	569	0	784	0	804	0
Basketball	1,856	2,340	2,754	1,778	180	214	660	588
Beach Volleyball	0	89	0	6	0	9	0	17
Bowling	0	124	0	72	0	11	0	16
Cross Country	2,484	2,734	421	358	391	387	383	418
Equestrian	0	93	0	0	0	1	0	8
Fencing	10	25	1	4	2	8	15	17
Field Hockey	0	631	0	15	0	13	0	82
Football	8,287	0	8,943	0	614	0	1,640	0
Golf	1,834	1,139	73	21	84	77	479	324
Gymnastics	0	97	0	8	0	9	0	16
Ice Hockey	163	80	0	0	0	1	22	17
Lacrosse	2,004	1,945	117	94	81	72	302	209
Rifle	17	13	1	0	0	0	3	2
Rowing	27	340	0	10	2	61	23	87
Rugby	24	51	0	5	5	4	15	27
Sailing	10	0	0	0	0	0	4	0
Skiing	46	62	0	0	0	0	25	19
Soccer	3,285	5,438	443	259	1,001	672	1,906	967
Softball	0	4,599	0	356	0	490	0	546
Swimming	1,041	1,436	41	19	88	91	330	307
Tennis	729	1,067	87	160	133	117	800	723
Track/Indoor	3,471	3,825	1,435	1,157	305	296	615	643
Track/Outdoor	3,950	4,288	1,870	1,517	596	531	773	768
Triathlon	0	14	0	0	0	2	0	0
Volleyball	260	3,595	21	574	96	269	90	530

(Continued)

Table A3.3.   (*Continued*)

Sport	White		Black		Hispanic		Other	
	M	**W**	**M**	**W**	**M**	**W**	**M**	**W**
Water Polo	87	139	5	2	19	19	36	48
Wrestling	1,396	0	203	0	148	0	199	0

Note: Abbreviations are National Collegiate Athletic Association (NCAA), Men (M), and Women (W). Other student athletes include American Indian/Alaskan Native, Asian, Native Hawaiian/Pacific Islander, Two or More Races, and Nonresident Alien. Swimming includes diving and synchronized swimming.

Source: "Sport Sponsorship, Participation, and Demographics Search," http://www.web1.ncaa.org cited 8 March 2017.

Table A3.4.   Men and Women Student Athletes, by Race and Sport, NCAA Division III, 2015–2016.

| | Race | | | | | | | |
| | White | | Black | | Hispanic | | Other | |
Sport	M	W	M	W	M	W	M	W
Baseball	11,708	0	280	0	695	0	782	0
Basketball	4,362	4,658	2,515	1,210	234	226	651	586
Beach Volleyball	0	28	0	1	0	0	0	1
Bowling	4	80	0	7	0	4	0	2
Cross Country	4,734	4,971	362	275	352	310	486	558
Equestrian	11	493	0	10	2	6	0	45
Fencing	137	136	7	11	14	29	72	88
Field Hockey	0	3,122	0	69	0	56	0	249
Football	17,003	0	5,430	0	1,261	0	2,102	0
Golf	2,912	1,293	33	18	55	45	265	200
Gymnastics	14	253	1	20	0	6	1	35
Ice Hockey	1,815	1,172	27	3	32	16	410	145
Lacrosse	6,900	4,927	253	161	148	185	502	438
Rifle	8	7	1	0	2	1	5	7
Rowing	719	952	13	27	43	65	138	274
Rugby	30	46	2	1	2	13	16	12
Sailing	158	0	3	0	6	0	90	0
Skiing	182	172	1	0	2	1	9	14
Soccer	8,672	9,006	914	349	1,358	705	1,347	818
Softball	0	6,530	0	176	0	416	0	524
Squash	177	160	10	11	9	17	93	67
Swimming	3,289	4,120	104	74	211	179	630	651
Tennis	2,689	2,983	148	219	220	194	634	558
Track/Indoor	6,653	6,242	1,359	823	412	280	876	797
Track/Outdoor	7,166	6,700	1,428	894	517	359	966	855
Triathlon	3	3	0	0	1	1	0	1

(Continued)

Table A3.4. (*Continued*)

Sport	White		Black		Hispanic		Other	
	M	**W**	**M**	**W**	**M**	**W**	**M**	**W**
Volleyball	746	5,598	86	395	94	305	112	613
Water Polo	207	182	2	1	32	40	52	40
Wrestling	2,012	0	187	0	173	0	256	0

Note: Abbreviations are National Collegiate Athletic Association (NCAA), Men (M), and Women (W). Other student athletes include American Indian/Alaskan Native, Asian, Native Hawaiian/Pacific Islander, Two or More Races, and Nonresident Alien. Swimming includes diving and synchronized swimming.

Source: "Sport Sponsorship, Participation, and Demographics Search," http://www.web1.ncaa.org, cited 8 March 2017.

Table A4.1. Men's Federal Graduation Rate Trends, by Sport and Season, NCAA Division II, 2009–2016.

Sport	2009	2010	2011	2012	2013	2014	2015	2016
Fall								
Cross Country/Track	55	55	53	53	52	53	54	55
Soccer	50	51	52	52	53	53	52	53
Volleyball	42	40	40	46	54	54	56	54
Winter								
Basketball	46	46	46	44	44	45	45	46
Fencing	50	50	50	50	67	90	89	82
Football	43	43	43	42	41	41	41	40
Ice Hockey	51	51	50	50	53	57	64	66
Rifle	50	100	50	58	78	72	77	68
Skiing	47	46	42	43	52	59	57	58
Swimming	60	57	60	59	60	61	61	61
Wrestling	50	48	48	45	40	40	39	40
Spring								
Baseball	51	51	52	51	50	50	51	51
Golf	55	55	56	56	56	56	56	55
Lacrosse	59	57	56	57	54	53	54	51
Tennis	60	60	59	56	55	57	58	60
Water Polo	58	61	54	53	53	50	53	57

Note: Abbreviation is National Collegiate Athletic Association (NCAA). Data is four-class averages, in percent, by reporting year such as 2015 representing 2005–2008 cohorts and 2016 the 2006–2009 cohorts. The sample is sixteen sports.

Source: "Federal Graduation Rate Trends for Division II Men's Sports," http://www.ncaa.org cited 16 March 2017.

Table A4.2. Women's Federal Graduation Rate Trends, by Sport and Season, NCAA Division II, 2009–2016.

Sport	2009	2010	2011	2012	2013	2014	2015	2016
Fall								
Cross Country/Track	64	65	66	66	64	63	64	65
Field Hockey	80	77	79	75	77	78	78	76
Soccer	64	63	63	62	62	63	64	65
Volleyball	61	62	62	62	64	65	65	65
Winter								
Basketball	60	60	61	60	59	60	58	58
Bowling	69	83	76	59	61	62	63	61
Fencing	100	100	100	100	100	100	87	91
Gymnastics	63	62	53	51	58	66	71	74
Ice Hockey	65	64	59	60	65	66	70	74
Skiing	54	57	60	57	66	77	77	78
Swimming	73	74	74	72	69	70	70	72
Spring								
Crew	50	53	55	63	64	69	72	72
Golf	64	64	65	66	65	63	64	64
Lacrosse	79	76	76	74	72	74	72	71
Softball	63	63	62	61	61	61	61	62
Tennis	65	67	66	67	68	68	69	68
Water Polo	52	67	67	57	54	65	64	68

Note: Abbreviated is National Collegiate Athletic Association (NCAA). Data is four-class averages, in percent, by reporting year such as 2015 representing 2005–2008 cohorts and 2016 the 2006–2009 cohorts. The sample is seventeen sports.

Source: "Federal Graduation Rate Trends for Division II Women's Sports," http://www.ncaa.org cited 16 March 2017.

Table A5.1.   Total Expenses, NCAA Division III, by Men and Women Sports, Fiscal Year 2014.

Sport	With Football		Without Football	
	Men	**Women**	**Men**	**Women**
Baseball	144	NA	115	NA
Basketball	153	136	115	95
Crew	NA	112	NA	67
Equestrian	NA	84	NA	70
Fencing	60	53	51	34
Field Hockey	NA	101	NA	81
Football	428	NA	NA	NA
Golf	38	34	28	36
Gymnastics	135	125	NA	44
Ice Hockey	190	156	204	150
Lacrosse	141	99	116	75
Rifle	26	0	0	0
Skiing	42	34	91	57
Soccer	101	95	87	77
Softball	NA	99	NA	70
Swimming	67	69	75	70
Tennis	37	34	31	27
Track and Field	95	92	33	32
Volleyball	67	99	40	60
Water Polo	63	68	100	90
Wrestling	110	NA	78	NA

Note: NCAA is National Collegiate Athletic Association. Amounts are median values in thousands of U.S. dollars. Track and Field includes cross country. Data excludes Other Sports. NA is 'not applicable'.

Source: "Total Expenses by Sport, NCAA Division III With Football, Fiscal Year 2014," http://www.ncaa.org cited 30 April 2017, and "Total Expenses by Sport, Division III Without Football, Fiscal Year 2014," http://www.ncaa.org cited 30 April 2017.

BIBLIOGRAPHY

ARTICLES

Anas, Brittany. "CU-Boulder to Enter Student-Athlete 'Pay for Play' Debate." *The Daily Camera* (20 June 2011): 1.

"Are College Athletes Being Mistreated?" *Florida Times Union* (5 April 2014): B.8.

"Athletic Scholarships Have a Huge Impact on Black Student Graduation Rates." *The Journal of Blacks in Higher Education*, 20 (Winter 2004): 68.

Auerbach, Nicole. "Athletes' Stipends Mostly go to Food, Rent." *Arizona Republic* (6 January 2016): C.9.

Baird, Katherine. "Dominance in College Football and the Role of Scholarship Restrictions." *Journal of Sport Management*, Vol. 18, No. 3 (July 2004): 1.

Baker, Ashley, and Billy Hawkins. "Academic and Career Advancement for Black Male Athletes at NCAA Division I Institutions." *New Directions for Adult and Continuing Education* (Summer 2016): 71–82.

Blackistone, Kevin. "Can College Athletics be Reformed? Blame '39 TV Game for Crisis." *Dallas Morning News* (8 December 2003): 1.

Blanchard, Joy. "The Supreme Court and the NCAA: The Case for Less Commercialism and More Due Process in College Sports." *Review of Higher Education* (Spring 2013): 406–408.

Bowen, Daniel, and Collin Hitt. "History and Evidence Show School Sports Help Students Win." *Phi Delta Kappa* (May 2016): 8.

Brand, Myles. "Academics First: Reforming Intercollegiate Athletics." *Vital Speeches of the Day*, Vol. 67, Issue 12 (1 April 2001): 367–71.

Brand, Myles. "Show Colleges the Money, University Sports in Need of Some Commercialism." *Chicago Tribune* (6 April 2005): 1–2.

Briggs, David. "Universities Deal With New Cost-of-Attendance Stipend for Athletes." *TCA Regional News* (5 July 2015): 1.

Campo-Flores, Arian. "School President Hits Back at NCAA Over Shapiro Scandal." *Daily Bankruptcy Review* (22 March 2013): 1.

"Carolina Congressman Cardenas Introduces Law to Help Protect Collegiate Student-Athletes Academic Progress." *Congressional Documents and Publications*, Washington, D.C. (20 November 2013).

"College Athletics Build to Business Success." *Wall Street Journal* (12 March 2012): B7–B10.

Comeaux, Eddie. "Innovative Research Into Practice in Support Centers for College Athletes: Implications for the Academic Progress Rate Initiative." *Journal of College Student Development*, Vol. 56, No. 3 (April 2015): 274–279.

Deal, Colin Jeffery, and Martin Camire. "An Examination of University Student-Athletes' Motivations to Contribute." *Journal of College and Character*, Vol. 17, Issue 2 (2016): 116–129.

Decock, Luke. "Battle Lines Between UNC, NCAA Never More Sharp." *Charlotte Observer* (26 May 2017): 2B.

Ferrell, Scott. "Area Colleges Adjust to NCAA Academic Reforms." *The Times* (18 January 2005): C.1.

Fouriezos, Nicholas. "UGA Football Scandal." *Atlanta Journal* (17 October 2014): B.1.

Fowler, Gavin. "Stipends a New Factor in NCAA Sports." *University Wire* (1 June 2016): 1.

Gaither, Steven. "New NCAA Eligibility Standards Come Under Scrutiny." *Diverse Issues in Higher Education* (11 April 2013): 7–8.

Gay, Jason. "The Power Shift in College Sports." *Wall Street Journal* (10 October 2015): D6.

Gehrke, Joel. "House Democrats Probe NCAA Neglecting College Athletes' Educations." *The Examiner*, Washington, D.C. (20 May 2014).

Greenstein, Teddy. "NCAA OKs Tough Reform Measures Based on Academic Standards." *Knight Ridder Tribune News Service* (29 April 2004).

Greenstein, Teddy. "NCAA Puts Number on Academic Reform; Goal of New APR Formula: Hold Schools, Athletes Accountable." *Chicago Tribune* (1 March 2005): 1.

Gurney, Gerald, and Jerome Weber. "Rethinking the NCAA's Academic Reform." *American Association of Collegiate Registrars and Admission Officers*, Washington, D.C. (2007).

Henderson, Mike. "AD Mark Coyle Discusses Fallout From Football Sex Assault Scandal." *University Wire* (21 February 2014): 1.

Higgins, Ron. "Coaches, AD's Question Academic Reforms." *The Commercial Appeal* (18 June 2003).

Hobson, Will. "NCAA President: Major Changes Needed to Restore Public Trust." *Charlotte Observer* (31 October 2017): 4B.

"How to Become a Scholarship Athlete." *USA Today* (December 2010): 2.

Hutton, Ted. "NCAA Adopts Landmark Academic Reform Package." *Knight Ridder Tribune News Service* (10 January 2005).

Hutton, Ted. "NCAA Board Adopts Strict Academic Reform." *Knight Ridder Tribune News Service* (10 January 2005).

"Is Racism the Main Factor in Opposition to Not Paying College Athletes?" *Journal of Blacks in Higher Education* (18 January 2016): 1.

Jayakumar, Uma, and Eddie Comeaux. "The Cultural Cover-Up of College Athletics: How Organizational Culture Perpetuates an Unrealistic and Idealized Balancing Act." *The Journal of Higher Education*, Vol. 87, No. 4 (July/August 2016): 488.

Jium-hau, Huang, *et al.* "Sexual Risk-Taking Behaviors, Gambling, and Heavy Drinking Among U.S. College Athletes." *Archives of Sexual Behavior* (June 2010): 706–13.

Kane, Dan. "North Carolina's Response Challenges NCAA's Jurisdiction in Academic Scandal." *Charlotte Observer* (26 May 2017): 1B, 2B.

Kerkhoff, Blair. "Wall of Shame: A Rundown of the 10 Scandals That Have Rocked — and Sullied — College Athletics." *Pittsburgh Post* (4 September 2011): D.1.

Korn, Melissa. "Troubled Campus Gets a New Leader." *Wall Street Journal* (25 May 2017): A3.

Kuwada, Robert. "Boeh Discusses Recent NCAA Reforms." *McClatchy-Tribune Business News* (30 October 2011).

"Latest Academic Progress Rates Data Shows That Academic Reform is Taking Hold." *US Federal News Service*, Washington, D.C. (1 March 2006).

Lewis, Fred. "UH Will Raise the Bar on Its Student-Athlete Stipends." *Honolulu Star* (25 June 2016): 1.

Lords, Erik. "Professors' Group Seeks to Reform College Sports." *The Chronicle of Higher Education* (7 April 2000): 1.

"Louisville Sex Scandal." *University Wire* (22 October 2015): 1.

McDowell, Jacqueline. "Title IX Exclusion and Marginalization Needs to Change." *Diverse Issues in Higher Education* (14 January 2016): 1.

McKissic, Rodney. "Classroom Wake-Up Call: NCAA's Academic Reforms Hold Colleges Accountable for Student-Athletes' Academic Performances." *Buffalo News* (16 June 2005): 1.

Meyer, Sandra. "NCAA Academic Reforms: Maintaining the Balance Between Academics and Athletics." *Phi Kappa Phi Forum* (Fall 2005).

Miller, Cameron. "Miller: What Role Did UNC Athletes Play in the AFAM Academic Fraud Scandal?" *University Wire* (4 November 2014): 1.

"Moran Introduces NCAA Reform Bill." *Congressional Documents and Publications*, Washington, D.C. (1 December 2014).

"NCAA: Division I Graduation Rates Remain at All-Time Highs." *The Hispanic Outlook in Higher Education* (25 January 2010): 31.

"New Rules for Student Athletes." *The Charlotte Observer* (4 March 2015): 2B.

Newman, Jonah. "At Tops Athletics Programs, Students Often Major in Eligibility." *Chronicle of Higher Education* (18 December 2014): 1.

Oden, Kimberly. "Winning Combination: How Counselors and Student-Athletes Can Team Up." *Journal of College Admission*, No. 231, (Spring 2016): 19.

O'Shaughnessy, Lynn. "Seven Ways to Capture a Sports Scholarship." *Penton Media, Inc.* (January 2011): 66–67.

O'Shaughnessy, Lynn. "Sports Scholarships Don't Come Easy." *Penton Media, Inc.* (November 2014): 50.

"Reform and College Sports." *Knight Ridder Tribune News Service* (31 December 2003): 1.

"Report: College Athletes Earn Degrees at Record Rates." *Charlotte Observer* (9 November 2017): 3B.

Rettig, Jean, and Hu Shouping. "College Sport Participation and Student Educational Experiences and Selected College Outcomes." *Journal of College Student Development*, Vol. 57, No. 3 (May 2016): 428–446.

Robinson, Doug. "UCLA's $280M Deal Adds to NCAA Hypocrisy." *Deseret News* (28 May 2016): 1.

Ross, Brooke. "Fielding Offers." *Junior Scholastic* (17 March 2014): 1–2.

Sack, Allen. "College Athletes Are Students First and Should Not be Paid." *Deseret News* (16 March 2008): G.3.

Sanderson, Allen, and John Siegfried. "Enough Madness: Just Pay College Athletes." *Chicago Tribune* (3 February 2016): 22.

Sanserino, Michael, and Sam Werner. "Cost of College Athletics May Rise Amid Challenges." *TCA Regional News* (10 June 2014): 1.

Schlossman, Brad Elliott. "Breaking News: UND to Pay All Scholarship Athletes Stipends in 2016–17." *TCA Regional News* (2 September 2015): 1.

Schneider, Robert. "Developing the Moral Integrity of College Sport Through Commercialism." *Physical Culture and Sport* (2010): 30.

Schoof, Renee. "NCAA VP: Don't Pay Athletes in College." *Charlotte Observer* (20 May 2015): 2A.

Schultz, Jeff. "NCAA Can't Reform With so Many Private Agendas." *TCA Regional News* (24 May 2014).

"SEC Faculty Leaders Urge Reform of Intercollegiate Athletics." *U.S. Newswire* (2 May 2003).

Selb, Nick. "Foreign Athletes Face Unique Challenges." *University Wire* (5 November 2013): 1.

Stern, Carol Simpson. "The Faculty Report in the Reform of Intercollegiate Athletics." *Academe* (January/February 2003): 64–70.

Stuart, Reginald. "Dollar$ and Sense." *Diverse Issues in Higher Education* (16 February 2012): 9–11.

Sullivan, Tim. "Confessions of a UC Coach and 'Slimeball'." *Cincinnati Enquirer* (27 December 2015): C.1.

Terlep, Sharon. "The NCAA's Drug Problem." *Wall Street Journal* (20 March 2015): D8.

"The Pros and Cons of Making Major Reforms in the American Collegiate Athletic System." *Congressional Digest*, vol. 94, issue 6 (June 2015): 8.

Thomas, P.L. "Invisible Young Men: African-American Males, Academics, and Athletics." *English Journal* (September 2014): 75–78.

Thomasson, Dan. "Greed is True College Bowl Champion; Money is Motivation." *Beaumont Enterprise* (5 January 2011): A.7.

Tonkin, Oliver. "Oliver Tonkin, Paying Student-Athletes Will Harm Academic Institutions." *University Wire* (23 October 2014): 1.

"Top Five Conferences to Allow Aid for Athletes' Full Bills." *The Charlotte Observer* (18 January 2015): 9B.

Tracey, Marc, and Dan Barry. "Baylor's Pride Turns to Shame in Rape Scandal." *New York Times* (10 March 2017): A.1.

Tucker, Hank. "ESPN Analyst, Former Duke Player Bilas is Body's Loudest Critic." *Charlotte Observer* 12 July 2017): 4B.

"UND Athletes Receive New Stipend." *University Wire* (8 September 2015): 1.

Williams, Mara Rose. "College Athletics: Professors Place Low Priority on Reforms Emphasizing Academics." *McClatchy-Tribune Business News* (15 October 2007).

Williams, Mitchell, and Kevin Pennington. "Community College Presidents' Perceptions of Intercollegiate Athletics." *The Community College Enterprise* (Fall 2006): 91–104.

Witosky, Tom. "Deck: Colleges; Critics Propose NCAA Reforms." *Des Moines Register* (27 March 2000): C.5.

Wolverton, Brad. "NCAA Considers Easing Demands on Athletes' Time." *The Chronicle of Higher Education* (8 January 2016): 1.

"You're a Student Not in to Sports? Too Bad." *Charlotte Observer* (2 December 2015): 26A.

Zimmerman, Michael. "Measuring the Impact of College Athletics on Athletes: A Work in Progress." *Phi Kappa Phi Forum* (Summer 2016): 16.

BOOKS

Bowen, William. *Reclaiming the Game: College Sports and Educational Values* (Princeton, NJ: Princeton University Press, 2003).

Brooks, Dana, and Ronald Althouse. *Diversity and Social Justice in College Sports: Sport Management and the Student Athlete* (Morgantown, WV: Fitness Information Technology, 2007).

Brown, Barry. *The Student-Athlete Playbook: Success in the Classroom, Sports & Life* (Atlanta, GA: Bar-Red Entertainment Group, 2009).

Cheville, Julie. *Minding the Body: What Student Athletes Know About Learning* (Portsmouth, NH: Heinemann, 2001).

Crowley, Joe. *In the Arena: The NCAA's First Century* (Indianapolis, IN: National Collegiate Athletic Association, 2006).

Fertman, Carl. *Student-Athlete Success: Meeting The Challenges of College Life* (Burlington, MA: Jones & Bartlett Learning, 2008).

Fizel, John, and Rodney D. Fort. *Economics of College Sports: Studies in Sports Economics* (Westport, CT: Praeger, 2004).

Hart, Algerian, and F. Erik Brooks. *The Student Athlete's Guide to College Success* (Westport, CT: Greenwood Publishing, 2016).

Isenberg, Marc, and Richard Rhoads. *The Student Athlete Survival Guide* (Camden, ME: International Marine/Ragged Mountain Press, 2000).

Jozsa, Frank P., Jr. *College Sports Inc.: How Commercialism Influences Intercollegiate Athletics* (New York, NY: Springer, 2013).

Kissinger, Daniel, and Michael Miller. *College Student-Athletes: Challenges, Opportunities, and Policy Implications* (Charlotte, NC: Information Age Publishing, 2009).

Mahiri, Jabari and Derek Van Rheenen. *Out of Bounds: When Scholarship Athletes Become Academic Scholars* (New York, NY: Peter Lang Inc., International Academic Publishers, 2009).

Porto, Brian. *The Supreme Court and the NCAA: The Case For Less Commercialism and More Due Process in College Sports* (Ann Arbor, MI: University of Michigan Press, 2012).

Schoem, David, and Shelly Kovacs. *College Knowledge for the Student Athlete* (Ann Arbor, MI: University of Michigan Press, 2011).

Shulman, James, and William Bowen. *The Game of Life: College Sports and Educational Values* (Princeton, NJ: Princeton University Press, 2001).

Yost, Mark. *Varsity Green: A Behind the Scenes Look at Culture and Corruption in College Athletics* (Palo Alto, CA: Stanford Economics and Finance, 2009).

Zimbalist, Andrew. *Unpaid Professionals: Commercialism and Conflict in Big-Time College Sports* (Princeton, NJ: Labyrinth Books, 2008).

INTERNET SOURCES

"A Whole New Ball Game? The Push to Reform — and Scale Back — Collegiate Athletics is Gaining Yardage." http://www.bloomberg.com, cited 27 May 2017.

"After the Game." www.ncaa.org, cited 12 May 2017.

Allen, Frederick. "When Colleges Recruit Athletes, Everyone Loses." http://www.forbes.com, cited 3 May 2017.

"An Economic Argument for the Paying of College Athletes." http://www.sportsbookreview.com, cited 11 May 2017.

"ASR Trends for Division II Men's Sports." http://www.ncaa.org, cited 16 March 2017.

"ASR Trends for Division II Women's Sports." http://www.ncaa.org, cited 16 March 2017.

"Average APRs by Sport for Men's Teams." http://www.ncaa.org, cited 16 March 2017.

"Average APRs by Sport for Women's Teams." http://www.ncaa.org, cited 16 March 2017.

"Average Athletic Scholarship Per Varsity Athlete." http://www.scholarshipstats.org, cited 8 May 2017.

"Average Eligibility Rates by Sport for Men's Teams." http://www.ncaa.org, cited 16 March 2017.

"Average Eligibility Rates by Sport for Women's Teams." http://www.ncaa.org, cited 16 March 2017.

"Average Federal Graduation Rates and ASRs for Division III Men's Sports (Voluntary Schools)." http://www.ncaa.org, cited 21 April 2017.

"Average Federal Graduation Rates and ASRs for Division III Women's Sports (Voluntary Schools)." http://www.ncaa.org, cited 21 April 2017.

"Average Federal Graduation Rates and ASRs for Division III Student-Athletes by Race/Ethnicity Group (Voluntary Schools)." http://www.ncaa.org, cited 16 March 2017.

"Average Federal Graduation Rates for the Division III Student Body and Student-Athletes by Race/Ethnicity Group (Voluntary Schools)." http://www.ncaa.org, cited 16 March 2017.

"Average Retention Rates by Sport for Men's Teams." http://www.ncaa.org, cited 16 March 2017.

"Average Retention Rates by Sport for Women's Teams." http://www.ncaa.org, cited 16 March 2017.

Barkhorn, Eleanor. "Athletes Are More Likely to Finish High School Than Non-Athletes." http://www.theatlantic.com, cited 2 May 2017.

Brown, Gary. "NCAA Graduation Rates: A Quarter-Century of Tracking Academic Success." http://www.ncaa.org, cited 1 April 2017.

Carter, Andrew. "Why NCAA Had no Penalties for UNC in Long-Awaited Report on Academic Scandals." http://www.newsobserver.com, cited 25 October 2017.

"College Athletic Scholarship Limits." http://www.scholarshipstats.com, cited 4 May 2017.

"College Athletics — History of Athletics in U.S. Colleges and Universities." http://www.education.stateuniversity.com, cited 28 March 2017.

Comeaux, Eddie. "Rethinking Academic Reform and Encouraging Organizational Innovation: Implications for Stakeholder Management in College Sports." http://www.researchgate.net, cited 2 May 2017.

"Cost of Attendance Q&A." http://www.ncaa.org, cited 9 May 2017.

Cutting, Gary. "The Myth of the Student-Athlete." http://www.opinionater.blogs.nytimes.com, cited 12 May 2017.

"Federal Graduation Rate Trends for Division II Men's Sports." http://www.ncaa.org, cited 16 March 2017.

"Federal Graduation Rate Trends for Division II Women's Sports." http://www.ncaa.org, cited 16 March 2017.

"Five Reasons Student Athletes Struggle Academically." http://www.gradesfirst.com, cited 12 May 2017.

"Difference Between NCAA, NAIA and NJCAA." http://www.sportsrecruitingusa.com, cited 28 March 2017.

"Division I." http://www.ncaa.org cited, 23 March 2017.

"Division I Academic Progress Report." http://www.ncaa.org, cited 6 March 2017.

"Division I Academics." http://www.ncaa.org, cited 6 March 2017.

"Division II." http://www.ncaa.org, cited 23 March 2017.

"Division II Academic Philosophy." http://www.ncaa.org, cited 6 March 2017.

"Division II Academic Success Rate." http://www.ncaa.org, cited 6 March 2017.

"Division III." http://www.ncaa.org, cited 23 March 2017.

"Division III Academics." http://www.ncaa.org, cited 6 March 2017.

"Division III Men's Sports (Voluntary Schools)." http://www.ncaa.org, cited 16 March 2017.

"Division III Women's Sports (Voluntary Schools)." http://www.ncaa.org, cited 16 March 2017.

Entman, Liz. "Elite College Athletes Should be Paid: Economists." http://www. news.vanderbilt.edu, cited 10 May 2017.

"Federal Graduation Rate Trends for Division II Men's Sports." http://www.ncaa. org, cited 16 March 2017.

"Federal Graduation Rate Trends for Division II Women's Sports." http://www. ncaa.org, cited 16 March 2017.

"14 Surprising Facts About Being a College Athlete." http://www.bestcollegesonline. com, cited 5 May 2017.

Frank, David. "5 Facts About Full-Ride Scholarships." http://www.athleticscholarships. net, cited 5 May 2017.

Ganim, Sarah. "CNN Analysis: Some College Athletes Play Like Adults, Read Like 5th-Graders." http://www.cnn.com, cited 12 May 2017.

"Graduation Success Rate Trends for Division I Men's Sports." http://www.ncaa. org, cited 13 April 2017.

"Graduation Success Rate for Division I Women's Sports." http://www.ncaa.org, cited 13 April 2017.

Greenlee, Craig. "Student-Athletes Making Their Voices Heard on Controversial Issues." http://www.diversseducation.com, cited 23 May 2017.

"Group Seeks to Reform Market-Driven College Athletics." https://www.asanet. org, cited 27 May 2017.

Gurney, Gerald. "Now We Must Reform Athletics Reform." http://www.chronicle. com, cited 29 May 2017.

"History of the NAIA." http://www.naia.org, cited 27 March 2017.

"History: The Drake Group, Inc." https://www.thedrakegroup.org, cited 27 May 2014.

Hosick, Michelle Brutlag. "D1 Council Adopts Academic Integrity Proposal." http://www.ncaa.org, cited 22 May 2017.

Hosick, Michelle Brutlag. "NCAA Releases Academic Progress Report for Coaches." http://www.ncaa.org, cited 29 May 2017.

"How Colleges Figure 'Cost of Attendance.'" http://www.collegedata.com, cited 8 May 2017.

"How OTL Completed Its Investigation." http://www.espn.com, cited 23 May 2017.

Hruby, Patrick. "Why the NCAA's New Reforms Won't Fix College Sports." http://www.theatlantic.com, cited 5 July 2017.

"Improve Your Chances for an Athletic Scholarship." http://www.collegescholarships. org, cited 3 May 2017.

Irick, Erin. "Report: National Collegiate Athletic Association." http://www.ncaa. publications.org, cited 23 March 2017.

Isenberg, Marc. "A Few Ways NCAA Could be There for Student Athletes." http://www.sportsbusinessdaily.com, cited 16 March 2017.

Johnson, Dennis, and John Acquaviva. "Point/Counterpoint: Paying College Athletes." http://www.thesportjournal.org, cited 14 May 2017.

Johnson, Greg. "Gallup Study Measures Long-Term Life Outcomes of Former Student-Athletes." http://www.ncaa.org, cited 10 May 2017.

Kerkhoff, Blair, and Tod Palmer. "They're Not Paychecks, But Major College Athletes Got Extra Scholarship Stipends for First Time This School Year." http://www.kansascity.com, cited 9 May 2017.

"Knight Commission Calls for College Sports Reform." http://www.knightfoundation. org, cited 1 June 2017.

"Knight Commission on Intercollegiate Athletics; Knight Commission Calls for College Sports Reform, Recommends Public Transparency of Finances and New Financial Incentives: Restoring the Balance: Dollars, Values, and the Future of College Sports Reveals Huge Disparities Between Spending on Athletics and Academics." http://www.knightcommission.org, cited 30 May 2017.

Lapchick, Richard, and DaWon Baker. "The 2015 Racial and Gender Report Card: College Sports." http://www.nebula.wsing.com, cited 16 March 2017.

Lavigne, Paula. "Lawyers, Status, Public Backlash Aid College Athletes Accused of Crimes." http://www.espn.com, cited 23 May 2017.

Lemmons, Malcolm. "College Athletes Getting Paid? Here Are Some Pros and Cons." http://www.huffingtonpost.com, cited 13 May 2017.

Levine, Joshua, *et al.* "Pluralistic Ignorance Among Student-Athlete Populations: A Factor in Academic Underperformance." https://www.link.springer.com, cited 13 May 2017.

"Managing Student-Athletes' Health Issues." http://www.ncaa.org, cited 28 May 2017.

"Men Student Athlete Participation." http://www.naia.org, cited 26 April 2017.

Mulhere, Kaitlin. "Student Athletes More Likely to Thrive After College Than Non-Athletes, Survey Says." http://www.time.com, cited 12 May 2017.

"NAIA Colleges and Universities." http://www.playnaia.org, cited 27 March 2017.

"NAIA Eligibility." http://www.playnaia.org, cited 3 May 2017.

"National Collegiate Athletic Association." http://www.britannica.com, cited 28 March 2017.

"National Collegiate Athletic Association: History." http://www.thefreedictionary.com, cited 28 March 2017.

"National Junior College Athletic Association." http://www.njcaa.org, cited 19 March 2017.

"NCAA Approves Academic Reforms." http://www.chronicle.augusta.com, cited 28 May 2017.

"NCAA Emerging Sports Timeline." http://www.ncaa.org, cited 21 March 2017.

"NCAA Goals Study of the Student-Athlete Experience: Initial Summary of Findings January 2016." http://www.ncaa.org, cited 13 May 2017.

"NCAA Sports Sponsorship and Participation Rates Report 1981–82 — 2014–15." http://www.ncaa.org, cited 13 March 2017.

"NCAA Sports Sponsorship and Participation Rates Report 1981–82 — 2015–16." http://www.ncaa.org, cited 13 March 2017.

"NCAA Sports Sponsorship 1981–82 — 2015–16: Average Number of Teams Per Institution." http://www.ncaa.org, cited 28 March 2017.

"NCAA Sports Sponsorship 1981–82 — 2015–16: Divisions I, II and III Men's Teams Overall Average Squad Size." http://www.ncaa.org, cited 28 March 2017.

"NCAA Sports Sponsorship 1981–82 — 2015–16: Divisions I, II and III Women's Teams Overall Average Squad Size." http://www.ncaa.org, cited 28 March 2017.

"NCAA Study of Student-Athlete Social Environments." http://www.ncaa.org, cited 13 May 2017.

"New Guide Released for Emerging Sports." http://www.ncaa.org, cited 21 March 2017.

"NJCAA History." http://www.njcaa.org, cited 18 March 2017.

"NJCAA Participation Figures-Men's Division." http://www.njcaa.org, cited 18 March 2017.

"NJCAA Participation Figures-Women's Division." http://www.njcaa.org, cited 18 March 2017.

Nocera, Joe. "A Way to Start Paying College Athletes." http://www.nytimes.com, cited 12 May 2017.

Oppenheimer, Daniel. "Why Student Athletes Continue to Fail." http://www.time.com, cited 12 May 2017.

"Pac-12 Passes Reforms for Athletes." http://www.espn.com, cited 29 May 2017.

"Pac-12 Universities Adopt Sweeping Reforms for Student-Athletes, Guaranteeing Scholarships, Improving Health Care, and More." http://www.pac-12.com, cited 29 May 2017.

Peebles, Maurice. "7 Common Reasons Why Student Athletes Should be Paid (According to Jay Bilas)." http://www.complex.com, cited 12 May 2017.

Pennington, Bill. "Expectations Lose to Reality of Sports Scholarships." http://www.nytimes.com, cited 5 May 2017.

"Play Division I Sports." http://www.ncaa.org, cited 3 May 2017.

"Play Division II Sports." http://www.ncaa.org, cited 3 May 2017.

Power, Clark. "Athletics vs. Academics." http://www.huffingtonpost.com, cited 7 March 2017.

"Rationalize Sports Recruiting: UC Regents Approve Reforms to Student-Athlete Policies." http://www.dailycal.org, cited 3 May 2017.

"Restoring the Balance: Dollars, Values, and the Future of College Sports." http://www.knightcommission.org, cited 30 May 2017.

"Results From the 2015 Goals Study of the Student-Athlete Experience." http://www.ncaa.org, cited 13 May 2017.

Romo, Professor Lynsey. "Study Offers Insight Into Challenges College Athletes Face." https://www.news.ncsu.edu, cited 28 May 2017.

"SEC Faculty Leaders Urge Reform for Athletics." http://www.scout.com, cited 5 July 2017.

Shipman, Matt. "Study Offers Insights Into Challenges College Athletes Face." http://www.news.ncsu.edu, cited 10 May 2017.

Soloman, Jon. "NCAA, Conferences Agree to Pay \$208.7 Million in Cost of Attendance Settlement." http://www.cbssports.com, cited 12 May 2017.

Soloman, Jon. "10 Ways College Athletes Can Get Paid and Remain Eligible for Their Sport." http://www.cbssports.com, cited 12 May 2017.

Soloman, Joe. "Pac-12 Adopts Reforms Hoping to Help College Athletes." http://www.cbssports.com, cited 28 May 2017.

"Sport Sponsorship, Participation and Demographics Search." http://www.ncaa.org, cited 8 March 2017.

"Sport Sponsorship, Participation, and Demographics Search." http://www.web1. ncaa.org, cited 8 March 2017.

Stanger, Melissa, and Emmie Martin. "50 Colleges Where the Students Are Both Smart and Athletic." http://www.businessinsider.com, cited 7 March 2017.

Staurowsky, Ellen. "A Brief Historical Perspective on Intercollegiate Athletics." http://www.humankinetics.com, cited 28 March 2017.

"Staying on Track to Graduate." http://www.ncaa.org, cited 6 March 2017.

"Student-Athletes." http://www.ncaa.org, cited 13 May 2017.

"Summary of Division III Academic Success Rates." http://www.ncaa.org, cited 6 March 2017.

"The Facts About 'Guaranteed' Multi-Year NCAA DI Scholarships." http://www. informedathlete.com, cited 5 May 2017.

"The Role of the Faculty in the Governance of College Athletics." http://www. aaup.org, cited 5 July 2017.

"The Student-Athlete, Academic Integrity, and Intercollegiate Athletics." http:// www.acenet.edu, cited 5 July 2017.

"The Student-Athlete Playbook — Book Review." https://seriousreading.com, cited 3 August 2017.

Thelin, John. "Here's Why We Shouldn't Pay College Athletes." http://www.time. com, cited 12 May 2017.

"Time for Accountability in Sports: Corrupt Collegiate Athletics Overshadow Faltering Academic Mission." https://www.thefreelibrary.com, cited 29 May 2017.

Toporek, Bryan. "For College Athletes, Concern About Balancing Sports, Academics." http://www.edweek.org, cited 7 March 2017.

"Total Generated Revenues and Expenses by Sport, Division I-Football Bowl Subdivision, Fiscal Year 2014." http://www.ncaa.org, cited 30 April 2017.

"Total Generated Revenues and Expenses by Sport, Division II With Football, Fiscal Year 2014." http://www.ncaa.org, cited 30 April 2017.

"2016 Athletic Scholarship Averages for NCAA I Teams by Sport." http://www. scholarshipstats.org, cited 5 May 2017.

"2016–17 NJCAA Eligibility Rules." http://www.njcaa.org, cited 3 May 2017.

"Vision, Mission and Goals." https://www.thedrakegroup.org, cited 27 May 2017.

Welch, Jarad, and Brad Marshall. "Should Student Athletes be Paid to Play?" http://www.usatoday.com, cited 12 May 2017.

Wolverton, Brad. "NCAA Says It's Investigating Academic Fraud at 20 Colleges." http://www.chronicle.com, cited 12 May 2017.

"Women Student Athlete Participation." http://www.naia.org, cited 26 April 2017.

Yankah, Ekow. "Why N.C.A.A. Athletes Shouldn't be Paid." http://www.newyorker.com, cited 13 May 2017.

Zagger, Zachary. "College Player Compensation Issue Rages On Despite Reforms." http://www.law360.com, cited 26 May 2017.

Zirin, Dave. "An Economist Explains Why Athletes Should be Paid." http://www.thenation.com, cited 12 May 2017.

Zola, Warren K. "Time for Transformative Change in Intercollegiate Athletics." http://www.huffingtonpost.com, cited 10 July 2017.

INDEX

Academics-Sports Controversies,
  x, 6, 159–194
    Academic Motivation and
      Performance, 163–168
    Pay-for-Play, 169–170
    Oppose Pay-for-Play, 170–173
    Support Pay-for-Play, 173–176
    Pay Proposals, 176–178
    Player Scandals, 178–186
    Other Topics, 186–194
Athletics Environment, 6, 121–157
    Commercializing College
      Sports, 122
    Financial Data, 122–127
    Events and Facilities, 127–130
    Student Athletes, 130–131
    Education Standards, 131
    NCAA Division I, 131–132
    NCAA Division II, 132–133
    NCAA Division III, 133
    NAIA, 133
    NJCAA, 133–134
    Scholarships, 135–149
    NCAA, 135
    NAIA, 135–136

NJCAA, 136
Cost of Attendance, 149–154
Athletes Environment Summary,
  154–157
Atlantic Coast Conference (ACC),
  150, 215

Baylor University, 181–183
Big Ten Conference, 150, 215
Big 12 Conference, 150, 215
Brand, Myles, 128, 176–177, 198,
  198n3, 199–200, 207n18, 210, 212,
  221

Cable News Network (CNN), 167,
  167n4
*College Sports Inc.: How
  Commercialism Influences
  Intercollegiate Athletics,* 7n1, 43n1
  see also Jozsa, Frank P., Jr.

Emmert, Mark, 168, 214, 225–226
Entertainment Sports Programming
  Network (ESPN), 173, 174n7, 182,
  184

Football Bowl Subdivision (FBS),
123, 152
Football Championship Subdivision
(FCS), 125

Gallup, 155, 155n20, 156
Grade Point Average (GPA), 44, 83,
88, 93, 132–133, 199

Indiana, Indianapolis, 44
Intercollegiate Athletic Association of
the United States, 8

Jozsa, Frank P., Jr. vii, 7n1, 43n1
see also College Sports Inc.:
How Commercialism Influences
Intercollegiate Athletics

Knight Commission, 10, 196,
203–205, 221

National Administrative Council
(NAC), 37
National Basketball Association
(NBA), 202
National Football League (NFL), 148,
173, 202
North Carolina State University
(NCSU), 154–155

Pacific 12 Conference, 150, 215

Reforms: Academics-Sports, 6,
195–228
NAFCAR/Drake Group,
195–197
Reform Movement, 197–203
Knight Commission, 203–205

NCAA Reforms, 205–208
Academic Progress Report,
208–214
Conference Reforms, 214–217
School Reforms, 217–222
Scholarship Reforms, 222–225
Government Proposals, 225–228

Schools Sports Programs, 5, 7–42
National Collegiate Athletic
Association, 11–12
Sports Period I, 12–15
Sports Period II, 16–20
Men's Sports Programs, 20
Division I , 20–24
Division II, 24–25
Division III, 25–27
Women's Sports Programs, 27
Division I, 27–30
Division II , 30–31
Division III , 32–33
National Association of
Intercollegiate Athletics, 36–38
National Junior College Athletic
Association, 38–39
Sports Programs, 39
Men's Division, 39–41
Women's Division, 41–42
Southeastern Conference, 150, 177,
215
Student Athlete Population, 5, 43–82
National Collegiate Athletic
Association, 45
Sports Period I, 45–49
Sports Period II, 49–54
Men Student Athletes, 54
Division I, 54–57
Division II, 57–58

Division III, 58–60
Women Student Athletes, 60
Division I, 60–63
Division II, 63–65
Division III, 65–67
SAs Race, 67
Divisions I–III, 67–69
Division I, 69–70
Division II, 70–71
Division III, 71–73
National Association of
    Intercollegiate Athletics, 73–77
National Junior College Athletic
    Association, 77–82
Student Athletes Academic
    Performances, 5, 83–120
    Division I , 84
    Academic Progress Report,
        84–90
    Graduation Success Rate, 90–95
    Eligibility Rates, 95–97
    Retention Rates, 97
    Division I, 97–99

Division II, 99–100
Academic Success Rate,
    100–106
Federal Graduation Rate, 106
Men's FGRs, 106–109
Women FGRs, 109–112
Division III, 112–114
Men Athletes, 114–117
Women Athletes, 117–119

Title IX, 13–15, 19, 42, 140, 146n15,
    147, 171

United States (U.S.), 10, 43, 121
University of Florida, 184–186
University of Georgia, 180–181
University of Hawaii, 151–152
University of Kansas, 130–131
University of Louisville, 182
University of Miami, 181
University of North Carolina-Chapel
    Hill, 127, 174n7, 179–180,
    180n11